Appalachia in Regional Context

D1520186

Appalachia in Regional Context

Place Matters

Edited by
DWIGHT B. BILLINGS
and
ANN E. KINGSOLVER

UNIVERSITY PRESS OF KENTUCKY

Editorial and Sales Offices: The University Press of Kentucky
663 South Limestone Street, Lexington, Kentucky 40508-4008
www.kentuckypress.com

bell hooks's poems titled by the numbers 11, 16, 18, 40, 56, and 57 appear with permission
from her collection *Appalachian Elegy: Poetry and Place* (University Press of Kentucky,
2012). The editors appreciate this powerful contribution to considerations of place.

Cataloging-in-Publication data is available from the Library of Congress.

ISBN 978-0-8131-7532-4 (hardcover : alk. paper)
ISBN 978-0-8131-7534-8 (epub)
ISBN 978-0-8131-7533-1 (pdf)

ISBN 978-0-8131-7913-1 (pbk.: alk. paper)

This book is printed on acid-free paper meeting the requirements of the American
National Standard for Permanence in Paper for Printed Library Materials.

Manufactured in the United States of America.

Member of the Association
of University Presses

Contents

Numbered poems from Appalachian Elegy *by bell hooks appear on pages 1 ("11"), 109 ("16"), 153 ("18"), 131 ("40"), 177 ("56"), and 69 ("57")*

11.
no crops grow
when dense clay dirt
packed solid
defies
all manmade
intent to destroy
let a blessing come here
let earth
heal and rejoice
she has here
mother of grace
and constancy
wild roses bloom
scatter these hills
with beauty
that does not linger
offering still the promise of healing
and return

—bell hooks

Introduction

Place Matters

Dwight B. Billings and Ann E. Kingsolver

This volume has grown out of myriad conversations. In Appalachian studies, broadly, people from around the world have discussed what it means to think about, represent or be silenced, and act in a *region,* exchanges that are akin to many other regional studies conversations about place and displacement, identities, voices, ecological and political histories, and imagined futures. More specifically, this collection was shaped by forty years of conversations in the Appalachian Center and Appalachian studies at the University of Kentucky, where a lecture series titled Place Matters was organized in 2011 and 2012 in which many of the authors participated.[1] This book is by no means comprehensive in voice or scope, but it is inspired by groundedness of praxis in place, and by the practice of equitable listening, in Appalachian studies, across disciplinary and academic or community boundaries, among others, which is a skill needed now more than ever. Appalachia as a place—the oldest mountain region in the world—has figured in various imaginings as a homeplace, a place of expulsion, a place of extraction, a literal and literary headwaters, America's internal homogeneous, intolerant other, and a place of intense biodiversity and centuries-old connections to global diasporas and place-based agency and imaginative organizing.

There is a groundswell in the twenty-first century to connect past discussions of what it means to conceptualize Appalachia as a region, as Batteau discussed, of who Appalachians are, as Turner and Cabbell documented, and of what it means to organize as Appalachians to discuss more inclusively decided and sustainable futures in Appalachia.[2] Within the broad, collaborative conversation between scholars, activists, and artists that Appalachian studies comprises, place matters in particular because what has brought most participants to that broad coalition is organizing in and around a *place* to contest misappropriations of resources, power, and agency and misattributions of isolation and intolerance.[3] Scott, Obermiller, and Berry observe in their essay "Making Appalachia: Interdisciplinary Fields and Appalachian Studies" that "Appalachian studies places a high value on local and regional knowledge, dialogical scholarship and writing, and a critique of how authority (including technocratic/scholarly authority) delegitimates and dismisses local knowledge, thereby disempowering communities, families, and individuals in the region."[4] As Stephen Fisher and Barbara Ellen Smith have argued, "We live in a world of many Appalachias";[5] how place is invoked, by whom, for what reason, matters. The phrasing of this book's subtitle is, of course, an homage to Cornel West's book *Race Matters;*[6] the use of "place matters" here is not meant to displace attention from racism and white supremacy as a violent form of othering in the Appalachian region and across the United States. Racialized discrimination requires constant focus and is included in this volume's discussion. This project is not intended to participate in the kind of painful silencing expressed in the Kentucky legislature's recent passage of Blue Lives Matter legislation, increasing penalties for violence against police officers, in response to the Black Lives Matter movement. Instead, we see othering by class, language, region, gender, and other dimensions of identity as rooted in the long-term denial of human equality justified through a racializing lens in the United States.

The essays in this volume are joined by the poems of bell hooks, first published in her book *Appalachian Elegy: Poetry and Place,*[7] and art—as Haywood, Kirby, and Pen also convey in their chapter—is a powerful way of expressing connection to and disconnection from place, in many languages and forms. Voices rooted in the region do not always focus their words or craft *on* the region, and it is not necessary to be from Appalachia to create work about it. Crystal Wilkinson, Silas House, and Nikki Giovanni are writers from or living in the Appalachian region, for example, whose work sometimes, but not always, explicitly discusses that connection to place.[8] As participants pointed out in the Symposium on Affrilachia: Celebrating the Artistic and Intellectual Contributions of African Americans to Appalachia, held at the University in Kentucky in 2011, voices from urban and northern regions of Appalachia—including that of the playwright August

Wilson, whose work is set in Pittsburgh—are often left out of discussions of Appalachian art and literature. There are many ways in which individuals choose to contextualize their work.

This volume contests the too-ready pigeonholing of Appalachia as a regional topic rather than a generally applicable one, because that can mislead readers about an ability to relate *across* experiences in and of place. The project of discussing Appalachia in context, or contexts (as one anonymous reviewer noted), in this book is to consider the many ways in which the region is being, and has been, constructed by many processes and voices, and how that shapes discussions of the future of the region. Themes, voices, political projects, and the soil and water itself all travel. Migrants from Hungary to the coal camps of the early nineteenth century brought economic and political ideas that led to the creation of Himlerville, a worker-owned coal-mining collective in Kentucky, in the middle of a landscape of absentee-owned capitalist extraction. Indigenous residents of Appalachia resisted the nation-state's violent land grab under Andrew Jackson, and indigenous Appalachians are not a historical "stage" in a chronology of Appalachia; instead, they are among the active voices in the region currently imagining its future. There are diverse histories and voices in the region, and as bell hooks describes in her chapter, those can be simultaneously affirmed and silenced in people's experiences. Narrative, performative, and visual arts are one way in which the invisibility and inaudibility of diverse experiences and Appalachia's global connections have been powerfully contested, as in the community-devised theater performance of *Las Voces de los Apalaches* (Appalachian Voices) at the University of Kentucky in 2014. Introduced musically by the band Appalatin, those gathered onstage shared their own and others' stories about their experiences as both Latin@s and Appalachians. There are so many storytellers and stories to tell in Appalachia, by generation, class, and the many ways in which we construct selves, family, and community; those diverse perspectives are *all* the voices of Appalachia.

Considerations of Appalachia, through whatever contextual lens, must take up at some point questions about how place matters. Why organize around a thirteen-state region in which north-south, urban-rural, state-county identities may be much more salient to residents than a coherent Appalachian identity? Has it not been imposed on residents of the region through map makers, politicians conceptualizing poverty as somehow spatially and culturally inherent, and media representations of Appalachia as the United States' internal "other" (or the voice of the Trump voter in the 2016 elections, even though the most vibrant turnout was for Bernie Sanders)? The rise of a focus on Appalachia by scholars and activists was intertwined with the Civil Rights, environmental, and labor movements in this country, as political and economic perspectives—brought, in part, to the United States through international workers who built the mining labor force in Appalachia—were applied to think historically and inclusively about power, agency, and voice in the eastern mountains of the United States. Place certainly mattered to Myles Horton, who helped start the Highlander Folk School (a center for place-based critical pedagogy) in Tennessee in 1932. As he participated in a conversation about Appalachia in 1968, he said, "I think the better way to learn about the power structure and to investigate it is to try to do something in a local way which will illuminate the problem for you."[9] Local and global are intertwined throughout this volume, as they are in the larger conversations in the Appalachian region and in Appalachian studies.

The chapters in this volume, then, explore this praxis of place from interdisciplinary perspectives, and in a global context. As bell hooks writes in her chapter, "humane globalization . . . begins with our living local." Place matters, more than ever, in relation to the construction of identity and meaning, politics and policy, citizen activism, creative expression, and in scholarship, research, and teaching. Appalachia was fueling global capitalist expansion in the nineteenth century,[10] but as the authors here note, that hyperconnectivity to the global through extractive industries has somehow resulted in the region's being portrayed repeatedly and very inaccurately as "unplugged" from capitalist globalization and in need of connection through development programs sponsored by the Appalachian Regional Commission and capitalist investors. In talk about globalization, it is sometimes claimed that now "the world is flat."[11] Like an Iowa cornfield or a mountaintop removal site in the Appalachian coalfields, the bumpy, recalcitrant friction of the local, it is often argued by neoliberal capitalist enthusiasts, has been smoothed over—and for the good of all. But that is not the case. Certainly people, money, products and services, information and ideas, military troops and killing drones flow across spaces at greater speeds than in the past, but they do so from place to place. One-sided talk about information technologies that shrink time/space distances and augment top-down, corporate globalization has the effect of eclipsing—even denying—the continuing importance of place. Yet people still live and die in places, leave places, and move to new places. Culture transcends localities but also resides in places and is worked up in new ways there. And people struggle to flee places, stay in places, defend places, improve places, and sometimes try to make them more healthy, safe, sane, and just. At the same time, some people try to keep other people out of "their" places—often violently—and some people simply ruin places, their own and others'. What we mean by the praxis of place is that *place,* as much as anything, is *action* more than passive context. It is about what people *do*—in one way or another, in concert, contestation, or consternation—as they try to make sense of and live with the nearby and distant forces in their lives. Yet the nearby and the distant are often reified and opposed as binary oppositions, and they are differentially valorized. In value terms especially, place often comes up short. Contributors to this volume, however, show why that mode of valorization is problematic, or downright wrong, and thus why and how *place matters.*

It has often been proclaimed—in electoral rhetoric, for example, until the most recent election—that globalization portends an entirely new and better world and that local places must thus adapt to its demands by becoming shape-shifters, reconfiguring their identities, cutting taxes and easing government regulations, opening borders, contorting to entice external capital investments, and so on—or else be left behind to wither in the dust of change. But globalization is not natural, inevitable, totalizing, or univocal. Its imagined "demands" do not represent a singular force of history.[12] Its various forms and potentialities—some positive, some negative—are enacted through a multiplicity of decentered economic, geographical, political, cultural, and discursive processes. Hegemonic discourses, however, naturalize neoliberal forms of capitalist globalization and uncritically promote a particular form of globalization as the way the world is and must be. They downplay the continuing importance of local places.[13]

The first three contributors to this volume—Ann Kingsolver, Barbara Ellen Smith, and John Pickles—all begin by reviewing extensive literatures that contest this binary opposition between local places and global processes, which, in John Pickles's words, dismiss place as "static, the dead, the inert, the immobile, even as parochial, backward, or antimodern." In the formulations they target for criticism, the global is seen as dynamic, ascendant, expansive, universal, open, inclusive, and agentive, whereas place is devalued as necessarily static, decadent, constricted, particularistic, bounded, exclusive, and dependent. Each author challenges this binary opposition as well as the either/or logic of the local versus the global by stressing their interrelationship. Stepping back from their own long-term studies of global/

local activism, each author refuses to essentialize or romanticize place—acknowledging how place-based thinking and politics can sometimes be exclusionary and reactionary—while showing empirically how place affords a crucial standpoint for understanding far-reaching global processes. They also examine how place-based politics, economic development, and activism can potentially challenge, resist, and sometimes defeat neoliberal capitalist globalization's negative effects by acting locally, thinking globally, and linking up to distant places with concerns of mutual interest.

Ann Kingsolver is a cultural anthropologist who has been studying how people understand capitalist logic and practice and act on those interpretations from the perspective of the particular geographical places they occupy and the work they do there. Advocating what Arif Dirlik calls "critical localism,"[14] Kingsolver puts place at the center of her historical and ethnographic analyses, bringing a long-term and comparative perspective to conveying critiques of capitalist globalization by variously situated individuals in the United States, Mexico, and Sri Lanka affected by transnational policies (like the North American Free Trade Agreement) and transnational industries (such as tobacco and tea). Concepts she has contributed to a larger conversation on Appalachia in a global context are "placing"[15] (drawn from the way people use place as a verb to situate one another, processes, and ideas relationally and continually) and "strategic alterity,"[16] referring to the specific ways in which non- or low-wage workers (and places where they reside) are devalued through capitalist logic in order to legitimate their exploitation. She sees conversations *across* places as vital.

Barbara Ellen Smith, a sociologist, contends that "place is becoming politicized in important ways that deserve attention from those who believe a more socially just world is possible," especially by those on the Left who—she says—too often view place-based politics as inadequate, futile, and reactionary. Affirming the theorizing of Doreen Massey, she advances a view of place that is relational and "extraverted."[17] Along with Steve Fisher, Smith has published a vital collection of original essays on contemporary, place-based organizing in Appalachia.[18] Reporting on this body of work, she identifies three place-based strategies that point toward a *global politics of place*, which she describes as "making space," "crossing space," and "transgressing space" and illustrates each with successful examples from Appalachia. Each of these organizing strategies challenges one of the most important threats to place: spatial closure. Smith identifies spatial closure as a manifestation of the global political logic of neoliberalism in which once-common spaces are enclosed and public spaces are privatized or diminished, processes she describes metaphorically as a prison "lockdown."

John Pickles, a geographer, examines opposition to such "lockdowns" as the political defense of the "commons," in which place-based activism takes center stage. As the locus of natural and social life worlds, place, according to Pickles, "provide[s] an operative context of common understandings, institutions, and practices that sustain the life of a community and provide the necessary conditions for any politics, whether of reaction and exclusion or hope and inclusion." Quoting the scholars of Appalachia Herbert Reid and Betsy Taylor, Pickles defines the "commons" as shared access to the "generative matrices [of embodied life] co-constituted from earth, air, water, nutrients, energies, and co-evolved creatures."[19] From opposition to mountaintop removal mining to forest environmentalism, commons activism has a long history in Appalachia.[20] Pickles provides theoretical guidelines for how to think about this commons activism in relation to Occupy, Rights to the City, global labor, and European autonomization movements and the theoretical debates they have inspired.

The place-based struggles over work and livelihood, community organizing, and the defense and expansion of the "commons" described in the first three chapters of this volume have to do with power. The political scientist John Gaventa—whose highly acclaimed book, *Power and Powerlessness*,[21] was a foundational study in the early Appalachian studies movement—suggests a new, multidimensional conceptualization of power in his contribution to this volume. He begins with a discussion of the how the places in which he has lived and worked—the Appalachian United States and Canada in North America, and countries in the United Kingdom and Africa—have influenced his understanding of what he calls the "power of place" and the "place of power." Local places, he says, exist in complex and far-reaching webs of power. The most effective efforts at place-based social transformation ultimately operate on each of three dimensions. They must (1) challenge three *forms of power* (visible, hidden, and invisible); (2) work across three *spaces of power* (invited, closed, and claimed); and (3) address three *levels of power* (local, national, and global). Readers familiar with Gaventa's early model of "three faces [forms] of power" will undoubtedly appreciate the greater complexity of his expanded conceptualization of power dynamics and—as in the case of Barbara Ellen Smith's formulation—the challenges that effective place-based organizing must confront.

Both Gaventa and Smith write about the importance of "creating," "claiming," and "transgressing" space in place-based politics, but community organizations are not the only agents that must do so. Mary Gray, an ethnographer, media studies scholar, and author of the pathbreaking book *Out in the Country,*[22] examines how LGBT youth effectively create queer visibility in rural places, using examples from Kentucky (chapter 5). Such places, as Gray points out, are typically "othered" in popular culture as forbiddingly inhospitable to queer life—places to escape rather than inhabit and transform, even though, she finds, many rural LGBT youth do not see it that way at all. Gray analyzes how television programs such as *Queer as Folk* suggest that the "good gay life" can be obtained only in large urban places where a critical mass of gay people live, where certain streets and neighborhoods can be "owned" ("gayborhoods"), and where metropolitan economies afford enough disposable income to support gay lifestyles, organizations, and politics. Despite the lack of such urban infrastructures and resources, however, Gray describes how rural LGBT youth creatively affirm at once their non-heteronormative identities and local belongings, enlist supportive allies, pool limited financial resources, and—most important—assert their visibility by queering seemingly unlikely quasi-public spaces such as Walmart parking lots and church-sponsored recreational areas, and by posting their actions on the Internet and social media. Here too, place matters, and it need not be locked down.

Another way of exploring being "out in the country"—in this case, to gather wild greens—is offered in chapter 6 by Elizabeth Engelhardt, a literature and cultural studies scholar who focuses on southern foodways. She explains, through an interdisciplinary lens, that it was more than taste, tradition, and affordability that drew people to gather wild greens in the early twentieth century. Pellagra was a deadly dietary disease that ravaged thousands of Southerners (especially women and children) in textile mill towns along the borders of Appalachia at that time. Engelhardt notes that though scientific evidence would much later reveal that eating wild greens did not actually cure pellagra—ultimately, it was the vitamin niacin (not present in wild greens) that would do so—it was the *process* of going out into the country to forage the commons for wild greens that in fact was curative for nonmedical, cultural, and social reasons. Gathering wild greens, she contends, challenged unbalanced diets and the overreliance on newly available processed foods along with the regimentation of corporatized clock time and the unhealthy conditions of factory life, consumerism, and commodification in the new industrial villages of the South by "a process of nurturing, unstructured time, and sustaining food practices." It was the foodways, not the food itself, that mattered. Engelhardt arrives at this conclusion from a provocative analysis of Depression-era novels about southern mill town life and completes her essay with the insight that wandering and gathering in wild places may well be an avenue for escaping the potentially dead zones of higher education that threaten the humanities today.

Places can become dead or deadly not only because of the ravages of unregulated industrialization, as in those early mill towns, but also when they become energy sacrifice zones for fossil fuel extraction—as Gaventa describes in Nigeria or Appalachia.[23] This can be true despite the vibrancy of opposition and resistance that is often found in those places, as described in previous chapters. Carol Mason (chapter 7), a humanities scholar in gender and women's studies, deploys Achille Mbembe's concept of "necropolitics" to explore how death is managed politically—in popular culture and in real life—in such zones.[24] Mason compares how anxieties about economic change and its resulting threats to masculinity are managed by mass media in the reality television series *Buckwild* (which focuses on marginalized and precarious youth in the coalfields of southern West Virginia), in the popular series *Mad Men* (which depicts the vanishing lifestyle of 1950s advertising men), and in Rebecca Scott's ethnographic study of how people, especially men who do not oppose mountaintop removal coal mining in Appalachia, adapt to living in such deadly zones.[25] Mason's point, of course, is not to condone depictions of place as dead but rather to prompt a discussion of the ways in which, as she puts it, "we live in the midst of a deadly world we cannot deny."

As challenging as life may be in many places, place nonetheless provides fertile soil for artistic creativity. The contributors to chapters 8 and 9 offer autobiographical reflections on the role of place in their lives and art. The renowned social theorist and author bell hooks reflects on how a strong sense of place—rural Kentucky—has always shaped her thinking and writing, even though she is not commonly thought of—but identifies as—a Kentucky writer (chapter 8). Recalling early memories of farms, tobacco fields, pigs, and her African American elders' relationship to the land and its healing powers, hooks says that her soul is "imprinted with the hills of Kentucky." In her youth, she split her time between those hills and the apartheid world of western Kentucky, went to graduate school on the West Coast, and lived in New York for many years before returning to Kentucky to make her home in the college town of Berea, nestled in the foothills of the Appalachian Mountains. hooks's story about these spatial, intellectual, and spiritual journeys reveals that we often make our homes only by leaving them and find our places only by reclaiming them.

John Haywood is a painter, tattoo artist, and old-time banjo player. Rich Kirby is also an old-time musician and a longtime member of Appalshop, the famed multimedia center in Whitesburg, Kentucky, where he helped found the June Appal record label. Haywood grew up in a coal-mining family in eastern Kentucky, studied painting at the graduate level in Louisville, and returned to eastern Kentucky, where he owns an art gallery and tattoo parlor. Kirby grew up in New York City but spent summers with his grandparents in central Appalachia, where he has now lived for many years. Haywood and Kirby perform and record with an old-time music group, Rich and the Po' Folk. They got together at the University of Kentucky to discuss how place matters in their art. Their lecture in the Place Matters series, "Somewheres on the Track: Place, Art, and Music in Eastern Kentucky," which forms the basis of their chapter with Ron Pen in this volume, combined musical performance with projections of Haywood's evocative paintings of people and places in the eastern Kentucky coalfields (chapter 9). After being influenced from many cultural directions and having at least one foot in urban environments, their decisions to settle in rural Appalachia were, like that of bell hooks, conscious choices to reclaim place and make their home in its varied artistic traditions.

The final chapter of this book examines pedagogies of place. Seven scholars—Dwight Billings, Gina Caison, David A. Davis, Laura Hernández-Ehrisman, Philip Joseph, Kent C. Ryden, and Emily Satterwhite—discuss the pitfalls and promises of teaching regional studies in or on Appalachia, Native American lands, the South, regional dialects, the Southwest, and New England. Their papers were first presented in a roundtable titled "Teaching Region" at the 2012 annual conference of the Southern Atlantic Modern Language Association, organized by Margaret McGehee and Emily Satterwhite and later revised for this book. Each author responds to questions posed by Satterwhite on best practices for teaching regionalism; reasons to be cautious about regionalism/nationalism and the potential privileging of rootedness (or multigenerational experience of place) over new immigrants' contributions to place; the value of a regional lens in a transnational context and in enabling a critical examination of hegemonic hierarchies of scale (internationalism over localism, city over country); and in what ways regionalism is both complicit in celebrations of whiteness and allied with ethnic studies in critiquing dominant views. The authors, when gathered, compared notes on whether and how region still matters to students they encounter, what role they think region should play in contemporary pedagogy, and how they might leverage interests in regional inequities and uneven geographic development to provoke insights into other varieties of social injustice.

The discussions of "Teaching Region," like the other essays in this collection, show why place matters—especially when recognized "not as the grounded specifics of locale," as the two feminist geographers writing as Gibson-Graham state, "but as the unmapped possibilities that are present in every situation—if only we are ready to encounter them."[26] This volume is informed by and encourages those encounters.

Notes

1. Dwight Billings, who has been involved with the Appalachian Studies Program at the University of Kentucky since its inception, facilitated the launch of the Place Matters lecture series as codirector of the Appalachian Studies Program with Ron Eller and Ron Pen in 2011. Ann Kingsolver, after being invited from the University of South Carolina to give the first lecture, later joined the University of Kentucky to direct the Appalachian Center and Appalachian Studies Program and organized the second year of lectures. Mary Anglin, Keiko Tanaka, Patricia Ehrkamp, Hsain Ilahiane, Erik Reece, Randall Roorda, Srimati Basu, and Shannon Bell contributed to the Place Matters lecture series as discussants, and their contributions—as well as those of all participating from the audience, and all the Appalachian studies faculty, staff, and student affiliates—were significant to the conversations leading to this book. The editors appreciate the support of this intellectual project by Dean Mark Kornbluh and the staff of the College of Arts and Sciences, and by the Appalachian Center's staff members over those two years; Pam Webb's and Shane Barton's contributions were especially crucial. Dwight Billings edits the Place Matters series for the University Press of Kentucky, also stemming from the 2011–2012 Place Matters lectures and discussions; this book is not the first published in that series, but it reflects the conversations framing it.

2. See Allen W. Batteau, *The Invention of Appalachia* (Tucson: University of Arizona Press, 1990); William H. Turner and Edward J. Cabbell, eds., *Blacks in Appalachia* (Lexington: University Press of Kentucky, 1985); Helen M. Lewis's career reflections on organizing (*Helen Matthews Lewis: Living Social Justice in Appalachia,* ed. Patricia D. Beaver and Judith Jennings [Lexington: University Press of Kentucky, 2012]); and, on work toward a sustainable future, Stephanie McSpirit, Lynne Faltraco, and Connor Bailey, eds., *Confronting Ecological Crisis in Appalachia and the South: University and Community Partnerships* (Lexington: University Press of Kentucky, 2012).

3. See Dwight B. Billings, Gurney Norman, and Katherine Ledford, *Back Talk from Appalachia: Confronting Stereotypes* (Lexington: University Press of Kentucky, 2000).

4. The essay appears in Chad Berry, Phillip J. Obermiller, and Shaunna L. Scott, eds., *Studying Appalachian Studies: Making the Path by Walking* (Urbana: University of Illinois Press, 2015), 22.

5. Fisher and Smith, "Placing Appalachia," in *Transforming Places: Lessons from Appalachia,* ed. Stephen L. Fisher and Barbara Ellen Smith (Urbana: University of Illinois Press, 2012), 1.

6. Cornel West, *Race Matters* (Boston: Beacon Press, 1993).

7. bell hooks, *Appalachian Elegy: Poetry and Place* (Lexington: University Press of Kentucky, 2012).

8. See, for example, Crystal Wilkinson's *Blackberries, Blackberries* (London: Toby Press, 2000), Silas House's *Clay's Quilt* (Chapel Hill, NC: Algonquin, 2001), and Nikki Giovanni and Cathee Dennison's edited volume, *Appalachian Elders: A Warm Hearth Sampler* (Blacksburg, VA: Pocahontas Press, 1991), in relation to their full body of work.

9. Myles Horton, "Study the Power Structure," in *The Myles Horton Reader: Education for Social Change,* ed. Dale Jacobs (Knoxville: University of Tennessee Press, 2003), 100.

10. Mary Beth Pudup, Dwight B. Billings, and Altina L. Waller, eds., *Appalachia in the Making: The Mountain South in the Nineteenth Century* (Chapel Hill: University of North Carolina Press, 1995).

11. Thomas Friedman, *The World Is Flat* (New York: Farrar, Straus & Giroux, 2005).

12. Its proponents also typically overestimate its extent. See David F. Ruccio, "Globalization and Imperialism," *Rethinking Marxism* 15 (January): 75–94, for a demonstration that today's levels of international trade, finance, production, and migration have, in fact, not surpassed those of 1870 to 1913.

13. Attention to place has also been displaced—at least temporarily—by scholarly reactions against the essentialist approaches to place and region in monolithic, Cold War–era area studies. But new multidisciplinary studies that view global issues in local contexts—as done by the contributors to this volume—brought new attention to place in positive terms. See, for instance, Bruce Cummings, "Boundary Displacement: Area Studies and International Studies during and after the Cold War," www.mtholyoke.edu/acad/intrel/cummings2.htm, and Schafer Wolf, "Reconfiguring Area Studies for the Global Age," in Saïd Amir Arjomand, ed., *Social Theory and Regional Studies in the Global Age* (Albany: State University of New York Press, 2014), 145–178.

14. Arif Dirlik, "The Global in the Local," in *Global/Local: Cultural Production and the Transnational Imaginary,* ed. Rob Wilson and Wimal Dissanayake (Durham: Duke University Press, 1996), 21–45.

15. Ann E. Kingsolver, "Contested Livelihoods: 'Placing' One Another in 'Cedar,' Kentucky," *Anthropological Quarterly* 65 (1992): 128–136.

16. Ann E. Kingsolver, "Farmers and Farmworkers: Two Centuries of Strategic Alterity in Kentucky's Tobacco Fields," *Critique of Anthropology* 27.1 (2007): 87–102.

17. Doreen Massey, *Space, Place, and Gender* (Minneapolis: University of Minnesota Press, 1994).

18. Fisher and Smith, *Transforming Places.*

19. Herbert Reid and Betsy Taylor, *Recovering the Commons: Democracy, Place, and Global Justice* (Urbana: University of Illinois Press, 2010), 12. Also see Pickles's essay "Collectivism, Universalism, and Struggles over Common Property Resources in the 'New Europe,'" in *The Global Idea of "the Commons,"* ed. Donald M. Nonini (New York: Berghahn Books, 2007), 26–40.

20. In addition to Reid and Taylor, see especially Jefferson C. Boyer, "Reinventing the Appalachian Commons" in Nonini, *The Global Idea of "the Commons,"* 89–114; and Kathryn Newfont, *Blue Ridge Commons: Environmental Activism and Forest History in Western North Carolina* (Athens: University of Georgia Press, 2012).

21. John Gaventa, *Power and Powerlessness: Quiescence and Rebellion in an Appalachian Valley* (Urbana: University of Illinois Press, 1980). On Appalachian studies as an academic and social movement, see Berry, Obermiller, and Scott, *Studying Appalachian Studies.*

22. Mary L. Gray, *Out in the Country: Youth, Media, and Queer Visibility in Rural America* (New York: New York University Press, 2009).

23. See Julia Fox, "Mountaintop Removal in West Virginia: An Environmental Sacrifice Zone," *Organization and Environment* 12.2 (1999): 163–183. For the life-affirming practices of resistance to this deadly form of mining, see Shannon E. Bell, *Our Roots Run Deep as Ironweed: Appalachian Women and the Fight for Economic Justice in Appalachia* (Urbana: University of Illinois Press, 2013).

24. Achille Mbembe, "Necropolitics," trans. Libby Meintjes, *Public Culture* 15.1 (2003): 11–40.

25. Rebecca Scott, *Removing Mountains: Extracting Nature and Identity in the Appalachian Coalfields* (Minneapolis: University of Minnesota Press, 2010).

26. J. K. Gibson-Graham, *The End of Capitalism (As We Knew It): A Feminist Critique of Political Economy* (1996; repr., Minneapolis: University Press of Minnesota, 2006), xviii.

1

"Placing" Futures and Making Sense of Globalization on the Edge of Appalachia

Ann E. Kingsolver

Comparative Spatial and Temporal Perspectives on How "Place Matters"

Regional studies programs—often beleaguered for political, economic, and epistemological reasons within universities—can constitute useful interdisciplinary communities for thinking critically about capitalist logic and practice.[1] And by further comparing perspectives across regions, it is possible to reflect on how "place matters" in studying capitalist globalization. I write as a cultural anthropologist; the central method in our toolkit is engaged listening. For the past thirty years, I have been listening to how people make sense of globalization and act on what they see as its effects on their lives and work. This long-term project in political economic and interpretive ethnography started in my home community of Nicholas County, Kentucky (Kingsolver 2011), with dissertation research between 1986 and 1989 and ongoing listening to how people saw livelihoods and identities affected by coming changes in the tobacco and textile industries that could be seen as related to all that gets glossed as "globalization." I wanted to follow the way residents imagined the future over several decades; in some ways, then, this long-term project has been a history of the future on the edge of Appalachia.

Conversations in Nicholas County led me to do two comparative projects to explore facets of how people in particular places make sense of global processes. The first project was in Mexico and the United States and addressed how people situated differently by occupation, citizenship, ethnic and/or racial identity, class, gender, age, rural-urban status, and political perspectives interpreted the North American Free Trade Agreement, or NAFTA (Kingsolver 2001). I was interested in how people could have strong views about a 2,000-page document to which few had access, in how people attributed NAFTA with agency over their lives, and in the way that economic anxieties translated into xenophobia. California Proposition 187, later ruled unconstitutional, was passed in the same year as NAFTA (1994), and it constituted the beginning of the most recent wave of anti-immigrant legislation across the United States. Capitalist logic is integrally tied to the process of strategic alterity—or the selective devaluing of a group of people on the basis of racialization or national or cultural citizenship, for example, naturalizing their position as the non- or low-wage workforce and enabling the free marketeers to do business. Economic nationalism (see Frank 2000) and particular immigrant groups being selectively targeted for hate speech, violence, and anti-immigrant legislation have grown even stronger in the two decades since then.

Regions—whether multinational, urban-rural, or U.S. North-South—are often invoked in public discourse as uniform sites of tolerance or intolerance, sources of one another's economic woes, or zones warranting protection or exclusion (Kingsolver 2010). Regional stereotypes demand constant contestation in order to render visible the diversity of views, voices, and histories within them (see Billings, Norman, and Ledford 1999). Those regional stereotypes are tenacious, though, and it can be difficult to break through them. Appalachians, for example, are often depicted in popular culture as homogeneous and isolated, when the region has been engaged deeply with the global economy for centuries through extractive industries, which in turn brought together very diverse labor forces that have shaped the identity of the region.

I took what I learned about capitalist logic and strategic alterity through conversations about NAFTA back to Nicholas County, and I thought about the non-wage and low-wage workforce that has facilitated the illusion of

Jeffersonian independence for small-scale tobacco farmers, though *farmer* itself is not a stable identity category, except through stereotypes (Kingsolver 2015, 2007). Over the past two hundred years, there has been a succession of strategically "othered" workers in the burley tobacco fields of Nicholas and other Kentucky counties at the labor-intensive points in the production cycle, particularly setting, cutting, and hanging the crop. The first of those non-wage or low-wage workforces facilitating family farming was enslaved Africans, a captive immigrant labor force. I learned that one in six residents of Nicholas County at the time of its founding was an enslaved African—a history that had been all but erased by the time of my childhood, when we were taught in integrated schools that slavery had existed only in the flatlands of western Kentucky. That unpaid or low-paid workforce was replaced by those with other identities, also largely unacknowledged as part of what made tobacco farming possible on small farms in the county: immigrant workers from a number of nations in the nineteenth century, seasonal migrants from farther up in the mountains, women and children in farming households, non-cash kin and neighbor-based labor exchange networks, and most recently new immigrants from Latin America who have been hired through the H2A visa program and also outside that system.

The neoliberal capitalist logic of Milton Friedman (1962) and others emphasizes the free marketeer's independence. That makes it difficult for a tobacco farmer to conceptualize, first, his or her dependence on low-wage or non-wage labor and, second, the fact that he or she is a worker for a global industry, taking on most of the risks of production, at that. My second transnational project compared explanations of globalization by those working in the tobacco industry in Kentucky and by those working in the tea industry in the mountainous region of Sri Lanka, where I interviewed people for seven months in 2004. This genealogy of a longer-term comparative project on interpretations of globalization is provided to explain the source of the later examples in this chapter. The discussion here is primarily of work in Kentucky, but I am engaged currently in a collaborative project in which participants across a number of global mountain regions who have been socially and economically marginalized are comparing notes and strategies.

Globalization can be used to refer to so many processes that it is like the air—everywhere, but hard to touch. Here is one of many working definitions that I find useful in talking with people about it: "Contemporary globalization is the increasing flow of trade, finance, culture, ideas, and people brought about by the sophisticated technology of communications and travel and by the worldwide spread of neoliberal capitalism, and it is the local and regional adaptations to and resistances against these flows" (Lewellen 2002, 7–8).

In all the conversations I have had with people about the processes glossed as globalization over the years, most have talked about it as having both positive and negative aspects. As Farhang Rajaee (2000, 96–97) puts it, "Globalization operates as a two-edged sword. It emancipates but also represses, and it brings together and unites but also divides and forms new hierarchies." The time-space compression David Harvey (1991) discusses— or the global reach facilitated by new technologies—does not reach everyone equally, and we have seen neoliberal capitalist policies increase inequalities within and across nations rather than bringing equality through the free market, as Milton Friedman envisioned in *Capitalism and Freedom*. The ironies of unequal application of global communication technologies were expressed eloquently by Mr. Gowreesan, who lost his family in the 2004 tsunami that killed over 30,000 people in Sri Lanka: "A whole generation of ours has been wiped out. Why was no one able to foresee this huge disaster? They say it's a global village and that the world has shrunk. But we didn't know of something that happened over three hours ago. Is this the era of information? We were watching the cricket in New Zealand on the day of the incident. Yet we didn't know about something important for us. Is this globalisation?" (TamilNet 2005).

It seemed unfathomable to him that there could be international broad-casting of a sports event but no advance news of the offshore earthquake that had rocked the coast of Indonesia hours before on December 26, 2004, and led to the tsunami in the Indian Ocean that resulted in almost 300,000 people missing or dead and over a million and a half being displaced. In Mr. Gowreesan's community, anguish was further compounded by the fact that while men were gathered to watch the cricket match on television, it was disproportionately women and children who were lost to the tsunami; many had been gathering fish that were left on the sand by the initial out-sweep of ocean water that preceded the deadly tsunami wave.

Globalization, then, is no panacea, and neither is a counterfocus on the local. Arif Dirlik (1996, 22), advocating a "critical localism," points out that the local should not be seen as an antidote to the global, but should be seen "as a site both of promise and predicament." On the one hand, there are local movements to resist the disastrous effects of global capitalism, such as the Chipko environmental movement organized in India (Guha 1989). On the other, the local can *also*—Dirlik notes—"serve to disguise oppression." In Kentucky, on the county level, for example, some repeated assaults might go unprosecuted for years because of the way power works in relation to social networks in the local justice system, and survivors may need to go to another jurisdictional level to get a hearing. Neither the local nor the global should be romanticized, nor perhaps seen in opposition to each other. Wilson and Dissanayake (1996, 7–8) have pointed out that global/local is not an either/or, but a "both/and." Stuart Hall (1988, 27) has suggested that as the nation-state is waning, regions have simultaneously gone above and below "the nation-state, the national economies, the national cultural identities, to something new" that is both "global and local in the same moment."

In relation to the focus of this book, how does "place matter" in thinking about the local and the global? Arturo Escobar (2001a, 141) notes that "place has dropped out of sight in the 'globalization craze' of recent years, and this erasure of place has profound consequences for our understanding of culture, knowledge, nature, and economy." He critiques the way that the global/local construction associates the global "with space, capital, history and agency while the local, conversely, is linked to place, labor, and tradition—as well as with women, minorities, the poor and, one might add, local cultures" (Escobar 2001a, 155–156). Wanda Rushing (2009, 20–21) argues that "place mediates the impact of global and local processes" because it is "uniquely situated in networks of *global* relations and cultural flows, as well as embedded in *local* history and culture." Rushing (2009, 18) further observes that "place itself is caught in the crossfire [between localization and globalization]. Both perspectives treat place more as a bystander than as an agentic player in social life." Regional or place-based interdisciplinary studies can help us think about both space and time as contingent, socially constructed, and situated within power relations. Rushing argues that "place can be seen as a crucible of cultural, social, and political interactions that occur within global flows of trade, migration, and epidemics and not as a space of stasis. These interdependent processes connect real people and places to the past, present, and future while integrating the global and local, as well as the urban and rural, in positive and negative ways" (Rushing 2009, 188).

How does place matter as we talk about globalization? How do the workers going into factories in foreign trade zones in several different countries to handle the same pieces of cloth that will become a garment on the rack at a Walmart experience where they *are*? What smells, sights, and memories do they experience as they enter the factory that have to do with what *place* they are in? And how are those workers involved in negotiating place *itself*? Like Rushing, David Harvey sees place as constructed constantly and actively: "Places are constructed and experienced as material ecological artifacts and intricate networks of social relations. They are the focus of the imaginary, of beliefs, longings, and desires. . . . They are an intense focus of discursive activity, filled with symbolic and representational meanings, and they are a distinctive product of institutionalized social and political-economic power" (Harvey 1996, 316).

Feminist critiques by Alison Blunt and Gillian Rose (1994), and J. K. Gibson-Graham (1996, 2005) point out the way globalization has been mapped and discussed in traditional patriarchal imaginings from imperial conquest and ownership of colonial territories to current discussions of the *penetration* of capital into marginalized regions. What else has been naturalized with capitalist logic of globalization that might be recognized or contested if "place" is moved to the center of analyses? What about the environment? Marcel Proust (1948 [1896]) wrote, "We have nothing to fear and a great deal to *learn* from trees," but how many people are listening? Where are the voices of the trees and streams in talk of globalization? Examples may be found in Chipko activists in India protecting long-term resources, and in Kentuckians for the Commonwealth and Kentucky Rising activists speaking up on behalf of the water being polluted by mountaintop removal mining runoff and coal ash sludge, but, most often, consideration of the long-term, the social bottom line, and the environment lose out in global capitalist logic. How did it ever come to make sense that corporate rights to minerals under the land took priority over collective and individual rights to the trees and homes and farms on top of it?

The social and environmental consequences of resource extraction in Appalachia, and the redistribution of the economic gains from that activity, can be compared with the same processes in other regions. Tunde Agbola and Moruf Alabi (2003, 272), for example, write about the environmental destruction of the Niger Delta region of Nigeria through the extraction of oil: "Long term sustainable development cannot occur in a situation of deteriorating environmental circumstances." The same point was made by Chico Mendes (1989) and other activists in the Amazonian rainforest. How do we think about accountability for a region's natural and social resources and the possibility of even *having* a place to make plans about, through whatever development discourse prevails? Attention to place can facilitate the reexamination of capitalist logic through its constantly calling *any logic or claim* into question. Place is, as Dirlik (2001, 18) says, "the location . . . where the social and the natural meet, where the production of nature by the social is not clearly distinguishable from the production of the social by the natural." And as Doreen Massey (1994, 5) reminds us, "The identities of places are always unfixed, contested, and multiple."

Fellow residents of Nicholas County, Kentucky, who make theory just as everyone else does in order to navigate social life, taught me that place is a verb. We all "place" ourselves, others, actions, and ideas differently according to the social context (Kingsolver 1992). In the globalization literature, there is often reference to "local knowledge." But local knowledge is not simple to contextualize when you take "placing" into account. "Insider" and "outsider" can be fairly fluid identities, but they can also be fixed in particular strategic moments. This can be seen at the national level as cultural citizenship expands and contracts with responses to political or economic crises (as when Japanese Americans were forced into internment camps, or anti-immigrant discourse and legislation ramps up), and it happens at the local level, as well. In Nicholas County, I have seen people and their ideas valued, devalued, localized, and distanced through intricate forms of "placing" the same person as an insider or outsider. Social science researchers as well as the researched, or those who collaborate with us, are "placed," often as both insiders and outsiders, as Kirin Narayan has pointed out: "The loci along which we are aligned with or set apart from those we study are multiple and in flux. Factors such as education, gender, sexual orientation, class, race, or sheer duration of contacts may at different times outweigh the cultural identity we associate with insider or outsider status" (Narayan 1993, 671–672).

Here is an example of how *placing* matters, in terms of both people and ideas. Tom Hensley worked very hard in the 1980s to organize a regional food system across county lines in Kentucky; he spoke with farmers' groups, chambers of commerce, Rotary Clubs, and anyone else who would listen. He lined up contracts with Kentucky Fried Chicken for locally produced chicken (most of theirs came from Georgia, it turned out) and cabbage for coleslaw, loans for vertically integrated vegetable processing plants, and locally controlled trucking for the regional food collective. He got the support of USDA representatives for what he called his Kentucky First campaign. But he never won support from fellow farmers in Nicholas County and surrounding counties because he and his ideas couldn't be "placed" right—he was seen as an incomer, because he had been born in Harlan and married into Nicholas County, and one local textile worker told me that Tom just did not have the local political support needed to pull something like that off. I would add that that was partly because of how he could be placed in terms of the ways in which local class processes and political processes intersected. Tom Hensley's Kentucky First campaign (arguably a forerunner of the current Kentucky Proud labeling) was an idea ahead of its time, and although he died before he could see them, he would be delighted to see the current attention to local food systems in Kentucky and the Kentucky Proud (kyproud.com) and Appalachia Proud labeling and marketing networks.

Tom Hensley wanted to organize agricultural producers into a collective that worked in this way:

> What it amounts to, the way I had it planned, is for the producers, the truck drivers that go to get the chicken and the people in the factory must all share in the profit. . . . So once these loans are paid off and everything is free and clear, we will still contribute, and what we'll use this contribution for then, we'll put it in the bank; we'll let it draw interest on each person's percentage of his contribution and that will benefit his retirement when he retires, and every person will have a piece of the pie. There'll be no big I's and little you's. (Hensley 1987, personal communication; quoted in Kingsolver 2011, 62)

In our many conversations, Tom told me he was a staunch capitalist, and that he did not like Roosevelt's New Deal policies. But he invented a plan for a Mondragón-like collective in which the emphasis on *place* in economic planning swamped capitalist logic, as far as I could see. And he envisioned a local economy in which there would be no "big I's and little you's." The local leader of the Chamber of Commerce at the time saw Tom's plan as impractical. He said this about it: "Isolationism on a state level is ridiculous and impossible to implement. He is completely and tea-totally ignoring the two basic economic principles of supply and demand—that you're gonna buy it where it's cheapest, no matter what. . . . His policies are that you buy it in Nicholas County. . . . Let the market decide what's going to happen."

The contradiction between what Tom Hensley saw as making economic sense and what the head of the Chamber of Commerce saw as making economic sense reflected different development discourses in which people participate hoping to make things better for their communities. Tom's logic was emphasizing social capital and place-based economies, and the head of the Chamber of Commerce believed that neoliberal capitalist logic would be the best way to improve living conditions for Nicholas Countians, which meant not restricting the market and encouraging capitalist investment from elsewhere rather than necessarily reinvesting locally. This thinking, in turn, made sense given the way in which chambers of commerce have been enlisted in capitalist development planning and factory recruitment since the 1940s. Just as economic nationalism can have its positive and negative ramifications (e.g., encouraging a local economy to resist international capitalist pressure to be drawn into further debt, as Jamaica and many other nations have attempted to do, on the one hand, or, on the other, the coupling of economic nationalism with xenophobia), consumer insistence on local-only rather than local-first movements can be problematic for local producers. Most farmers I have interviewed find it necessary to combine local and global marketing strategies to remain viable. There are *various* logics through which residents of any place argue the welfare of the community will be best served; the key is listening across them and finding any points of convergence between them. This applies whether we are talking about the World Trade Organization or the Nicholas County Industrial Development Authority. What gets discussed as globalization is always also local; decisions are made by individuals who can be "placed" in social, ideological, and physical contexts.

Arif Dirlik (2001, 34) advocates "placing" globalism "so as to counteract its mystification of its own location." Arturo Escobar has called place "the other" of globalization, further elaborating its critical potential noted by Dirlik: "Place, to begin with—like local culture—can be said to be 'the other' of globalization, so that a discussion of place should also afford an important perspective toward rethinking globalization and its relation to the question of alternatives to capitalism and modernity" (Escobar 2001b, 203).

Place-based movements, as Escobar and others argue, can provide not only short-term stoppage of the building of a dam, for example, but also the reconceptualization of economic life and the recalibration of value in relation to that. What is the economic worth, for example, of a human life? The value of the life of Jeremy Davidson, a child killed in his bedroom by a runaway boulder from a strip-mining site, was set at $15,000, which is what the mining company was fined for operating equipment in the dark and without a permit, according to Catherine Pancake's 2006 film *Black Diamonds*. His life was worth infinitely more than that to his family and community. As one woman said in the same film, "The ones who give the permits don't live here. *They* won't have to bury anybody."

It is not necessary to sign over one's agency to a particular logic, and globalization has been a logic used to justify a lot of inequality. One way that works is the assumption of capitalist globalization's uniformity and inevitability, as the two authors writing as J. K. Gibson-Graham (1996) noted, and place-centered thinking can help us work through counterexamples of that ubiquity. Who *constitutes* the non-wage or low-wage labor force facilitating global capitalist production—and how, and why, for example—is very different across regions, and those place-based distinctions can be documented, as they are in the comparison of tobacco and tea production in this chapter. James Peacock (2007) has looked at how place matters by examining the particular way in which globalization has played out in the U.S. South. Anna Tsing (2000) has argued that it may be just as big a mistake for scholars to endorse the concept of globalization unquestioningly as it was to endorse the project of modernity in an earlier era, an intellectual move that has now been critiqued. Place-based thinking can provide a conceptual lever similar to the role postcolonial theory provided in questioning the aims of modernity and just whom those aims benefited and valorized.

In talking about "placing," it is important to recognize active displacing (cf. Stewart 1996), just as it was important to recognize the active development of underdevelopment (Frank 1966) in relation to modernity. As Rodman states, "The most powerless people have no place at all" (1992, 650). Think of the homeless, the displaced, and those who are denied citizenship by *any* nation (as many of those forming the tea workforce in Sri Lanka, discussed later in this chapter, were for four generations). In an Appalachian example, Sasha Waters, in her 2003 film *Razing Appalachia,* documented Mrs. Weekley's family cemetery having been bulldozed as part of mountaintop removal mining by Arch Coal. She had no *place* to remember her mother. And when the overburden from the mining covered up the stream by which the Burgesses carved initials on trees in one generation and caught crawdads in another, all those family memories—part of what constitutes place and the stories that can be used to relate us to place—were gone. People can be marginalized not only by place, but also by *voice.* Place and voice are very much intertwined.

Economic and social marginalization is a common experience across many places, and it can be useful in contesting capitalism's inequitable logic and practice—as strategic essentialism (Spivak 1987)—to emphasize that shared global experience of marginalization at certain moments. In other moments, focusing on the unique ways in which power is organized in specific places becomes a useful strategy. As J. K. Gibson-Graham (2005, 132) wrote, "Place signifies the possibility of understanding local economies as *places* with highly specific economic identities and capacities rather than simply as *nodes* in a global capitalist system" (emphases in original). Local and global are both/and instead of either/or when it comes to citizens' actions. Saskia Sassen (2008, 371) refers to this as a "multiscalar politics of the local," and Wendy Harcourt (2003, 78) describes the particular kind of organizing that can be done across localities as "meshworks"—"created out of the interlocking of heterogeneous and diverse elements brought together because of complementarity or common experiences." Shirin Rai (2002) further advocates such work as a "politics of engagement" that can recognize the differences between activists who may have some convergent goals in addressing what they see as some of the negative effects of capitalist globalization. There has been increasing South-South organization of economic infrastructure, which W. E. B. DuBois and others advocated in the Pan-African Congresses of the first half of the twentieth century, as a way to destabilize neocolonial arcs of control of resources and labor forces considered dependent or marginal (or both) in the Europe- and U.S.-centered modernization era. Place-based counter-capitalist meshworks do not have to have completely similar identities or goals to work together—just some strategically convergent interests, exactly like capitalist business deals. John Gaventa (2001, 276), writing about global citizen action, has suggested that we turn around the saying "think globally, act locally" to *instead* "think locally" and "act globally." "Global action occurs," he says, "when citizens link across borders in *campaigns of mutual concern.*"

Organizing above and below the nation-state, as Hall (1988) alluded to, has been a strength of globalizing communication technologies and transnational social and political organization, *paralleling* the organization of linked economic processes that appear to cohere as "the global market" but are not nearly as coherent as the name suggests. Here are some examples of organizing above and below the nation-state. In Europe, the formation of the European Union gave Catalán and Basque regional communities a transnational forum for critiques of the Spanish nation-state. And the appeals of the Madres de la Plaza de Mayo in Argentina to the international community to bring pressure on the military dictatorship because of its human rights violations contributed to ending the murders and disappearances of Argentinians by their own government. Global communications can have a range of local effects that might be interpreted very differently according to one's vantage point. The current efforts to bring broadband Internet access to every county in Kentucky, for example, mean that mountaintop removal mining can be more readily documented for the national and international community on websites like ilovemountains.org, Amazon.com can build shipping warehouses in rural Kentucky, an Appalachian farmer can sell her organic tobacco to European consumers through the Internet, and workers for urban tech companies can telecommute from rural counties, perhaps displacing some local residents while others appreciate the influx of capital.

There are no blanket positive or negative effects here, and multiscalar processes as well as different discourses about what would benefit a region most are in play. Because a locality is also jurisdictionally part of a state and a nation-state, there can be conflicting goals—some of which reflect capitalist or noncapitalist (longer-term, place-based) logics. In several Kentucky counties over the past four decades, for example, local residents have fought to stop importing radioactive wastes to be disposed of (with inadequate safety measures) in garbage dumps in their communities, only to find out that legally they could *not* stop the flow of hazardous waste because it would have interfered with trans-state commerce laws put on the books over a century before for the benefit of the railroad barons laying rails across state lines. So the toxic garbage had special protection while the community members did not.

A place can be looked at through multiple scales of spatial and political jurisdiction, then, and also, of course, through multiple temporal scales. In Nicholas County, by looking at the census rolls over two hundred years, it is possible to think about the long history of connections to global economic organization and migration. Two major stories of global capitalist history in rural Kentucky have largely been erased in dominant community and textbook narratives. One involves the land grab by the new United States of Native American territory, from the Appalachian Mountains west, because the British Proclamation Line of 1763 recognizing Native American title to those lands was no longer honored after the Revolutionary War (see Dunaway 1995). Another major history is that of enslaved Africans in rural Kentucky. Although dominant narratives in Nicholas County assert that there was no slavery in eastern Kentucky, I found through archival research that one in six residents at the time of the county's founding was an enslaved Kentuckian and that in the hemp processing plant, one of the largest industries in the county in 1828, all thirty workers were enslaved (cf. Perrin 1882). "Placing" involves remembering that history, and so many others.

In the 1980s I used to sometimes drive around Nicholas County with older residents and a tape recorder to learn how every individual maps the same space differently. Even if we all live within the same political borders of a county, we may each live in a different *place,* because place is experiential. A stark example of that was when Ms. Lorrain Irvin pointed out a steep hillside to me one day, a pasture for cattle and, like much of the land, too steep to plow and not in woodlands, and said that she remembered quite a few families who used to live there. That whole small community was decimated by the 1918 flu epidemic, she said. Her memories made me see the county differently—concretizing that loss that I would never have mapped onto the landscape. All of us live in different places, but it is possible to weave strategic meshworks between us, through convergent goals. The reasons, however, may be very different—one person may want to organize local food systems because of worry about a carbon footprint, and another may want to do so because of fear of terrorists contaminating the food supply.

Residents of places that have occupied the national imagination as somehow "exceptional" face a great challenge when there is a need to appeal to national or international solidarity, as Lolis Eric Elie (2007), a metro columnist for the *Times-Picayune* who lost his home along with so many others in New Orleans after Hurricane Katrina, commented. He stated that people in other regions of the United States felt they were insulated from such slow responses by the federal government because they were more integral to the nation than New Orleans was, given its exceptional status—or "social apartness," as Martha Menchaca (1995) might put it. Appalachia shares that exceptional status in the U.S. imagination, as many have argued well (e.g., Batteau 1990), and that may be why responses across the United States to the destruction of Appalachian forest reserves and communities because of mountaintop removal mining have been far less intense than U.S. consumer demands to stop the destruction of Amazonian forest reserves and communities. Maybe selling "stop killing the mountains" coffee would help. Forming meshworks between marginalized regions within the United States—Native American nations' reservations, Appalachia, and Puerto Rico, for example—could constitute a useful forum. Similarly, forming meshworks between residents of Appalachia and Amazonia to appeal to the United Nations for the protection of biosphere reserves would exemplify collaboration above the level of the nation-state, as has happened in the European Union.

In Appalachian studies, as in Native American studies, African American studies, and Latino/a studies, there have long been excellent critiques of exceptionalist narratives, of the attribution of economic inequality to cultural rather than structural or relational factors, and of the pernicious persistence of stereotypes (cf. Billings, Norman, and Ledford 1999). Within that body of critical literature is the noting, again and again, that there is tremendous diversity within any category of identity. In Appalachia, for example, the urban tends to drop out of representation of the region in popular culture even though the urban population is larger than the rural population, according to the Appalachian Regional Commission (www.arc .gov/appalachian_region/TheAppalachianRegion.asp). Turner and Cabbell's 1985 volume, *Blacks in Appalachia,* countered dominant representations of Appalachians in popular culture as white, and there have been other similar interventions, but those homogeneous depictions have persisted. In a parallel example of regional stereotyping, when I was studying NAFTA, some U.S. listeners would not believe me when I said that Mexico's impetus in promoting NAFTA was to attract Mexican millionaires back to the Mexican market from investing in the European Union; it was hard for them to imagine Mexican millionaires, given the widespread images in the United States of low-wage Mexican workers poised on the border to invade this country and steal jobs as soon as NAFTA was passed. Such regional imaginaries go in many directions, and they can be deterrents to the kind of "campaigns of mutual concern" John Gaventa referred to, which are vital in relation to globalization. One way to study the ways in which place-based notions of identity are constructed and contested is to look at how people navigate them in border zones.

A Tobacco Town on the Edge of Appalachia

Nicholas County, Kentucky, where I've been listening to stories about globalization for more than thirty years, is on the *edge* of Appalachia, where that region meets the Outer Bluegrass. In ecology, edge zones are the most productive of biomass—where a forest meets a meadow, for example, or in an estuarial wetland between a river and the ocean. In terms of human places, edge zones can either have lots of options for being "placed"—to strategic advantage—or be marginalized on all sides. Nicholas County is on a bioregional border in a border state. Kentuckians, in conversation, might "place" ourselves as Southerners, Northerners, or Midwesterners, depending on the social context. Similarly, Nicholas Countians might "place" ourselves in the Bluegrass or in Appalachia, depending on the circumstances. I have been told by local realtors that wealthy people from the Bluegrass buy land in Nicholas County to have a place to hunt in Appalachia, and wealthy people from Appalachia buy land in Nicholas County to have a place in the Bluegrass to pasture horses. Nicholas Countians go on mission trips to Appalachia up in the mountains, and Ohio young people come on mission trips to Appalachia in Nicholas County. Being on the edge like that makes it possible to see the contingency of place, and how political even the constitution of what we think of as bioregions can be. In 2008 the U.S. Congress legislated that Nicholas County belongs to Appalachia, and the county became party to the Appalachian Regional Commission, or the ARC. This took a good deal of lobbying, and the county judge-executive was assisted in this bid by the staff of the Bluegrass Area Development District; being placed as part of Appalachia came about through working the edges, much as many Nicholas Countians might supplement cash-based activities with non-cash resources found in the fencerows, like blackberries to make into jam and sell at farmers' markets or cedar trees to take to the next county and sell to be made into pet litter. Being on the edge can also mean edgy, as in contesting the ways in which one is constructed.

What does it mean to Nicholas Countians to be part of Appalachia? Many are not aware of the change in status from outside to inside the ARC. For most residents of the region, county identity is most salient, and *Appalachian* is just not an identity label in use. Counties are not only significant for identity, but they are very discrete economic and political units—thinking regionally has not been common practice. There have been periods when the state has encouraged competition between counties, and some periods when cross-county cooperation has been encouraged. An example of the former was the All-Kentucky Cities competition, which served to compile information about county resources and workforces as part of a larger state-led development discourse focused on attracting industrial investment to the state. An example of the latter are the Area Development Districts providing support for seeking grants for infrastructure, including ones through the ARC. There is an infrastructure crisis in many rural Kentucky counties, as water systems and other systems go bankrupt because the small tax bases of each county cannot support them, so regional collaboration is on the rise these days. Recently, the hospital in Nicholas County, which had been autonomous for sixty years, was first taken over by a regional health-care network and then closed. Residents have to go to another county to seek that level of care. The U.S. government, which has not had a strong record since the New

Deal era of investing in regional strategies, has recently increased funding through the Appalachian Regional Commission for regional communications and marketing networks. The ARC co-chair, Earl Gohl, remarked, "Initiatives like these build the region's entrepreneurial ecosystem and contribute to making Appalachia the next great investment opportunity in America" (Sebastian and Brislin 2015).

If you go to the website of the Appalachian Regional Commission (arc. gov) and look up the latest economic map (e.g., Appalachian Regional Commission 2016), you will see the counties recognized as Appalachian counties by the ARC, spread across thirteen contiguous states in the eastern half of the United States. On the one hand, the ARC gives these counties a political entity to belong to beyond the state, which could mean leverage, as in the Basques appealing to the European Union; on the other, it imposes a problematic modernist developmental framing of county identities. Nicholas County is on the edge. On these multicolor maps portraying economic status, the red counties are called "distressed"—they are clustered into what the ARC calls "the worst 10% of U.S. counties" in terms of economic status, and that crimson cluster is strongest in eastern Kentucky and at the very southwestern edge of the ARC-defined Appalachian region, in Mississippi. The "at-risk" counties are in peach—they're seen as the lowest performing 10–25 percent of U.S. counties, according to multiple economic indicators, and they tend to be scattered around the red counties. The counties in white are labeled "transitional"—or ready for "take off," to use Rostow's (1962) developmental terminology for the stages nations go through in globalization. Those counties portrayed in white are clustered largely in Pennsylvania and New York. The light blue counties are called "competitive," belonging to the highest performing 10–25 percent of U.S. counties economically, and the darker blue counties are labeled by the ARC "attainment" counties, having *attained* economic development and belonging to the "best 10% of U.S. counties" economically. The blue counties tend to be urban areas within the Appalachian region. This discussion of county economies reflects participation in *cash* economies and does not reflect many other resources, including knowledge, use of non-cash resources, barter economies, and social resources like kin-based child care.

There are many ways in which this annually produced map could be discussed. The citizens in the *rest* of the counties of each of these states have benefited from profits from resource extraction or global capitalist participation in the areas seen as most "remote" and "distressed" in the core of the

Appalachian region, which can turn the development of underdevelopment sideways: those in what are constructed as the economically "developed" regions of each state marginalizing Appalachian counties socially may have actually been *less* tied to the global economy than the Appalachian counties. The development of underdevelopment, as André Gunder Frank argued, is an *active,* not a *passive* process. As Jane Nadel-Klein suggests (1991, 502), global economic processes have *made* local communities in many places: "I suggest that it might be helpful to look at localism not as paradox but as irony: global processes call localities into existence, but make no commitments to their continued survival. The irony lies in the fact that the local identity is an unintended result of the global division of labor.... An explicit link between place and political economy enables us to see how localism remains a highly salient, creative category, not merely a plaint to be invoked on behalf of those who live in out-of-the-way places."

We can think about this in relation to John Sayles's 1987 film *Matewan,* which shows that international migrant communities were intentionally brought in to constitute transnational towns of workers for the coal companies. Their language barriers were probably imagined by the management as a way to reduce the chances of labor organizing, but many workers brought with them, of course, international labor organizing ideologies and strategies. As mentioned in the introduction to this volume, one group of workers from Hungary organized a coal-mining community as a worker collective, in stark contrast to the corporate-owned coal camps around them.

On the ARC map, as I noted, the majority of the "distressed" counties of Appalachia, flagged in red, are in Kentucky. The first interpretation of this concentration that might spring to mind, on the basis of popular culture, would be that these are the counties most affected by global resource extraction through participation in the coal industry. My own interpretation is that the counties of Kentucky are smaller in size and population than those in most of the region and cannot sustain an economy and infrastructure at that scale. Billings and Blee argue in *The Road to Poverty* (2000, 207)—their long-term analysis of Clay County, Kentucky—that these counties became "distressed" through reliance on subsistence agriculture that could not quite support all households, thus creating a surplus labor force of low-wage workers. Still, agriculture has been a consistent activity in eastern Kentucky. Of the forty-five ARC counties in Kentucky producing burley tobacco in 1997, thirty-six were "distressed." In other words, the vast majority of "distressed" counties in Kentucky were producing burley tobacco for the global market.

In 1997, according to an ARC report (Wood 1998, 7), Kentucky produced 63 percent of the burley tobacco grown in the United States, and 33 percent of that burley crop in Kentucky was grown in Appalachian counties. Nicholas County has been one of the major burley-producing counties by small-scale producers, meaning that instead of huge, full-time tobacco farms that consolidated a lot of leased land when the federal tobacco program applied (now phased out under the federal tobacco buyout authorized by H.R. 4520), Nicholas Countians produced a lot of burley tobacco in small plots of a few acres on the tops of ridges or in river bottoms as part of a mixed livelihood strategy. That strategy has also included working in the textile and garment factories until they closed, or commuting to jobs in other counties (in the Toyota assembly plant, for instance).

Talking Futures in the Shadow of Tobacco and Tea Leaves

Commodity studies have been a common way to study capitalist globalization since Sidney Mintz (1985) studied sugar. There are resonances between the totalizing strategies controlling workers' lives and labor in the coal camps and the way Mintz describes the British capitalists investing in both the early textile mills and the colonial plantations on which stimulants—coffee, tea, tobacco, and sugar—were produced that were used to facilitate workers adapting to repetitive, boring, long days of factory work and encouraging worker indebtedness through paying them in gin and scrip.

In my long-term research, I have followed the low-wage labor forces in two marginalized mountain regions that produce two of these stimulant crops for today's low-wage workforces in the global factory. Workers in Appalachia produce tobacco for a growing global market for cigarettes—in China, for example. Workers in Sri Lanka produce tea for export, to Bangladesh, for example, where—as in China—the bulk of garment factory growth has been since the expiration of the MultiFibre Arrangement in 2005. How are the working conditions in Appalachia for the global tobacco industry and the working conditions in the hill country of Sri Lanka for the global tea industry similar, and how are they different? How does "place matter" in the comparison?

One way to situate people and place in relation to the production of these two global commodities, tea and tobacco, is historically. Early Kentuckians, reliant on river travel, considered seceding from the Union and becoming part of Spain to make it easier to get tobacco and other products to global consumers by going downriver to eventually travel the Mississippi to the Spanish-controlled port of New Orleans, instead of the more difficult prospect of taking the hogsheads of tobacco over the mountains and east (Shannon 1976, 28). Thomas D. Clark, in his book *Agrarian Kentucky* (1977, 15–16), describes this river traffic and commodity trade two centuries ago:

> By the turn of the nineteenth century the rapidly expanding com-
> modities trade returned almost $2.25 million. . . . While farmers,
> housewives, distillers, and cordwainers produced growing mounds
> of commodities, untrained boatwrights labored about creek mouths
> fitting and mauling green timbers into tightly caulked cargo boxes
> to transport those farm products downstream. The lumbering west-
> ern river "arks" were made of heavy, sawn timber pegged together
> with wooden pins and gaping seams rammed tight with hempen
> oakum. . . . The Kentucky boats were laded with corn in the shuck
> and in barrels, tobacco packed in 1200 pound hogsheads, whiskey,
> brandy, and cider royal, hempen rope and bagging, salt port, tubs
> of lard, piggins of butter, hides, barrels of soap, and tons of flour.
> Each passing year the country boats grew larger and more elaborate.

Participating in a global market is nothing new for Kentuckians. As part of colonial Virginia, tobacco served as a currency across the Atlantic, and early Kentuckians—as noted—were trying to figure out whether to link up to the global commodity trade through Spain or England. Kentucky has always been engaged in global networks, trading early in both tobacco and the enslaved Africans who constituted part of the labor force for its production.

Comparative historical research makes it easier to see that long-term patterns in the organization of the agricultural sector in particular places are related to global conversations among transnational political and economic elites. One of the major long-term patterns that I have seen transnationally, and that is relevant to the production of tobacco and tea, is the shift from privatization to nationalization (or at least protectionist policies) and repri-vatization over the past century and a half.

In Mexico, a century ago, President Porfirio Díaz believed—much like the Nicholas County head of the Chamber of Commerce I mentioned ear-lier—that the future of economic well-being for his community (national, in this case) lay in attracting capital investment from elsewhere. So he invited European capitalists to buy large tracts of land, which became export plantations. The Mexican Revolution resulting in the new constitution of 1917 was largely about reorganizing land ownership and establishing a more place-based orientation of the economy. Workers who had had little option but to work for subsistence wages or less on the foreign-owned plantations now had access to nationalized and community-controlled *ejido* plots for subsistence agriculture so they would have more livelihood options and would not again have to constitute a dependent labor force for the global market. To make way for NAFTA, in 1993, *ejido* lands were reprivatized—along with many state-owned industries—in keeping with a neoliberal capitalist logic of development through the free market.

If we compare this cycle of nationalization and reprivatization with tobacco production in Kentucky, there are some similarities. While President Porfirio Díaz was courting transnational capital in Mexico, the American Tobacco Company (or the Tobacco Trust)—established in 1899 by James Buchanan Duke—was becoming a monopoly in the transnational tobacco trade, in which Kentucky burley (2 million pounds of it, in 1890) was mixed with tobacco produced in Turkey and other nations and sold to global consumers of tobacco. When the trust became a monopoly, it started lowering the prices paid to producers of tobacco, and—just as in Mexico—there was popular revolt. In 1908 burley tobacco producers went on strike. The strike was first announced in Nicholas County, and it became what Tracy Campbell (1992, 77) has called "the only large-scale agricultural strike in America." Thirty-five thousand farmers refused to plant their tobacco crops. Antitrust legislation broke up the tobacco monopolies in 1911 enough for prices to begin increasing for small-scale tobacco farmers. The populism of this era, largely erased in Kentucky history, was recorded in the landscape. My grandfather, who grew up as one of over a dozen children in a tenant-farming household producing tobacco crops in Nicholas County, told me that early in the twentieth century there were local tobacco warehouses: one was called the Red Star Warehouse, and another was called The People's Warehouse.

When the Depression hit the United States, the 1933 federal Agricultural Adjustment Act, the 1938 Farm Price Stabilization Program, and the Federal Commodity Credit Corporation set up what was known by participants as the tobacco program, or the quota system. Tobacco production was not nationalized, but it had a regulated market protecting small farmers from getting too low a price for tobacco, the point being to keep them on their land through the Depression and beyond. And the quota system (first tying production levels to acreage, then to poundage) ensured that many farmers would be getting *some* cash income from tobacco rather than one or two growers taking over *all* the production. That tobacco program lasted until the 1998 Master Settlement Agreement and the Fair and Equitable Tobacco Reform Act of 2004, which reprivatized the tobacco industry so that farmers are once again directly contracting with multinational tobacco companies, much as they did a century ago. My point here is that tobacco policy and its effects on the edge of Appalachia—transferring most of the market risk to the lowest-wage workers in the industry—is related to much larger global capitalist patterns, paralleling privatization, nationalization, and reprivatization in Mexico, and also in Sri Lanka.

Here is a brief overview of the tea industry in Sri Lanka, and how conditions compare with tobacco production in Appalachian Kentucky. Sri Lanka, an island nation off the southern tip of India, was colonized by the Portuguese, then the Dutch, and then the British, as Ceylon; it remained a British colony until independence in 1948. Its strategic importance to global trade in the colonial era was as a port on the European-Asian trade route, and as a producer as well in the spice trade. Pepper and cinnamon are still grown in small quantities for export, and rubber and coconut plantations have waned in significance with the restructuring of those industries. The main British colonial plantation was coffee until there was a coffee blight, and then tea, which has to be grown at least six hundred feet above sea level, so tea plantations were established in the central Upcountry, or mountain, region. By 1933, the year the Agricultural Adjustment Act was passed in the United States establishing the federal tobacco program, there were 478,000 acres of tea being grown in the Upcountry of Sri Lanka for the global market (providing stimulants, as Kentuckians were, for people all around the world), and the 400,000 workers in the labor-intensive tea crop in Ceylon were indentured Tamil laborers from India. As is the case in many postcolonial nations, the demographics of Sri Lanka are related to its colonial history; the majority of Sri Lankans identify as Sinhalese (speaking the Sinhalese language and being primarily Buddhist), and Tamils are the main minority group (speaking the Tamil language, shared with much of southern India, and identifying mostly as Hindu); the other minority groups are Muslim and Christian. Upcountry Tamils, discriminated against by lowcountry Tamils, trace their history to the many indentured laborers the British brought (often under deceptive contracts) to work on the plantations in the mountains, their lodgings and right to work and travel being owned by the company. At the time of independence, the Sri Lankan constitution established

Buddhism as the state religion, and the Sinhalese ethnicity and language as primary national identities. The ethnic war lasting from the early 1980s until 2009 was largely between the Sinhalese majority and Tamil minority over the possibility of a separate Tamil state in the north and east of the island.

The indenture contracts were moving workers between India and Ceylon, both British colonies, but when India and Sri Lanka became independent, *neither* state wanted to grant citizenship to the Tamil labor force on Sri Lankan tea plantations—India did not want to repatriate them because they had almost no capital or property, and the Sri Lankan Sinhalese majority did not want to grant more minority Tamils voting rights. So most of the Upcountry Tamil population remained stateless for four generations, being offered the option of Sri Lankan citizenship only a few years ago. Because tea plantations have been total institutions, Upcountry Tamils were considered the property or wards of the estates into the twenty-first century, and if the estate management was sloppy, there might be whole communities with no records of births, marriages, or deaths, so establishing citizenship has been a challenge for some.

Like Appalachian tobacco growers, workers in the Sri Lankan tea industry are producing a bulk product; the value-added processing happens elsewhere—only instead of its happening in, say, coastal North Carolina, tea is being packaged and advertised by Lipton (a major buyer) outside the country altogether, and that is where the bulk of the money in the tea industry is, too. In 2003 Sri Lanka produced 310 million kilos of bulk, processed tea. It takes 4.5 kilos of green leaf to make 1 kilo of bulk tea for the global market, where it sells for $1.80 or so. A company like Lipton increases the value of tea by eight times just by packaging and distributing it on the world market. Of the tea grown in Sri Lanka, 90 percent is for export. "A commodity that was alluring because of its very distance from the familiar would be slowly transformed into the signifier of a quotidian and very English definition of civil manners, genteel taste: the penultimate icon of civilization itself. Indeed, hidden in such consummate navigations from 'strange' to 'familiar' are the histories of empire: the mappings of exoticism, the continuous struggles over symbol and sign, and the cultural cartographies of conquest" (Chatterjee 2001, 21).

As Piya Chatterjee notes, the British tea habit depended on the work of colonial producers. Today, tea is among the top three sources of foreign capital in Sri Lanka. The others are garment manufacturing and remittances from domestic workers, mostly migrating to Middle Eastern countries. As one retired Sri Lankan planter said to me, the nation's economy rests on the backs of its women, since women are the primary labor force in all three of those industries.

The tea plant is a bush, *Camellia thea,* related to the camellia. A secret that Chinese growers guarded from British buyers for some years before the British got plants and started plantations themselves is that green tea, black tea, orange pekoe, and other kinds of tea all come from the same plant. The difference is in the way it is rolled, cut, and dried in processing. The bushes can live for around a century, and among managers in the Sri Lankan tea industry, one complaint is that the nation's tea bushes are old and cannot compete with the younger, productive bushes in the newer tea industry in Kenya and the tea industry in Vietnam, newer still. One tea industry official worried, in an interview I did with him, about what a free trade agreement would enable in terms of the "mixing" and labeling of different nation's tea leaves: "Under this agreement, people can bring low-quality tea as bulk from India and other countries and mix and send them back to other countries as Ceylon tea. That is a danger. That kind of threat is there." I have heard such statements (some more overtly xenophobic than others) about threats to the national purity of the crop in conversations with people in both the Sri Lankan tea industry and the U.S. tobacco industry.

In Sri Lanka, women workers on tea estates pluck only the new growth from the top of the bushes and throw them into the sacks on their backs. They pick to meet a quota, or "norm," and are paid under two dollars (U.S.) a day for picking between twelve and twenty-five kilos (or sixty pounds) of tea leaves. When there is a drought, there is no new growth, and women do not get paid. In the Hinduism practiced on the tea estates, Amman, goddess of water, is the principal deity. She is said to have come as an indentured worker from India and to care for the residents of the tea estates. Tea pluckers may be the only wage earners in their families. When the tea estates were nationalized in the 1970s, men were given jobs on the estates as well, doing soil stabilization and replacing the tea bushes. With reprivatization of the tea estates in 1992, viable estates were purchased by investors and nonviable estates were taken under state management because of the resident labor forces. Workers told me that the nationalized era was better, since they had better benefits, food distribution, clinics, and schools on the estates in those days. With reprivatization, men and boys generally migrate long distances to urban centers to work in the backs of restaurants or driving trishaws, and women have become a captive labor force for garment factories built in very remote areas beside tea estates, which is comparable to the low-wage, farm-based female labor force for small garment factories built across Appalachia in the mid-twentieth century. Women working in the textile industry in both Kentucky and Sri Lanka have been affected by the end of the Multi-Fibre Arrangement, as factories suddenly closed in the twenty-first century.

One woman living on a tea estate and working in a garment factory explained to me in 2004 the dilemma faced by many low-wage workers across the world who do not earn a living wage: "However we work . . . the salary will be the same: 121 rupees per day. Salary is 121 rupees, but a packet of baby formula is 140 rupees, so one day's salary is not enough to feed the baby. We can't give nutrition to our children." A tea agricultural extension worker told me that he thought Sri Lanka had made a mistake investing in industries like garment factories rather than value-added agricultural industries, since agriculture was the basis of the nation's production. Some are starting to believe that about Appalachia, in place-based economic planning facilitated, for example, by the Community Farm Alliance in Kentucky, and some young people are exploring innovative ways to make a living in sustainable agriculture (such as partnering with elders for non-cash transfer of farm land and niche marketing, which remains, however, fairly limited by proximity to consumers, investment capital, and debt loads—especially student loans).

I was told by many middle-aged managers and researchers in the tea industry that the industry would be in crisis because young people in rural areas would choose not to enter into agricultural work, opting for computer or factory jobs in cities instead. At the time I was talking with people about globalization in Sri Lanka, youth unemployment was high—over 30 percent—and there were very high rates of youth suicide. I organized a workshop in which young people from the tea estates gathered to talk (in three languages) about their views of the future. Some talked about feeling abandoned by the state, as there were no schools or clinics in their tea-growing communities. Many said they would like to stay in their communities to start common welfare programs (called *shramadhana*), and that they would prefer living and working in the agricultural sector if they were paid a living wage and had job security. They saw their communities as a resource, particularly what they saw as their unique Upcountry Tamil culture, like the Amman temples.

Hearing from the young people in the tea sector about their views of the future made me want to hear what young people in Nicholas County had to say about the future, given the restructuring of the global tobacco industry, so I sponsored an essay contest in Nicholas County for seventh, eighth, and ninth graders on their views of the future of their rural community. Like the young people in the tea sector of Sri Lanka, they stressed—in so many words—the beyond-the-market value of social capital (discussed by many scholars of Appalachia, including Billings and Blee, 2000). Ashlee Garcia, for example, wrote: "Nicholas County may not be the best place to work, but it is a great place to live. Most people would say that this town depends on its agriculture, but that isn't entirely true. . . . The future of our county depends on our residents. . . . The adults aren't the only ones who can change the future; the young adults and children can even help, because the young adults and children are the future" (quoted in Kingsolver 2011, 165–166).

To sum up the comparison of the Appalachian tobacco sector and Sri Lankan tea sector and invoke agency in an unusual heuristic, I believe we could think in Nadel-Klein's terms of the global commodity distributing the workforce on the landscape in both instances. Tobacco, as a major cash crop, organized many small communities along rivers and railroads in Appalachia, and the fairly captive labor force—like the workers on the tea estates in Sri Lanka—then supplied low-wage, often female labor for small factories in the garment sector as it moved through both contexts in its own global restructuring. Both workforces have been controlled through othering in some ways, through cultural citizenship, national citizenship, regional or ethnic stereotypes, and more. As both labor forces are no longer needed for tobacco, tea, or garment production, displacement is growing: through outmigration for work in other regions (women internationally and men domestically, in Sri Lanka), sending back remittances, taking on the risks of direct contracting with the global agricultural commodity industries on even more marginal land, and (in Kentucky) participation in what is arguably the largest economic sector: the informal drug economy. There is agency, certainly, in the ways that people make sense of and manage their engagement with the global, but the structural forces at play are so often rendered invisible in popular accounts of rural upland regions, like a recent popular television show implying that West Virginia schoolchildren were obese because they just did not make good decisions about food and exercise. Community organizations have become expert in using the language of childhood obesity and type 2 diabetes to access the funding stream from federal agencies that somehow is unavailable to address injustices like toxic sludge being dumped next to schools or potential rockfalls above schools created through mountaintop removal mining.

Finally, to address the imagined futures on the edge of Appalachia in this chapter's title, Nicholas Countians have tried and are trying a number of different strategies. Tobacco has been so entwined with identity and the organization of the local economy (drugstore bills, for example, being paid when the tobacco checks came in), even when cattle production largely subsidized tobacco production, that it seemed unlikely twenty-five years ago that a tobacco town could become, say, a tomato town. But there are a few large-scale fresh vegetable operations in the county, a growing number of farmers' markets and certified farmstands, and community-supported agriculture (most subscriptions come from urban centers). There is also some custom farming for the inner Bluegrass, such as supplying hay for horse farms. I see a strong tendency to commodify rurality, through urban residents wanting to purchase a piece of "community" by buying land in Nicholas County. Amish communities have grown in Nicholas County, and there is an exchange of agricultural knowledge and products between long-term residents and newcomers. Some local artisans are using the Internet to organize with other artisans across the region to find global markets. The commodification of history, through tourism in an out-of-the-way place (literally, since the residents of Carlisle, the county seat of Nicholas County, did not allow the highway to come through many years ago, thus by accident preserving its historical town square), has also been a strong discourse in community development plans. Those wanting to attract industries to occupy the empty factory buildings vacated when the underwear company left town have not had been able to find one single large employer to fill the space, but there are smaller local groups renting sections of the space, such as a beer cheese company. There is a small, successful machining shop that supplies the Toyota plant, two counties over. A number of farmers commute to Toyota, and they say it keeps them in farming.

An advantage of studying globalization through one county is seeing historical patterns and following multiple discourses and voices closely, as Billings and Blee (2000) also found in their research on Clay County, but the disadvantage is the loss of regional perspective. As I mentioned, county social and political identity is strong in Kentucky. One businesswoman in Nicholas County told me in 1999, "It seems like Kentucky could progress more socially and maybe economically, if they had less counties and more people grouped together.... Everybody is like a different little country over the border." With the unusually high number of counties in the state, the relatively small number of people living in each rural county makes it is difficult to provide basic infrastructure, or to have the scale of services for (and collective organizing by) those with special needs, gender-questioning or transitioning youth, and returning veterans with PTSD, for example, or multilingual services. Online collectives are one way to share experiences and services across county borders, but they can only go so far. As a place-based strategy, I think it is an interesting moment for cross-county planning—as rural workers migrate to urban centers for work and urban workers migrate to rural communities to live, for example. Like local/global, county/region is not an either/or, but a both/and. Area development districts and ARC regional identities may not capture the imagination of residents strongly, but other cross-county collaborations might.

Small towns do not seem to me to be dying out in Kentucky, even if the labor forces have outlived their purposes for particular global commodities like labor-intensive tobacco, coal, and garment production. During the 2008 economic crisis, a number of Nicholas Countians moved home because the social capital made a difference in their ability to piece together a livelihood in challenging times. Community matters, place matters, and diversity matters in the voices included in imagining the future of places like Nicholas County. Planning processes need to take into account the full formal and informal sectors (including remittances from outmigrants and the economic significance of the underground drug trade, for example), and *all* stakeholders—not just those of a certain literacy or class status, or racialized, ethnic, religious, gender, or linguistic identity. These are challenges that are easily mentioned but not easily addressed, but like Ashlee Garcia, I believe that by including young people as stakeholders in thinking about the future, it is possible to at least have that conversation.

References

Agbola, Tunde, and Moruf Alabi. 2003. "Political Economy of Petroleum Resource Development, Environmental Injustice and Selective Victimization: A Case Study of the Niger Delta Region of Nigeria." In *Just Sustainabilities: Development in an Unequal World*, edited by Julian Agyeman, Robert D. Bullard, and Bob Evans, 269–288. London: Earthscan Publications.

Appalachian Regional Commission. 2016. "County Economic Status by County, Fiscal Year 2017." Map. Accessed June 17, 2016. www.arc.gov/research/MapsofAppalachia.asp?MAP_ID=116.

Batteau, Allen W. 1990. *The Invention of Appalachia*. Tucson: University of Arizona Press.

Billings, Dwight B., and Kathleen M. Blee. 2000. *The Road to Poverty: The Making of Wealth and Hardship in Appalachia*. Cambridge: Cambridge University Press.

Billings, Dwight B., Gurney Norman, and Katherine Ledford, eds. 1999. *Back Talk from Appalachia: Confronting Stereotypes*. Lexington: University Press of Kentucky.

Blunt, Alison, and Gillian Rose, eds. 1994. *Writing Women and Space: Colonial and Postcolonial Geographies*. New York: Guilford Press.

Campbell, Tracy. 1992. "The Limits of Agrarian Action: The 1908 Kentucky Tobacco Strike." *Agricultural History* 66: 76–97.

Chatterjee, Piya. 2001. *A Time for Tea: Women, Labor, and Post/Colonial Politics on an Indian Plantation*. Durham, NC: Duke University Press.

Clark, Thomas D. 1977. *Agrarian Kentucky*. Lexington: University Press of Kentucky.

Dirlik, Arif. 2001. "Place-Based Imagination: Globalism and the Politics of Place." In *Places and Politics in an Age of Globalization*, edited by Roxann Prazniak and Arif Dirlik, 15–52. Lanham, MD: Rowman & Littlefield Publishers.

———. 1996. "The Global in the Local." In *Global/Local: Cultural Production and the Transnational Imaginary*, edited by Rob Wilson and Wimal Dissanayake, 21–45. Durham, NC: Duke University Press.

Dunaway, Wilma.1995. "Speculators and Settler Capitalists: Unthinking the Mythology about Appalachian Landholding, 1790–1860." In *Appalachia in the Making: The Mountain South in the Nineteenth Century*, edited by Mary Beth Pudup, Dwight B. Billings, and Altina L. Waller, 50–75. Chapel Hill: University of North Carolina Press.

Elie, Lolis Eric. 2007. Remarks at the meeting of the Society for the Anthropology of North America, New Orleans, April.

Escobar, Arturo. 2001a. "Culture Sits in Places: Reflections on Globalism and Subaltern Strategies of Localization." *Political Geography* 20: 139–174.

———. 2001b. "Place, Economy, and Culture in a Post-development Era." In *Places and Politics in an Age of Globalization*, edited by Roxann Prazniak and Arif Dirlik, 193–218. Lanham, MD: Rowman & Littlefield Publishers.

Frank, André Gunder. 1966. *The Development of Underdevelopment*. New York: Monthly Review Press.

Frank, Dana. 2000. *Buy American: The Untold Story of Economic Nationalism*. Boston: Beacon Press.

Friedman, Milton. 1962. *Capitalism and Freedom*. Chicago: University of Chicago Press.

Gaventa, John. 2001. "Global Citizen Action: Lessons and Challenges." In *Global Citizen Action*, edited by Michael Edwards and John Gaventa, 275–288. Boulder, CO: Lynne Rienner Publishers.

Gibson-Graham, J. K. 2005. "Building Community Economies: Women and the Politics of Place." In *Women and the Politics of Place*, edited by Wendy Harcourt and Arturo Escobar, 130–157. Bloomfield, CT: Kumarian Press.

———. 1996. *The End of Capitalism (As We Knew It): A Feminist Critique of Political Economy*. Oxford: Blackwell Publishers.

Guha, Ramachandra. 1989. *The Unquiet Woods: Ecological Change and Peasant Resistance in the Himalaya*. Delhi: Oxford University Press.

Hall, Stuart. 1988. "The Local and the Global: Globalization and Ethnicity." In *Culture, Globalization and the World System: Contemporary Conditions for the Representation of Identity*, edited by Anthony King, 19–39. Minneapolis: University of Minnesota Press.

Harcourt, Wendy. 2003. "The Impact of Transnational Discourses on Local Community Organizing." *Development* 46.1: 74–79.

Harvey, David. 1996. *Justice, Nature and the Geography of Difference*. Malden, MA: Blackwell.

———. 1991. *The Condition of Postmodernity*. Malden, MA: Wiley-Blackwell.

Kingsolver, Ann E. 2015. "Farming the Edges: Women's Natural Resource Management on Small Farms in Eastern Kentucky." In *Gender, Livelihood and Environment: How Women Manage Resources*, edited by Subhadra Mitra Channa and Marilyn Porter, 50–75. Delhi: Orient Blackswan.

———. 2011. *Tobacco Town Futures: Global Encounters in Rural Kentucky*. Long Grove, IL: Waveland Press.

———. 2010. "Talk of 'Broken Borders' and Stone Walls: Anti-immigration Discourse and Legislation from California to South Carolina." *Southern Anthropologist* 35.1: 21–40.

———. 2007. "Farmers and Farmworkers: Two Centuries of Strategic Alterity in Kentucky's Tobacco Fields." *Critique of Anthropology* 27.1: 87–102.

———. 2001. *NAFTA Stories: Fears and Hopes in Mexico and the United States*. Boulder, CO: Lynne Rienner Publishers.

———. 1992. "Contested Livelihoods: 'Placing' One Another in 'Cedar,' Kentucky." *Anthropological Quarterly* 65: 128–136.

Lewellen, Ted C. 2002. *The Anthropology of Globalization: Cultural Anthropology Enters the 21st Century*. New York: Praeger.

Massey, Doreen. 1994. *Space, Place, and Gender*. Minneapolis: University of Minnesota Press.

Menchaca, Martha. 1995. *The Mexican Outsiders: A Community History of Marginalization and Discrimination in California*. Austin: University of Texas Press.

Mendes, Chico, with Tony Gross. 1989. *Fight for the Forest: Chico Mendes in His Own Words*. London: Latin America Bureau.

Mintz, Sidney W. 1985. *Sweetness and Power: The Place of Sugar in Modern History*. New York: Viking.

Nadel-Klein, Jane. 1991. "Reweaving the Fringe: Localism, Tradition, and Representation in British Ethnography." *American Ethnologist* 18.3: 500–517.

Narayan, Kirin. 1993. "How Native Is a 'Native' Anthropologist?" *American Anthropologist* 95: 671–686.

Pancake, Catherine, producer and director. 2006. *Black Diamonds: Mountaintop Removal and the Fight for Coalfield Justice.* Oley, PA: Bullfrog Films.

Peacock, James. 2007. *Grounded Globalism: How the U.S. South Embraces the World.* Athens: University of Georgia Press.

Perrin, William Henry, ed. 1882. *History of Bourbon, Scott, Harrison and Nicholas Counties, Kentucky.* Chicago: O. L. Baskin & Co.

Proust, Marcel. 1948 [1896]. *Pleasures and Regrets.* Translated by Louise Varèse. New York: Crown Publishers.

Rai, Shirin M. 2002. *Gender and the Political Economy of Development.* Cambridge, U.K.: Polity Press.

Rajaee, Farhang. 2000. *Globalization on Trial: The Human Condition and the Information Civilization.* W. Hartford, CT: Kumarian Press.

Rodman, Margaret C. 1992. "Empowering Place: Multilocality and Multivocality." *American Anthropologist* 94: 640–656.

Rostow, W. W. 1962. *The Five Stages of Economic Growth.* London: Cambridge University Press.

Rushing, Wanda. 2009. *Memphis and the Paradox of Place: Globalization in the American South.* Chapel Hill: University of North Carolina Press.

Sassen, Saskia. 2008. *Territory, Authority, Rights: From Medieval to Global Assemblages.* Updated ed. Princeton: Princeton University Press.

Sayles, John. 1987. *Matewan.* New York: Cinecom International Films.

Sebastian, Terry, and Jennifer Brislin. 2015. "Kentucky Receives $6 Million in Federal Grants; Portion of Funding to Support E-commerce Opportunities, Training for Broadband." Accessed June 24, 2016. http://kentucky.gov/Pages/Activity-Stream.aspx?viewMode=ViewDetailInNewPage&eventID={07940 EAA-6BAE-42CE-B834-BD9E888D3B2B}&activityType=PressRelease.

Shannon, Jasper B. 1976. "Nicholas County in General." In *History of Nicholas County,* edited by Joan Wessinger Conley, 23–45. Carlisle, KY: Nicholas County Historical Society.

Spivak, Gayatri Chakravorty. 1987. *In Other Worlds: Essays in Cultural Politics.* London: Routledge.

Stewart, Kathleen. 1996. *A Space on the Side of the Road: Cultural Politics in an "Other" America.* Princeton: Princeton University Press.

TamilNet. 2005. "Navalady—A Village Turned Graveyard." January 8. Accessed June 21, 2016. www.tamilnet.com/art.html?artid=13910&catid=79.

Tsing, Anna. 2000. "The Global Situation." *Cultural Anthropology* 15.3: 327–360.

Turner, William H., and Edward J. Cabbell, eds. 1985. *Blacks in Appalachia*. Lexington: University Press of Kentucky.

Waters, Sasha. 2003. *Razing Appalachia*. Oley, PA: Bullfrog Films.

Wilson, Rob, and Wimal Dissanayake. 1996. "Introduction: Tracking the Global/Local." In *Global/Local: Cultural Production and the Transnational Imaginary*, edited by Rob Wilson and Wimal Dissanayake, 1–20. Durham, NC: Duke University Press.

Wood, Lawrence E. 1998. "The Economic Impact of Tobacco Production in Appalachia." Report. Washington, D.C.: Appalachian Regional Commission.

Note

1. This was the inaugural lecture in the Place Matters series at the University of Kentucky in 2011. A video of the lecture was published online through the University of Kentucky immediately (unlike the other lectures), making this text publicly available. There have been similar reviews of the cultural geography literature and excellent related discussions published by others since, but this chapter reflects the lecture as delivered originally in 2011.

2

Transforming Places

Toward a Global Politics of Appalachia

Barbara Ellen Smith

In this era of ruthless deracination called globalization, place attachments and the politics of place have become increasingly salient in collective mobilizations across the spectrum of political life. Whether making radical new claims to territory, cultural integrity, and political autonomy, as the Zapatistas did in Chiapas, defending established borders and the imagined community of the nation, as in many anti-immigrant mobilizations, seeking sustainable economies that do not harm the environment of specific places—in these and many other contexts across the globe, activists are mobilizing place-related demands, symbols, and affinities in complex and contradictory political directions. Never self-evident, never "given," place is coming alive as a potent force in the hands of those who are able to harness its emotive and symbolic powers for political organizing.

Let me acknowledge at the outset that place-based organizing has many critics, particularly from the Left. In this era of globalization, place connotes the local, the particular, indeed, the parochial and insular; place-based organizing therefore appears out of sync with the times, incapable of addressing the great transnational issues—climate change, war, immigration, the depredations of capitalism—that give substance to the term *globalization*. The Marxist geographer David Harvey, for example, offers a relatively sympathetic critique of what he terms, following Raymond Williams, "militant particularisms," the solidarities and visionary alternatives forged through continuity in place and local struggles against injustice and exploitation. But in the end, he finds these place-based efforts lacking in reach and influence, and he asks how they might be transformed "into something more substantial on the world stage of capitalism."[1]

Moreover, place attachments are inevitably at least in part about the past, about defense of a place that activists seek to preserve, and place-based organizing is therefore not only inward-looking in the sense of being localistic, but potentially backward-looking and reactionary. The political mobilization of nostalgia for the imagined places of the past is a recurrent theme in southern history, from Lost Cause rhetoric to defense of the "southern way of life" during the massive resistance of the Civil Rights era. Today defense of place reverberates powerfully through other reactionary political rhetorics, perhaps most prominently in the nativist condemnation of immigrants. Well before Trump in 2006, for example, in the small town of Rockfield, Kentucky, a sign posted alongside a burning cross in a Salvadoran family's yard read, "In my country, maybe. In my neighborhood, no way!!!"[2] Place-based organizing, then, is either localistic, inadequate in this global age, and doomed to failure, or, in its framework as defense of place, intrinsically reactionary and *deserving* of failure. The proliferation of transnational organizations addressing everything from sex trafficking to greenhouse gas emissions seems only to confirm the futility of local, place-based struggle.

I don't share this perspective. That is in part because over the past several years I have witnessed a proliferation of place-based struggles in Appalachia, which, taken together, tell me that place is becoming politicized in important ways that deserve attention from those who believe that a more socially just world is possible. Since moving to Virginia in 2005, I have had the good fortune to work with Steve Fisher on many projects, including a book, *Transforming Places,* which collects original essays about contemporary place-based organizing in Appalachia. I want to acknowledge Steve and our ongoing conversations, as well as the work of our contributors, as substantial influences on my comments; indeed, this paper, particularly the conclusion, draws directly from the last chapter of our book, which Steve and I wrote together.[3]

The challenging process of analyzing common themes and political lessons from the essays in *Transforming Places* has led me to the conviction that we are living in a vortex of contradictions regarding place and space in this age of globalization. On the one hand, as it is commonly observed, electronic technologies can connect us with people and issues across the globe in seemingly limitless ways; we can Skype friends in China, gain instantaneous access to news about Bahrain, enter seductive new landscapes playing computer games with people we have never met. This virtual space appears expansive, free, unbounded. But, on the other hand, we live simultaneously in an era of militarized checkpoints; a proposed expensive and deadly wall on the U.S.-Mexico border; surveillance cameras in traffic intersections, shopping malls, and other public sites; scanners and pat-down procedures at airports; loss of freedom in the name of freedom; privatization of parks, prisons, and government offices—an incremental shrinking and surveillance of public space. In racial politics, we have moved from a brief experiment in inclusion, at least for some, to what Pat Hill Collins calls a policy of containment—literal containment in the high and disproportionate incarceration rates of African Americans and Latinos, especially men.[4]

Even as we enjoy the many freedoms of virtual space, then, we are increasingly living in actual, material conditions of spatial closure, what might even be called, pursuing the prison as metaphor, a lockdown of public space. We can be signing online petitions opposing privatization of the Internet, while the local post office has shut down, the local library is on shortened hours, the neighborhood school has closed owing to consolidation, and the local parks (if you live in a city or town that has parks) are so unkempt, even dangerous, that few people use them anymore. This incremental shrinkage of public space may be traced to the overall political logic of neoliberalism, which, with its exaltation of radical individualism and the untrammeled operation of markets, has legitimated privatization of public assets and savage cutbacks in the social welfare functions of government. My arguments here recapitulate in a somewhat different register the insights of Herb Reid and Betsy Taylor in their wonderful book, *Recovering the Commons*.[5]

I am not suggesting here that all people, regardless of gender, class, race, and other dimensions of inequality, experience loss of public space in the same way; there is tremendous geographic and social diversity in the manifestations and consequences of this trend. Some, for example, have the wealth and desire to live in gated communities with their own parks and swimming pools, send their children to private schools, enjoy the amenities of country clubs, and so on. But those who live in rural Appalachia, especially those who live near sites of mountaintop removal and other forms of so-called development, find that the forests and open space that were once treated as a commons are increasingly cordoned off with fences, barbed wire, and "No Trespassing" signs; that their children can no longer play in the creek because of pollution; that high levels of noise and dust make daily life almost unlivable. These two examples, while intentionally contrasting, partake of the same spatial logic: public space is either nonexistent or, increasingly, so unlivable that it is avoided, which of course furthers its disappearance.

This leads me to the conclusion that today, *the production of inequality and the exercise of power are in fundamental respects about the production and control of space.* For critical geographers, this is hardly a new insight, but for some of us, at least for me, it provides an angle of vision that brings into focus certain dimensions of social inequality and movements for social change in both the past and the present.[6] Jim Crow segregation, for example, was clearly a spatial regime, which members of SNCC and others who engaged in civil disobedience implicitly recognized as they sat in at lunch counters and moved to the front of buses.

But what of today? What forms does the spatial exercise of power assume today, especially in Appalachia? It seems to me that we are living today, contra the expansive rhetoric of globalization and boundless freedoms of virtual space, in a regime of spatial closure. *Neoliberalism is a regime of spatial closure,* a regime that both produces and depends on the lockdown of public space. I come to this conclusion in part from studying neoliberalism, but even more so from thinking about common themes that underlie contemporary place-based organizing in Appalachia, much of which implicitly contests this spatial lockdown. What understandings of place and space are being mobilized in this activism? How can we conceptualize, theorize, and learn lessons from what is happening on the ground? Insofar as David Harvey's and others' critiques about the deficiencies of place-based organizing must be taken seriously, is it possible to identify a *global* politics of *place,* or is that a contradiction in terms?

In the rest of this paper, I pursue answers to these questions by moving back and forth between theorizations of space and instances of place-based organizing in Appalachia. I'll look first at some common understandings of place, drawing in particular on the current battle over mountaintop removal (MTR) and related theorizations of space. I chose MTR in part because this struggle is so profoundly important for the future of Appalachia and it has been studied by a number of other scholars on whose work I draw. In addition, this battle closely parallels struggles over land, nature, culture, and identity that are evident in locations across the globe, such as the Colombian Pacific, analyzed by Arturo Escobar, where the supply chains of capitalism—and the "coloniality of knowledge, power and nature" increasingly extend.[7] Finally, I draw more widely on examples of place-based organizing for social justice from the book that Steve and I edited as I conclude by seeking tentative answers to the questions that I posed about the spatial exercise of power and a global politics of place.

Theories of Space, Practices of Place

PLACE AS COORDINATES, SPACE AS GRID

The vernacular understanding of space for most people who have been trained to perceive the basic structure of reality, including space and time, within a Western cosmology is that it is simply a backdrop, the setting. Space is fixed, inert. We take it for granted. Events happen in space, but space itself is not produced. It simply is. Geographers call this "absolute space," the space of maps and Western cartography, which vacates heterogeneity by reducing all places to a standard measure as points on the surface of the Earth. This view of space is associated with scientific rationality and certain forms of knowledge about landmasses, oceans, the physical features of the Earth, which were greatly extended during the so-called Age of Discovery. This is not an innocent beginning.[8]

The social and political project implicit in this view of space is the domination of nature, the mastery of the Earth. The inertness of space and equivalent fixity among places "prepare" them for passivity, to be acted on, discovered, opened up, penetrated. My overtly gendered language intentionally invokes the masculinist imaginary at work here. It is also, of course, a capitalist imaginary, in which the purpose of place becomes its role in the process of "development," its potential contribution to a seemingly inevitable progression toward modernity.

This "commonsense" understanding of space and place is at work in the struggle over MTR, particularly in the justifications of its supporters, analyzed so brilliantly in Rebecca Scott's book, *Removing Mountains: Extracting Nature and Identity in the Appalachian Coalfields.*[9] Scott extensively examines MTR supporters' tendency to situate the ancient mountains of Appalachia within a national progress narrative that emphasizes American ingenuity, industry, resourcefulness, hard work; nature within this narrative is something to be used, conquered even, especially when it presents challenges to the extraction of its riches for human benefit. This elision of place and economic purpose is inscribed in the very nomenclature that most of us use to demarcate certain portions of Appalachia simply as "the coalfields." This naming of place also constitutes an identity claim for at least certain residents, for whom perceived attacks on the coal industry by opponents of MTR are viewed as assaults on their personhood.[10]

In the context of mountainous Appalachia, there is an additional logic of development. Insofar as the steep slopes and thick forests of the central coalfields thwart the construction of roads, cell phone towers, and other infrastructure, much less the shopping malls and big-box stores that are hallmarks of our consumer culture, they represent impediments to progress, "artificial" barriers as it were in the way of development and modernization. This attitude is summed up well in the argument that one hears quite routinely among promoters of MTR: "We need more flat land around here." Within this logic, the fact that MTR is about the extraction of coal becomes secondary to the imperatives of economic development; it is as if the mountains would need to be flattened regardless of the seams of coal that they contain, since they stand in the way of progress and modernity.

Lest this line of thinking be interpreted as shallow opportunism, it is quite important to keep in mind the socioeconomic context of Appalachia and the way the region is framed in relation to American nationhood. As we know, one finds in the hollows of southern West Virginia and eastern Kentucky the highest rates of white poverty in the country and, in certain instances, some of the highest rates of poverty, period. Moreover, within the national imaginary, Appalachia is a land of backward, inbred (always implicitly white) hillbillies whose very degradation—in the manner of most binary oppositions—functions to valorize the intelligence and culture of the normative, middle-class American, who is decidedly not from Appalachia. Understood within this socioeconomic and discursive context, supporters of MTR achieve distance from pejorative images of Appalachia and position themselves not as hillbillies but as normal Americans within dominant narratives of progress. A double meaning may thus be at stake in another common framing of MTR, in this instance referring to the supposedly reclaimed, flattened sites of former mining: "You wouldn't even know you're in West Virginia." (That is, it's so flat it could be Anywhere, USA, and presumably there are no hillbillies in sight.)

I offer this extended discussion of the logic of MTR's supporters (again, heavily indebted to Scott) to underscore the profound importance of how we conceptualize space and place. The very commonsense quality of the dominant understanding of space, as fixed backdrop, conceals an underlying political grammar that deeply structures our own language and world-view in accord with the imperatives of capitalist masculinity. Concealed by the very fact of its obviousness, its taken-for-grantedness, space is thereby depoliticized. If space is fixed and given, how could it be otherwise? What is the point of fighting over it?

PLACE AS THE PAST, SPACE AS "DEAD" (FOUCAULT)

Place acquires human meaning and emotional power in large part because of the past: the traces of memory, feeling, stories, and relationships that circulate through and become attached to specific places in our individual biographies and collective histories. As before, this conceptualization is deeply gendered: place often figures as a storied landscape of origin, our mother, our home. Although memory is fickle and stories change over time, these figurations of place tend to feature a past that is comforting in its familiarity and predictability, and in that sense unchanging, timeless. Theorizations of space that complement this understanding of place feature once again the fixity of space and position it as the opposite of time. In Foucault's formulation, space is "dead," "fixed," "undialectical," "immobile," whereas time is dynamic, dialectical, never still.[11]

Defense of place within this framework of understanding becomes defense of the past, and therein lies political trouble. For if the past is cherished in part for its familiarity and predictability, then defense of place-as-the-past tends to be grounded in homogeneity, exclusion of the other, and repudiation of change. This does not mean, of course, that all change is just and desirable, or that memories of a golden age cannot function to critique emergent exploitation and injustice. But, too often, as we see in the violent exclusions of ethnic conflict and fundamentalist nationalisms across the globe, the supposedly golden-age past to which some seek to return often spells terror and misery for others. Hence, the author Ernst Bloch wrote in the context of rising Nazism in Germany, "The primacy of space over time is an infallible sign of reactionary language."[12]

The struggle over MTR is again instructive in supporters' and opponents' mobilizations of divergent pasts to legitimate their claims to place; they allow us to examine more closely the political valences of place-as-the-past and to probe for potentially progressive rather than reactionary implications. Supporters of MTR, for example, tend to position themselves within the heteronormative and patriarchal elements of the bygone days of Fordism, that is, that period when working-class men, at least those who were white, were able to earn a "family wage" that supported a dependent, presumably "nonworking" wife and children.[13] This interpretation of the past replaces the fierce class conflict that occurred throughout much of the twentieth century in the bituminous coal industry with a morality tale of individual sacrifice and provisioning for others. Coal mining in whatever form is not simply a job that opponents of MTR seek to deny would-be workers, but a place-based moral economy in "which working-class people not only earn their bread but also bake it, break it, and eat it—all within divisions of labor, notions of worth, rituals of collectivity, claims to identity, and relations of power that they may contest and alter but rarely invent anew."[14] Unfortunately, the features of this moral economy resonate with wider neoconservative discourses of heterosexism, racism, and the erasure of class.

Industry groups like Friends of Coal seize on this story of sacrifice and claim it as their own by eliding the distinction between workers, those who actually mine the coal, and owners to emphasize the heroic contribution of the coal industry as a whole. As Shannon Bell and Richard York perceptively observe, coal companies intentionally embody the industry in their visual propaganda as a manly coal miner.[15] The West Virginia Coal Association, for example, calls on a gendered nationalism[16] and discourse of sacrifice for the sake of national well-being when it admonishes others to remember a certain version of the past: "Coal mining . . . has helped win our nation's wars and fueled an economy that is the envy of the world. Coal is West Virginia! Coal is America!"[17]

Opponents of MTR not surprisingly proceed from sharply contrasting visions of place-as-the-past. The place-based moral economy evident in many opponents' narratives envisions forests full of wildlife where one can hunt for ramps and ginseng, streams teeming with fish, large gardens that produce healthy and abundant food. The emphasis here is on use values and the direct consumption of nature by women as well as men rather than commodification of natural resources and the economic development that can presumably occur as a result of masculine employment. The intergenerational legacy of living on the land is a recurrent theme. Judy Bonds, for example, a leader in the anti-MTR movement from Boone County, West Virginia, recounted: "My first memories was of my father and grandfather plowing the field above my home. I remember the smell of the rich, beautiful black earth. That's how it is in Appalachia—you are the mountain and the mountain is you."[18] In the words of Jessie Lynne Keltner: "[If I could talk to all my neighbors about MTR], I'd try to remind them to remember their heritage, their families, how their ancestors worked these hillsides, walked these mountains. I'd encourage them to visualize their parents and their grandparents standing around on these mountains with their hoes and fiddles and mules, saying, 'Now you all need to stop this.'"[19]

It is important to note that not all opponents of MTR call on a pre-industrial legacy of land-based survival; some (possibly men in particular, though I am speculating here) position themselves within the intergenera-tional continuity of underground coal mining, which they depict as more dangerous, requiring more skill, and nobler than surface mining, especially MTR. In the words of Carl Shoupe, a third-generation coal miner, "These guys up here on top of these mountains pushing dirt around, they're not coal miners. I won't give them the respect of calling them coal miners. They're earth movers."[20]

Shoupe and others who call on the legacy of underground mining also tend, in sharp contrast to the historiography of individual male provisioning, to foreground class conflict. A former miner and mine inspector and cur-rent organizer with Southern Appalachian Mountain Stewards, Larry Bush recalls: "My dad preached union to me from the time I was big enough to listen. . . . Strikes. Picket lines. I've lived through it. I've been arrested, my wife's been arrested, thrown in jail because she was out there with us. . . . Growing up union taught me to respect people's rights."[21]

The conflicting political uses of place-as-the-past evident in the narra-tives of supporters and opponents of MTR suggest that the past need not be a reactionary resource. Rather, the question at stake is the *substance* of the social relations depicted in place-as-the-past and the political relationship of variously remembered pasts to present struggles. Intergenerational depen-dence on the land, for example, involves a living memory of noncapitalist economic activities that, as Julie Graham and Katherine Gibson argue, are critical to our capacity to imagine and create more just and equitable social relations.[22] Similarly, articulated memories of class conflict stand as a power-ful antidote to the fear and coerced silence that permeate the coalfields today. Nonetheless, the violently exclusionary and reactionary politics that rely so heavily for their appeal on certain imagined pasts stand as a strong caution for those who would mobilize the past to progressive ends. It seems to me that we must always be asking: Which past is invoked in defense of place-as-the-past, and whose past is thereby excluded? Above all, what visions of the future do these invocations of the past imply?

PLACE AS LOCAL, SPACE AS GLOBAL

The assertion that place is inherently local seems in one sense so obvious that it hardly merits mention. After all, every place, in the sense of geographic territory, is politically, topographically, and/or culturally bounded: there are town limits, county boundaries, city neighborhoods. There is Trestle Hollow, Big Branch, Harveys Creek. But, as we have already seen, the physical dimensions of territory are quite different from the imagined geographies of place. To what extent do those engaged in place-based organizing envision their aims and craft their strategies within localistic parameters?

Substantial political and theoretical debate lies behind the disparagement of place-based organizing as "merely" local.[23] Within the globalization rhetoric that names the age, the local tends to lose out as the low point on an implicit hierarchy of scale. The local is small, bounded, insular, interior, whereas the global represents a boundless, cosmopolitan exteriority. The opposition between global and local finds parallel in the binary contrast between space and place: space/the global is large, abstract, universal, "out there," whereas place/the local is small, tangible, particular, close by. Place is where the embodied person lives; space, or the global, is the locus of nonhuman systems and forces such as capitalism and neoliberalism that impinge on but so often escape the constraints of (and political demands emanating from) specific places. In the present era of global capitalism, David Harvey, for example, argues that space is the terrain of capital; labor and oppositional citizens' groups have on occasion been able to influence social relations in specific places, but never to command space.[24]

I find this formulation useful insofar as it points to the power-laden reality that those with wealth and position are able to initiate and coordinate social and economic activities, networks, and relationships across the globe; their capacity thereby to influence fundamental aspects of daily life—from the local supply of food to the allocation of national budgets for education—in far-flung places is great, and at present it certainly exceeds the countervailing efforts and capacities of those who would oppose them. Nonetheless, this opposition between global/local and space/place also tends toward reification of each element and a determinist conclusion: global processes always happen elsewhere (in space), and place is the passive victim of forces that are seldom if ever susceptible to local intervention. The futility of challenging such pervasive and apparently inevitable processes generates a political defeatism that of course serves the interests of those who benefit from certain trajectories of globalization.

As the feminist geographer Doreen Massey notes: "In 1998 Bill Clinton delivered himself of the reflection that 'we' can no more resist the current forces of globalization than we can resist the force of gravity." Massey then quips, "Let us pass over the possibilities of resisting the force of gravity, noting merely that this is a man who spends a good deal of his life flying about in aeroplanes." She also points out that "this proposition was delivered to us by a man who had spent much of his recent career precisely trying to protect and promote (through GATT, the WTO, the speeding-up of NAFTA/TLC) this supposedly implacable force of nature."[25]

An alternative perspective redefines the polar opposition between local and global, place and space, as deeply embedded, mutual interactions: virtually every place on the globe has long been shaped by and continues to participate in networks of relationship that stretch far beyond its boundaries; this of course includes Appalachia and the U.S. South, historically as well as presently, as scholars such as Wilma Dunaway and Peter Coclanis forcefully remind us.[26] At the same time, the global is continually *produced* through the activities of human beings in specific locales.[27] Processes of globalization, even as they may shape local ways of life, can "take place" only within—and are thereby everywhere dependent on—the contingencies, particularities, and potential resistance of specific locales. Distinctions between the global and the local, as well as between space and place, become more blurry from this perspective, as their coproduction comes into view.

How then might we best theorize place in this age of globalization, this age of instantaneous connection and virtual freedom combined with polarized social relations and spatial closure? The geographer Doreen Massey offers what is in my view the most insightful and useful theoretical formulation of a global sense of place, which has been oft-quoted:

> What gives a place its specificity is not some long internalized history but the fact that it is constructed out of a particular constellation of social relations, meeting and weaving together at a particular locus. . . . Each place . . . is, indeed, a *meeting* place. Instead then, of thinking of places as areas with boundaries around, they can be imagined as articulated moments in networks of social relations and understandings, but where a large proportion of those relations,

experiences and understandings are constructed on a far larger scale than what we happen to define for that moment as the place itself, whether that be a street, or a region or even a continent. And this in turn allows a sense of place which is extroverted, which includes a consciousness of its links with the wider world, which integrates in a positive way the global and the local.[28]

What does this "extroverted," relational sense of place look like, and what are its political ramifications? For starters, and specifically for Appalachian studies, Massey's formulation in my view forcefully repudiates the insider/outsider distinction that we have so long deployed as a key axis of identity and conflict and thereby debilitated our capacities of social analysis and political critique. I know of no better indictment of the analytical vacuity and political regressiveness of the insider/outsider dualism than the fact that the coal operators have managed to position themselves alongside coal miners and other "Friends of Coal" as insiders to Appalachia in the struggle over MTR. Miners and operators stand together within this field of representation, joint victims of environmental extremists who by definition must be outsiders to the region because, according to the logic of this binary constriction, they are "enemies of coal" and therefore presumably have no legitimate role or say in the region's future.

An extroverted and relational understanding of place also requires us to challenge the processes of privatization, militarization, securitization, and outright physical destruction of spaces once considered "commons," which are incrementally eradicating public space. Even as these processes lock us down and lock us out, they lay bare the production and control of space as a central arena for the exercise of power, and thereby render struggles over space and place more astutely, intensely political.[29] In countering this closure of space, as much place-based organizing in Appalachia seeks to do, organizers are drawing strength from the politically potent reality that place is inherently shared and in that sense collective; however, it is increasingly not public or democratic in the sense of accessible to or collectively governed by all. The tension between a deep sense of identity with place, especially when shared with others, and the private appropriation and even destruction of place forms a crucible of possibility that is just beginning to be realized. Organizing taking place on the ground in Appalachia today points us toward more extroverted understandings of place and from there toward a global politics of place.

Toward a Global Politics of Place

To return to the observation with which I began: we are living in a moment of acute contradiction in our experiences of place and space; the apparently boundless freedom of virtual space that is both an outcome of and prerequisite to contemporary globalization and the simultaneous, drastic erosion of actual, public space that I don't know what else to call but a lockdown. How are organizers contesting this spatial closure? There are three overall strategies exemplified in the organizing discussed in *Transforming Places:* (1) making space with and for each other through the creation of actual physical sites and social contexts where people in specific locales can meet one another as equals; (2) crossing space, creating horizontal relationships of solidarity across spatial, social, and ideological difference; and (3) transgressing space, refusing the politics of lockdown and the neoliberal closure of space through civil disobedience and above all, trespass. Let me examine each of these in turn.

Producing public space, in contexts where gathering places open to all have virtually disappeared, means in part creating actual physical sites where people can meet one another. I was struck, at a recent Appalachian studies conference, to learn about Amelia Kirby's and others' strategic initiative in Whitesburg, Kentucky, where, recognizing the absence of public space, they opened a bar named Summit City as an intentional "anti-oppression" space. For this young woman, running a bar where, as Kirby put it, "a lot of sexist dudes want to buy beer" was rife with moments of difficulty and contradiction, but her commitment is to "fight sexism in the real world of the coalfields" by creating a space where encounters across gender, race, ideology, and other forms of difference can occur.[30]

The group RAIL Solution offers an innovative example of making space not by establishing an actual physical site but by creating an imagined, shared place among people separated by spatial distance yet linked by proposals to privatize a space they claimed in common. RAIL Solution developed in response to the effort, launched by Halliburton Corporation among others, to create privatized truck lanes on I-81 in Virginia. RAIL Solution was able to turn this anonymous (but publicly financed) stretch of interstate highway into a shared place through, among other actions, a rhetorical strategy: "I-81, it's our Main Street." Calling on this symbol of small-town Americana, RAIL Solution framed the residents of small cities and towns along the I-81 corridor as an egalitarian collectivity and reinforced that solidarity through email and face-to-face meetings. In responding to that appeal, on the basis of an invented but highly strategic definition of shared place, supporters of RAIL Solution opposed the privatization of I-81 in part because, by their own accounts, they were inspired by belief in democracy, the desire to reclaim their political voice, and the possibility that, collectively, they could actually defeat a corporate giant.[31]

Another way of "making space" is to widen the purpose and constituency of nominally public institutions and existing social justice organizations, thereby opening them up to those who have been previously excluded.[32] Robert Gipe and his colleagues at the community college in Harlan County, Kentucky, have used music, performance, oral history, and visual arts to draw local residents into common projects, bridge deep social divisions, and build more inclusive and egalitarian social relations, thereby turning this state institution into more genuine public space.[33] In a more episodic and transitory fashion, certain local churches have become institutional spaces for supporting striking union members, distributing critical messages about nuclear weapons production, and creating farmers' markets in inner-city neighborhoods.

Social justice and cultural organizations can themselves make space and thereby create a form of public space.[34] This requires stretching their reach and accessibility so that new constituencies are able to participate and existing ones are able to do so more fully. Appalshop, the community-based media arts and education organization, incubated the youth-focused Appalachian Media Institute (AMI) to make its work more inviting to young people; youth who participate in AMI's programs use video to view, literally, their homes through new eyes and thereby potentially reinvent their place. In turn, these young participants tend to view AMI as a rare "safe space" for developing and expressing their personal and political identities.[35] The Center for Participatory Change in western North Carolina extended its grassroots support organizing to emergent Latino groups and leaders and in so doing transformed itself, learning, among other lessons, that "multilingual spaces are not optional."[36]

Other organizing *crosses* space, linking together place-based activists in one locale with those elsewhere. The Oak Ridge Environmental Peace Alliance offers an example of place-based organizing that crosses space to contest, in this instance, the militarization of space. Oak Ridge, Tennessee, is a company town created in 1941 by the federal government as part of the Manhattan Project; the Y12 plant in Oak Ridge produced the highly enriched uranium used in the bomb that destroyed Hiroshima. Contesting nuclear weapons production in Oak Ridge, which was the original goal of the Alliance, is not unlike opposing MTR in the coalfields: it is a lonely and dangerous position to take. Nonetheless, since its founding in 1988, the Alliance has deepened its base of support (sometimes of a clandestine nature) in Oak Ridge, extended its reach among college students in Knoxville and beyond, and developed extensive transnational networks among faith-based groups and individuals ranging from Catholic to Buddhist to New Age. In recent years, increasingly aware of connections among nuclear weapons production, militarism, institutionalized racism, and an array of unmet social needs, the Alliance intentionally extended its outreach to African American organizations and has lent its active support to antiracism organizing efforts in eastern Tennessee.[37]

Such organizing exemplifies Massey's vision of an "extroverted" sense of place and her formulation that "each place is . . . a meeting place," but it also raises a crucial if implicit question for place-based organizers: Of all the interconnected issues and constituencies with which we might deliberately intensify our relationships, which are the most strategic to pursue? Those who are skeptical of the political reach and influence of place-based organizing would tend to focus on the work of crossing space in the sense of moving up on a hierarchy of scale, creating links to activists addressing similar issues in other countries and continents. While such links are certainly not undesirable, Massey's theorization questions the disparaging association between place and localism and suggests that globally conscious place-based organizing may also mean building strategic *lateral* relationships that pursue the wider relations of power that are produced in and circulate through specific places and moments.

Organizing efforts on the ground exemplify this theorization: for activists in Jobs with Justice of East Tennessee, a community-based offshoot of the labor movement, involvement in immigrant rights organizing was a logical but strategic outgrowth of their support for a unionization drive among Latino workers in Morristown, Tennessee.[38] When Kentucky's Community Farm Alliance sought urban markets for its farmers' food products, the organization deliberately developed relationships with African American churches and organized distribution in low-income, African American neighborhoods as well as collaborating with "foodie" groups in Louisville.[39]

By intentionally creating horizontal relationships among peoples, places, and ideas that transcend social, spatial, and ideological barricades (such as those between immigrants and labor, peace, environmental, and antiracism activists, rural and urban, white and black), these groups, I would argue, are crossing space and in so doing creating a form of public space. They are bringing together those who would otherwise not encounter one another—certainly not as equals, and perhaps not at all—in a common social space, and they are thereby also creating a "countertopography," in the words of the geographer Cindy Katz.[40]

Electronic communication technologies play an obvious and important role in facilitating these linkages among people, places, and ideas; they also possess a more subtle but quite powerful potential to expose and politicize social relations and interconnections across geographic and social space. Innovative websites such as ilovemountains.org make visible the production, circulation, and consumption of commodities—in this instance, coal from MTR operations that is used in coal-fired utilities—and call individuals to account for their participation in economic relations that they may not recognize or may take for granted. The possibilities for similar sites to expose the operations of global capitalism, lay bare the economic relationships in which differently situated people are implicated, and call on viewers to join in political response are only beginning to be realized. Insofar as unjust power relations endure in part because those who benefit from them are able to naturalize and obscure the operations of power, the subversive potential of such uses of the Internet is enormous. It can be used to create diverse venues in which different forms of knowledge and potentially subversive information may be systematically shared and utilized to challenge dominant definitions of what is true and what is possible.[41]

Certain models of place-based organizing in urban settings outside Appalachia also reach in this direction. In New York, Los Angeles, and other major cities, nascent movements are combining an array of local labor unions and community-based organizations in powerful coalitions to demand the "right to the city," a goal that aims far beyond access to an expanded array of public services. In the words of Edward W. Soja, "Seeking the right to the city is a continuous and more radical effort at spatial reappropriation, claiming an active presence in all that takes place in urban life under capitalism."[42] Put somewhat differently by Don Mitchell, the "right to the city" is an effort to *produce* space that is public; it is in demanding the right to the city that public space is created over and against the claims of property, propriety, security, and privatization.[43] In Appalachia, there are stirrings, exemplified by the organizing I've mentioned and many more efforts beyond, that move toward similar production of space and that could become far more expansive and intentional. "The coal belongs to the people," Walter

Burton Franklin, a disabled coal miner of southern West Virginia, doggedly argued.[44] Perhaps the mountains do as well.

In conclusion, I want to recognize that the strategies of making space and crossing space do not *necessarily* mean direct challenges to privatization, securitization, and the processes of spatial closure. It is noteworthy, however, that several place-based organizing efforts in Appalachia are turning increasingly to the third strategy I mentioned: spatial transgression, specifically trespass, as intentional tactics to make vivid the conditions of lockdown. Mountain Justice, for example, links civil disobedience against MTR and other actions on the ground to a wider network of environmental activism that spans places, national borders, environmental issues, and social identities. For Mountain Justice, "claiming space" involves visible trespass into places that mountain-destroying corporations produce and presume to control (whether their urban corporate headquarters or the actual sites of MTR). The organization "jumps scale" in the sense that it does not build incrementally from local chapters toward ever higher levels of political influence (county, state, national); its tactics of civil disobedience have in the past antagonized counterpart organizations accountable to place-based constituencies, but now some members of these organizations, such as Kentuckians For The Commonwealth, increasingly turn to intentional trespass as well.[45] This, too, was evident at the 2011 Appalachian studies conference, where Jason Howard, who among others that year participated in an anti-MTR sit-in in Kentucky governor Steve Beshear's office, expected that civil disobedience would increasingly be used to protest MTR.

By trespassing on selected sites of private property and seats of power, contesting corporate practices that are destructive of place, inventing new places and place-based identities, and constructing spaces of encounter across social, ideological, and spatial distance, organizers in Appalachia are refusing to be locked down or locked out even if it means they are temporarily locked up. Drawing on varied place-based allegiances, they are opening up space, and thereby, to paraphrase Doreen Massey, opening up the future for us all.[46]

Notes

Portions of this chapter appeared as the conclusion to *Transforming Places: Lessons from Appalachia,* edited by Stephen L. Fisher and Barbara Ellen Smith (2012). Reprinted with permission from the University of Illinois Press.

1. The phrase "militant particularism" originated in the work of Raymond Williams. See David Harvey, *Spaces of Capital: Towards a Critical Geography* (New York: Routledge, 2001), 175.

2. Quoted in Barbara Ellen Smith and Jamie Winders, "'We're Here to Stay': Economic Restructuring, Latino Migration and Place-Making in the US South," *Transactions of the Institute of British Geographers* 33, no. 1 (2008): 60.

3. Barbara Ellen Smith and Stephen L. Fisher, "Conclusion: Transformations in Place," in *Transforming Places: Lessons from Appalachia*, ed. Stephen L. Fisher and Barbara Ellen Smith (Urbana: University of Illinois Press, 2012), 267–291.

4. Patricia Hill Collins, *Fighting Words: Black Women and the Search for Justice* (Minneapolis: University of Minnesota Press, 1998).

5. Herbert Reid and Betsy Taylor, *Recovering the Commons: Democracy, Place, and Global Justice* (Urbana: University of Illinois Press, 2010).

6. Henri Lefebvre's *The Production of Space* (Cambridge, MA: Blackwell, 1991) is a key text.

7. Arturo Escobar, *Territories of Difference: Place, Movements, Life*, Redes (Durham: Duke University Press, 2008), 4.

8. See Doreen Massey, *For Space* (London: Sage Publications, 2005); David Harvey, "Space as a Key Word," in Harvey, *Spaces of Global Capitalism: Towards a Theory of Uneven Geographical Development* (New York: Verso, 2006), 119–148.

9. Rebecca Scott, *Removing Mountains: Extracting Nature and Identity in the Appalachian Coalfields* (Minneapolis: University of Minnesota Press, 2010).

10. Ibid.

11. Michel Foucault, *Power/Knowledge: Selected Interviews and Other Writings, 1972–1977*, ed. Colin Gordon (New York: Pantheon, 1980), 70.

12. Ernst Bloch (1932), as quoted in Massey, *For Space*, 42.

13. David Harvey, *The Condition of Postmodernity: An Enquiry into the Origins of Cultural Change* (Cambridge, MA: Blackwell, 1989).

14. Barbara Ellen Smith, "Another Place Is Possible? Labor Geography, Spatial Dispossession, and Gendered Resistance in Central Appalachia," *Annals of the Association of American Geographers* 105, no. 3 (2015): 578–579.

15. Shannon Elizabeth Bell and Richard York, "Community Economic Identity: The Coal Industry and Ideology Construction in West Virginia," *Rural Sociology* 75, no. 1 (2010): 111–143.

16. Ibid. Bell, York, and Scott analyze support for MTR from different theoretical frameworks but complement one another's arguments in instructive and important ways.

17. West Virginia Coal Association, "Coal Facts 2010," 5.

18. Judy Bonds, "The Endangered Hillbilly," in *Something's Rising: Appalachians Fighting Mountaintop Removal*, ed. Silas House and Jason Howard (Lexington: University Press of Kentucky, 2009), 133.

19. Anne Shelby and Jessie Lynne Keltner, "Holy Ground," in House and Howard, *Something's Rising*, 244.

20. Carl Shoupe, "Union Made," in House and Howard, *Something's Rising*, 102.

21. Larry Bush, "The Gathering Storm," in House and Howard, *Something's Rising*, 257.

22. J. K. Gibson-Graham, *The End of Capitalism (As We Knew It): A Feminist Critique of Political Economy* (1996; repr., Minneapolis: University of Minnesota Press, 2006).

23. This theoretical discussion is drawn directly from Smith and Fisher, "Transformations in Place."

24. Harvey, *The Condition of Postmodernity*.

25. Massey, *For Space*, 5.

26. Wilma Dunaway, *The First American Frontier: Transition to Capitalism in Southern Appalachia, 1700–1860* (Chapel Hill: University of North Carolina Press, 1996); Peter Coclanis, "Globalization before Globalization: The South and the World to 1950," in *Globalization and the American South*, ed. James C. Cobb and Williams Stueck (Athens: University of Georgia Press, 2005), 19–35.

27. Doreen Massey, *Space, Place, and Gender* (Minneapolis: University of Minnesota Press, 1994); Saskia Sassen, *The Global City: New York, London, Tokyo* (Princeton: Princeton University Press, 2001); Gibson-Graham, *The End of Capitalism*.

28. Massey, *Space, Place and Gender*, 154–155; emphasis in original.

29. Reid and Taylor, *Recovering the Commons*.

30. Amelia Kirby, "AVs: Women and Activism in Appalachia," panelists' comments, Appalachian Studies Association annual conference, Richmond, KY, March 11, 2011.

31. Rees Shearer, "RAIL Solution: Taking on Halliburton on the Home Front," in Fisher and Smith, *Transforming Places*, 32–46.

32. Sonia E. Alvarez, "Afterword: The Politics of Place, the Place of Politics: Some Forward-Looking Reflections," in *Women and the Politics of Place*, ed. Wendy Harcourt and Arturo Escobar (Bloomfield, CT: Kumarian Press, 2005), 256.

33. Maureen Mullinax, "Resistance through Community-Based Arts," in Fisher and Smith, *Transforming Places*, 92–106.

34. Richard A. Couto with Catherine S. Guthrie, *Making Democracy Work Better: Mediating Structures, Social Capital, and the Democratic Prospect* (Chapel Hill: University of North Carolina Press, 1999).

35. Katie Richards-Schuster and Rebecca O'Doherty, "Appalachian Youth Re-envisioning Home, Re-making Identities," in Fisher and Smith, *Transforming Places*, 78–91.

36. Craig White, Paul Castelloe, Molly Hemstreet, Yaira Andrea Arias Soto, and Jeannette Butterworth, "Center for Participatory Change: Cultivating Grassroots Support Organizing," in Fisher and Smith, *Transforming Places*, 145.

37. Ralph Hutchison, "Stop the Bombs: Local Organizing with Global Reach," in Fisher and Smith, *Transforming Places*, 19–31.

38. Fran Ansley, "Talking Union in Two Languages: Labor Rights and Immigrant Workers in East Tennessee," in Fisher and Smith, *Transforming Places,* 164–179.

39. Jenrose Fitzgerald, Lisa Markowitz, and Dwight B. Billings, "Not Your Grandmother's Agrarianism: The Community Farm Alliance's Agrifood Activism," in Fisher and Smith, *Transforming Places,* 210–225.

40. Cindy Katz, "On the Grounds of Globalization: A Topography for Feminist Political Engagement," *Signs* 26, no. 4 (2001): 1213–1234.

41. Anita Puckett, Elizabeth Fine, Mary Hufford, Ann Kingsolver, and Betsy Taylor, "Who Knows? Who Tells? Creating a Knowledge Commons," in Fisher and Smith, *Transforming Places,* 239–251.

42. Edward W. Soja, *Seeking Spatial Justice* (Minneapolis: University of Minnesota Press, 2010), 96.

43. Don Mitchell, *The Right to the City: Social Justice and the Fight for Public Space* (New York: Guilford Press, 2003).

44. I worked with Walter Burton Franklin, now deceased from the disabling effects of working as an underground coal miner, in the context of the black lung movement during 1974–1976 in McDowell County, WV. This was one of his favorite sayings.

45. Cassie Robinson Pfleger, Randal Pfleger, Ryan Wishart, and Dave Cooper, "Mountain Justice," in Fisher and Smith, *Transforming Places,* 226–238.

46. Massey, *For Space,* 11.

57.
fierce grief shadows me
I hold to the memory
of ongoing loss
land stolen bodies shamed
everywhere the stench of
death and retribution
all around me
nature demands amends
spirit guides me
to take back the land
make amends
silence the cries of the lost
the lamentations
let them sleep forever sublime
knowing that we
have made a place
that can sustain us
a place of certainty
and sanctuary
                              —bell hooks

3

Place, Autonomy, and the Politics of Hope

John Pickles

The traditional Eurocentric order of international law is foundering today, as is the old *nomos* of the earth.
>—Carl Schmitt, *The "Nomos" of the Earth in the International Law of the "Jus Publicum Europaeum"* (1950)

A map of the world that does not include Utopia is not worth even glancing at, for it leaves out the one country at which Humanity is always landing. And when Humanity lands there, it looks out, and, seeing a better country, sets sail. Progress is the realization of Utopias.
>—Oscar Wilde, "The Soul of Man under Socialism" (1891)

Place is a crucial concept for any geographer, architect, or planner, and in recent years it has become increasingly important for many others. Along with key words like *space, location, proximity, distance, region, territory,* and *landscape, place* frames a conceptual field that shapes the ways these and other disciplines see the Earth and human activity on it. But for many the rich significance of such rhetorical and geographical forms of place as topos and locus was flattened by modernity's infatuation with time; place and space came to be seen as static, the dead, the inert, the immobile,[1] even as parochial, backward, or antimodern.[2] For others the spaces delimited by lines, fences, and borders produced the territorial state, itself a precondition for the emergence of capitalist development.[3] More recently these fixed territories of the state have themselves been reterritorialized by the expansion of empire, the globalizing of capitalist economies, and the rise of new powers. In turn, places have come under increasing threat from what Slavoj Žižek has called four fundamental antagonisms. The first three constitute "the 'commons,' the shared substance of our social being";[4] (1) ecological catastrophe; (2) the consequences of private property regimes, particularly evinced now in struggles over intellectual property; and (3) the socioethical implications of new techno-scientific developments (especially biogenetics). The fourth is the consequence of these forms of enclosure with the emergence of new kinds of place built on new forms of apartheid (walls, slums, enclosures). The first three affect the "practices of livability—with the generative powers of embodied life battening, hungering, eating, fearing, enjoying, sensing, resting, and playing with the generative matrices co-constituted from earth, air, water, nutrients, energies, and co-evolved creatures."[5] In this sense, place matters in two fundamental ways: as the condition of possibility of living well and as a concrete site for a politics of defense of a common set of resources, values, institutions, and practices, particularly against expanded forms of accumulation and dispossession.

As the destruction of traditional ways of life and natural environments has become more common, as deregulation of national and global economies has fueled accumulation by dispossession, and as markets have been increasingly disembedded from institutions and practices of social regulation, place has reemerged in recent years as a crucial rallying node: the defense of place as the site of experience, history, attachment, and meaning and the defense of the right to cultural survival. As Arturo Escobar has stressed, "There is a need for a corrective theory that neutralizes the erasure of place, the asymmetry that arises from giving far too much importance to 'the global' and far too little value to 'place.'"[6]

It is in this context that Doreen Massey reminded us that "Place Matters," and it matters in ways that are fundamental to the lived worlds of people everywhere.[7] Place matters to people living their everyday lives, making sense of the world around them, and struggling to defend or change the common spaces and resources that are fundamental to their existence. It matters most explicitly at times of rapid structural and social change, when one form of life is destabilized by the emergence of new forms of social and spatial organization. And it has come to matter in very specific ways as the national structures of economy, culture, and sovereignty have been deterritorialized by the combined effects of postcolonialism, technological change, and neoliberal globalization.

Place also matters in a slightly different way. It is the purely quotidian and often unacknowledged condition of possibility for movement, interaction, meaning, community, and survival. It is the material and symbolic context within which action unfolds, or—if we think in action theoretic terms with Werlen and Schatzki—it is the material and symbolic consequences of our actions.[8] Place, in this sense, is the locus of the lifeworld; the pregiven context of entanglements and commitments that make up the taken-for-granted of our lives.[9] Such places provide an operative context of common understandings, institutions, and practices that sustain the life of a community and provide the necessary conditions for any politics, whether of reaction and exclusion or of hope and inclusion.[10] We move from place to place, settle in place, materialize those movements and settlements, trade among places, dream of close and distance locales, work daily in proximity with others, and travel annually to distant places; we carve out regional economies and regional systems, and we defend territory often on the basis of landscape markers and visions that we come to identify as ourselves and as our society, which must be defended. In this sense, place and community are not purified concepts bounded spatially by the locality.[11] Location is important, but when we assert that "place matters," it is not a claim about the essential or unique character of a locality. Instead, place is a nodal point of a relational network that has effects. It is—as Doreen Massey so eloquently told us—the "throwntogetherness," the articulation and crystallization of relations and flows occurring at many scales.[12] Place functions as the material and symbolic horizon of my locale (home, neighborhood, village, region) and of the totality of institutional practices that give it meaning (the nation, the people, us-not-them). All of these—and many more—are the places of a particular life, structured collectively, and producing emergent new virtualities.

In what follows, I turn first to a brief methodological discussion of place to introduce key concepts of *context* and *conjuncture,* two ways of thinking about place that inform the remainder of the chapter. I then show how place has been marginalized by universal spatial logics of globalization, but how "place" is currently being reworked as embedded networks and resources, what Eddie Webster and his colleagues have called grounded globalization.[13] I ask where new ways of thinking about place and space might be emerging and what consequences they might have for the practice of politics. I then focus on the renewal of our understanding of place by turning to recent discussions of place as a site for the defense of the commons and new acts of commoning. The chapter concludes with a discussion of efforts on several continents to rework the relationship among place, commoning, and territory.

Place, Context, and Conjuncture

In recent years geographers, anthropologists, and cultural theorists have expanded our understanding of diverse and alternative modalities of power, economy, and life through their engagements with meanings of context in the new discourses of cultural economy, "open" and "heterodox" Marxism, and approaches to diverse economies, alter-globalizations, and alternative modernities. With these various discursive, social, and cultural turns in critical theory, we can now take as given that context matters. Yet, as Jamie Peck warns us, when turning to issues relating to the social, spatial, and scalar constitution of economic systems, identities, processes, and development paths, we too often leave "only fuzzily defined and untheorized 'context' in the background."[14]

In this section I focus on what we mean by context and, by so doing, I point to the always conjunctural nature of place.[15] For Grossberg, "a conjuncture is always a social formation understood as more than a mere context— but as an articulation, accumulation, or condensation of contradictions."[16] I want to build on this conceptualization to ask what a conjunctural reading of context might mean for an understanding of place. That is, I want to consider not "mere context" but context and place as always an articulation of relations and practices occurring at multiple spatial and temporal scales.

In his debate with Austin and Searle, Derrida spoke directly to the meaning of context, and it may be useful here to follow his argument a little. For Derrida there are only contexts, but these contexts cannot be "saturable or exhaustively determinable."[17] Context is not a given space or framework of objects and relations within which specific identities are formed and determined. It cannot be a conceptual space of relations that could, in principle, be filled out by the pursuit of more detailed research and writing. For Derrida, meaning is (temporarily) stabilized or fixed through the play of difference in an infinite chain of similarly unstable relations of signification—always fixed, but always open to deconstruction, reinterpretation, and reworking, to rewriting and reinscription.

The concept of the conjuncture was fundamental to refocusing critical theory and cultural studies on this understanding of the concrete, temporary, and contingent specificities of contexts.[18] For Stuart Hall this always open possibility contains the potential for real social transformation: "Its sense of context is always a complex, overdetermined and contingent unity. Contextualism in cultural studies is often defined by and as a theory of articulation, which understands history as the ongoing effort (or process) to make, unmake and remake relations, structures and unity (as well as differences). If reality is relational and articulated, such relations are both contingent (i.e. not necessary) and real, and thus, never finished or closed for all times."[19]

In thinking about place through this lens of context and conjuncture, I want to highlight four aspects of conjuncturalism. First, in this view place is always relational; as a historical reality places are produced through what Grossberg refers to as the constant struggle to make, unmake, and remake ("articulate") complex configurations.[20] Second, this commitment to complexity rejects reductionist or deterministic analyses and any attempt to impose direct and simple causality to explain how places are produced. Place is always produced by the articulation of multiple and often contradictory forces.[21] Third, and as a consequence, the conjunctural study of places is always about concrete socio-geo-historical formations, and the analysis of place is always strategic, not universal. Fourth, this notion of complex articulation means that there are no guarantees: the world did not have to become the way it is; it could always have been and can be otherwise.[22] But such "otherwiseness" is not an open possibility or something we can just choose. It is itself contingent on the relations and structures that constitute the "real" and on the social forces mobilized to this or that end. In this sense, life is the continuous actualization—construction and reconstruction—of effective structures that constitute specific geohistorical realities of power.[23] By rearticulating a context, conjunctural analysis seeks to open up further possibilities for struggle and articulation and thereby to shape the nature of the debate about the political. This same sensibility is reflected in Douglas Reichert Powell's study of critical regionalism, which stresses the importance and value of examining how regions, and Appalachia in particular, "are made and what they are made for."[24]

This was also Doreen Massey's understanding of place; it is the materialization of a conjuncture that sees a context as an articulation, accumulation, and condensation of different currents or circumstances occurring at different scales.[25] It has to be constructed as the complex product of multiple lines of force, determination, and resistance, with different temporalities and spatialities, what she refers to as power geometries.[26] A conjuncture need not have a specific national form, although it is always territorialized in some way. The unity of a conjuncture is never complete, stable, or organic, but is constituted by a particular problematic within the analysis itself.[27]

This is a thoroughly nonessentialist project, sensitive to the contextual and embedded nature of all cultural practices. Its primary goal is to describe and analyze the diverse forms of practice, embeddedness, and class processes at work in the new geographies of globalization. It asks how we can be attentive to the rhythms and contexts of everyday life, and to the diversity that constitutes this matrix of diverse and alternative ways of living (the deepening of contemporary capitalisms, the proliferation or demise of non-capitalisms, or their articulations in concrete regional economic geographies).[28] It is, I think, precisely what we mean by *place* and the fact that places are "always in the process of being made, always contested."[29] In the next section I focus more directly on some of the ways in which this contextual and conjunctural understanding of place has been flattened by particular representations and discourses of space.

Logics of Planetary Space

In *The Age of Planetary Space: On Heidegger, Being, and the Metaphysics of Globalization,* Mikko Joronen addressed the changing geographies of "place" and why place matters particularly at this historical juncture.[30] His is a detailed reading of Heidegger on space and being, and the implications of Heidegger's work for how we might think about globalization and the ways in which we dwell on the Earth today. He reads a Heidegger engaged with what we now call globalization, not merely as a geographical rescaling, but as the completion of a logic intrinsic to Western metaphysics—an abstract rationality and an "ontological-historical emergence of calculating ordering"[31] that produces the "world-as-picture" and enables increasing planetary management and control.

Contemporary debates about globalization are replete with such abstract logics and universal claims, flattening the meaning and value of place, subsuming its structures, dynamics, and possibilities to a universal calculus. This subsumption is particularly clearly illustrated in Ellen Meiskins Wood's otherwise poignant description of contemporary capitalism: "For the first time, capitalism has become a truly universal system. It's universal not only in the sense that it's global, not only in the sense that just about every economic actor in the world today is operating according to the logic of capitalism, and even those on the outermost periphery of the capitalist economy are, in one way or another, subject to that logic. Capitalism is universal also in the sense that its logic—the logic of accumulation, commodification, profit maximization, competition—has penetrated just about every aspect of human life and nature itself."[32]

For J. K. Gibson-Graham in *The End of Capitalism (As We Knew It)*, this kind of description of globalization and capitalism makes for bleak reading and depressing politics. By narrating the global in this way, capitalism is treated as an iron-cage mechanism from which there is no hope of release. As a result, corresponding to this overwhelming and distant image of a structured totality, individual community efforts to shape their own destinies are interpreted as defensive, running against the tide, and with little chance of success. Places may resist or try to shape their own futures, but they do so in a context in which the power relations they face are viewed as overwhelming, resistance is understood as temporary, and community struggles are limited to temporary defense of specific sites.

The results of this kind of totalizing view of global capitalism have been devastating for the evolution of community and regional economic development models and initiatives to create alternative economic development strategies. Assumptions about dominant "global" logics and weak "local" powers have given rise to selective policies and prescriptions that have been naturalized as "given" and "unquestionable"; local and corporate taxes need to be reduced to ensure entrepreneurial competitiveness and hold companies in place; employment strategies should favor technical training for and underwriting of high-tech jobs in an information economy; places need to compete through local and state giveaways to attract greenfield investments; state support for labor-intensive manufacturing has little place in public policy in the face of global competition; at the same time, speculative ventures to create global cities as mechanisms for renewed capital accumulation require the periodic dispossession of residential neighborhoods and livelihoods. In these scenarios, wages are said to be too high, benefits and insurance costs are prohibitive, competitive markets prevent locally based northern producers from surviving, and the remaining futures are ones that "require" a mix of vicious austerity politics and wholesale investment in the creative class while "non-networked" places are consigned to out-migration of skilled workers, in-migration of service workers, aging populations, and the growth of precarious work. Within this model of global capitalism, places and communities have been subsumed under the universal calculus of value and profit. But in the face of this dominant discourse it becomes crucial to ask, "How might we challenge the dominant script of globalization and the victim role it ascribes to workers and communities in both 'first' and 'third' worlds? For . . . to accept this script as a reality is to severely circumscribe the sorts of defensive and offensive actions that might be taken to realize economic development goals."[33]

The central thesis of *The Age of Planetary Space* is that thinking about globalization in terms of such forms of abstract rationality, ordering, calculation, and objectivity—what Heidegger called world-space or planetary space—has very specific origins and commitments. Calculative forms of space are always abstractions from the concrete specificities of everyday life and the spatiality of particular places. The age of planetary space represents itself as universal and necessary, but it does so only at the expense of concealing its own historical geography, its own existence as a kind of "local" knowledge.[34]

In *The "Nomos" of the Earth in the International Law of the "Jus Publicum Europaeum,"* Carl Schmitt similarly argued that political space is always sustained by geohistorical practices of order and localization (*Ordnung* and *Ortung*) that are themselves dependent on very specific kinds of places, legal regimes, and political economies.[35] Schmitt concentrated primarily on what he called the "second *nomos*," the spatial and political organization of the Earth imposed by the sixteenth-century colonial conquest of the New World and sustained by the seventeenth-century development of the European territorial nation-state system. This Eurocentric *nomos* comprised an increasingly global arrangement of land-appropriation and industrialization, of civilized Europeans and subject peoples, of territorial states and sea power. Following World War I the United States took over the "maritime existence" of the British Empire and began to impose a "new *nomos*," prolonging the destiny of Western planetary hegemony into what Schmitt called a regime of "total war." Like Heidegger, Schmitt saw this *nomos* of the Earth to be a universalizing claim based on a structure of power that was parochial and specific to the Euro-Atlantic.[36] Its spatial specificity becomes even clearer now that it is coming to an end and new forms of localization and order are emerging. These emerging forms are quite different from the Western coordinates of planetary space and its specific *nomos,* and they are redefining the meaning and effects of place, space, soil, land, field, terrain, territory, district, and other related spatial concepts.

These emerging meanings of place and space are not without their own problems. For example, Stuart Elden has warned of the dangers of the recent return to Schmitt's geopolitical analysis, suggesting that although *The "Nomos" of the Earth* was published in 1950, it was probably begun between 1942 and 1945. Thus, readers need to be aware of the ways in which his thinking and arguments are inflected by his political commitments to conservative *Volkish* conceptions of place.[37] With this caution in mind, the challenge, then, is to pay attention to new forms of globalization that might allow for different configurations of being-in-the-world and living alongside others and nature without falling prey to such conservative and politicized conceptions. Saying that "place matters"—in Heidegger's terms that we must live differently and must seek new ways of being-in-the-world, or in Schmitt's terms that a new *nomos* is emerging—is one thing. Activating change in those modes of being-in-place and the rules and laws that constitute them is something entirely different.

Provincializing Modernity

If place matters in these ways, then the task is to show how it matters and how this mattering challenges or changes the logics of global ordering. For Massey, "the story of the world cannot be told (nor its geography elaborated) through the eyes of 'The West' alone, as had so long been the case."[38] Far from being the universal view it had long claimed to be, this Eurocentric history of modernity must be understood as a local knowledge. Planetary and world space are not merely descriptions of the way we interact with each other across abstract space, but forms of local knowledge and culturally specific ideas whose claim to universality have erased other histories and continue to deny their possibility. To talk about alternatives to modernity—whether these be southern, indigenous, environmental, regional, or subaltern—is thus to disclose a discursive and practical space in which the idea of a single modernity has been suspended, where European or North Atlantic modernity has been provincialized and displaced from the center of the historical imagination. From this perspective, social movements struggling to defend or redefine place, and to sustain their environments and livelihoods, must do so by also rethinking their own understanding of the global.

In his criticism of Eddie Webster, Rob Lambert, and Andries Bezuidenhout's *Grounding Globalization,* Michael Burawoy suggested that their writing is representative of a broader turn in labor studies from Marx to Polanyi and from economy to society. Though Burawoy agreed with the need for more focus on worker struggles in value chains, he clearly felt uncomfortable with the strategic decisions of the authors and workers in the factories they studied to focus on the individual plant and worker mobilization. Burawoy asserted the need for a more "global" analysis. What he called the Polanyian retreat to marketization and society as sites of labor struggle are—he argued—clearly inadequate to the task of real social transformation. For Burawoy this represented an abandonment of a critical project of social transformation in favor of an approach that seems to be "largely trapped in localism."[39] The attack was surprising in its strength, and it led to a series of bemused responses from those attacked and others, particularly since nearly all understood their own work as a contribution to Burawoy's own call for greater levels of commitment to public sociology, and much of their writing was directly influenced by his detailed accounts of production politics on the shop floor in various places around the world. Indeed, Webster, Lambert, and the others who responded to Burawoy expressed their surprise that Burawoy, of all people, would take this absolutist view of the global over the embedded and local struggles of workers and communities in specific places.[40] In particular they pointed out how, in recent years, new attempts have been made to refigure the relationship between politics and capital in ways that define precisely such new roles for the labor movement in the context of the globalization of production and the off-shoring of jobs. The result has been the creation of important new spatial strategies that focus on the contingencies of particular sites to facilitate new organizing tactics that may have enormous transformative potential.

For Webster and his colleagues, as for Boaventura de Sousa Santos (each grounded in experiences of the global South), the need is for a critical utopia and a sociology and geography of emergent forms that aim "to identify and enlarge the signs of possible future experiences, under the guise of tendencies and latencies that are actively ignored by hegemonic rationality and knowledge."[41] These are projects that seek to produce new or different problematics, practices, and politics of place infused with possibility, hope, and responsibility.[42] At the heart of their project is a rethinking of the relationship between autonomy and place.

In our recent book, *The Anomie of the Earth,* Federico Luisetti, Wilson Kaiser, and I also focused on the growing number of convergences between practices of autonomy emanating from both European social movements and decolonial movements in the Americas.[43] These include indigenous, postcolonial, environmental, and regional movements. Each is, in its own way, producing new forms of reason, different conceptual vocabularies, and political imaginaries that are reconceptualizing traditional notions of place, locality, and region. This geopolitical shift may be part of a broader erosion of the centrality of the Euro–North Atlantic space and the autonomization of European, South American, and Asian regions. It is directed at a restructuring of neoliberal globalization, but it is also intended to be a transformative geopolitics that generates alternative practices and imaginaries. Organized around concepts of autonomy, terms such as *home, community, forms-of-life, nature,* and *the defense of commons* give new meaning to place, suggesting a variety of practices of decolonization and experimentation of modes of resistance to capitalist accumulation and its universalizing logics.[44] It is to these emerging formations that I turn next.

Place and the Practices of Commoning

How then are we to read and write *place* in the context of an ever more globalizing world? As Moulier Boutang has recently argued in *Cognitive Capitalism,* we first need good theory directed at the concrete circumstances of the day: "We need new sea charts. And we might risk the idea that it is our compasses that are obscuring the road ahead, and then draw the necessary consequences. So the problem is not to appeal to a superhuman will—or to its artificial or maniacal paradises—to get out of the hells into which reason has fallen. Rather let us throw overboard our outmoded navigational instruments. Let us abandon the old reason in order to build a new one."[45]

In *Rebel Cities* David Harvey suggested some ways of thinking about the commons as a foundational practice for a politics of urban space. For Harvey the "ambience and attractiveness of a city, for example, is a collective product of its citizens. Through their daily activities and struggles, individuals and social groups create the social world of the city, and thereby create something common as a framework within which all can dwell."[46] In this view, the commons is a form of relating and place-making based on social cooperation. Harvey insisted on this refreshing conceptualization of commons as a social practice beyond legal entailments. Rather than a specific thing or asset, commons as a verb consists in an unstable and malleable social relation between people vis-à-vis social and physical aspects of the environment considered necessary to their existence. There is, he says, a social practice of *commoning* that is "off-limits to the logic of market exchange and market valuations."[47] Such commoning involves active participation and taking back control of decision-making processes. As Harvey further suggested:

> The human qualities of the city emerge out of our practices in the diverse spaces of the city even as those spaces are subject to enclosure, social control, and appropriation by both private and public/state interests. . . . Public education becomes a common when social forces appropriate, protect, and enhance it for mutual benefit (three cheers for the PTA). . . . The struggle to appropriate the public spaces and public goods in the city for a common purpose is ongoing. But in order to protect the common it is often vital to protect the flow of public goods that underpin the qualities of the common. As neoliberal politics diminishes the financing of public goods, so it diminishes the available common, forcing social groups to find other ways to support that common (education, for example).[48]

Harvey insisted that it is difficult to identify what is an urban commons, and there is a fine line particularly between what we mean by public space and public goods on the one hand and the commons on the other. Public places and public goods might be essential for the possibility of a commons, but the production and sustaining of a commons requires real effort and political action on the part of a people. Without such effort and action, the commons are always in danger of enclosure. As a consequence, the commoning of places is both a defensive statement and a propositional enactment of a different kind of politics: an alternative mode of organizing resources.[49]

In his essay "In Defense of Conviviality and the Collective Subject," Manuel Callahan similarly suggested that a new social paradigm may be emerging that is based on the defense of place.[50] Exemplified by the Occupy movement and by autonomous European and Latin American movements, as well as struggles to defend and expand the Appalachian forest and waterway commons, stop mountaintop removal mining, and build diverse, non-capitalist economies,[51] this new social paradigm is predicated on a politics of conviviality aimed at community regeneration through the mobilization of new places of occupation and convergence, a spatial politics resisting the new enclosures and defending and redefining the commons in response to the broader crisis of post-Fordism and contemporary globalization. In his work on Boston's Occupy tent city, Jeff Juris pointed to just such communing practices and to the physicality of the practice of tenting as a struggle over space:

> [For occupiers] space is important, first, on a microlevel, as the occupations contested the sovereign power of the state to regulate and control the distribution of bodies in space . . . in part, by appropriating and resignifying particular urban spaces such as public parks and squares as arenas for public assembly and democratic expression. . . . #Occupy encampments were thus . . . physical sites of contention involving myriad embodied spatial struggles with the police and symbolic sites of contention over the meaning of space.
>
> On a second, macro, level, the occupations challenged the transformation of social space into abstract space under the calculus of exchange value that drives neoliberal capitalism. . . . In this sense, #Occupy camps, particularly when situated near financial centers, sought to redefine urban space in ways that contrast with dominant socioeconomic orders, embody utopian movement values, and give rise to alternative forms of sociality.[52]

In these contexts, the reorganizing of the relationship between public and private claims on urban places becomes a model of and for political citizenship and a mechanism to ensure the "right to the city"—and offers new models for producing and living in places.

The proxemics of place—the tightly interwoven networks of everyday existence, the complex exchange and trust relations that tie the economy together, the ebb and flow of people and goods throughout the day—produce webs of interaction that engender place. But the resulting interactional spaces of movements like Occupy not only laid claim to public-private space as the commons of a new community (the 99 percent), but also represented the power of place in producing new forms everyday life in networks of similar occupy movements and broader debates about the structure of societies in which the 1 percent controls disproportionate wealth in relation to the other 99 percent. In this sense, community and place are not predicated on what Michael Rustin has called "the idea of the autonomous, self-seeking individual as the foundational 'atom' of the human world," but on the quality and depth of the relations that sustain life.[53] Such a relational society is the foundation for all notions of community and the commons and essential to any functioning economy; it is a solidarity economy.[54]

Place matters because it provides temporary sutures of relations that structure the ways in which everyday experiences are organized.[55] Even experiences of the "global" were placed in context in this way by Occupy; global financial capital—the 1 percent and Wall Street—was put in its place. The global was shown to be a product of the interactional effects of local systems of communication and exchange among surprisingly small numbers of people and companies (albeit incredibly powerful). This placing certainly did not demobilize the power of capital or the state, but for a brief moment it did reveal their partial and numerically limited base and the fragmented nature of their claim to universality and hegemony.

These practices have their own complex temporalities and geographies, and they are anathema to the flattening and abstract logics of planetary space, Euro-Atlantic *nomos,* or the market. As Gustavo Esteva argued in discussing communal practices in southern Mexico: "In the same way that commons is a generic term for very different forms of social existence, the immense richness of the social organizations currently existing or being created in Latin America cannot be reduced to formal categories. . . . The Spanish *ejido* (the land at the edge of the villages, used in common by the peasants in the 16th century) is not identical to the British commons, to the pre-Hispanic communal regimes, to the modern Mexican *ejido,* or to the emerging new commons."[56] Such places and the commons they sustain "are the substantive grounds of collective life,"[57] and they depend on radically different ontologies.

In pointing to Gibson-Graham's preference to multiply the forms and practices of the commons, Jodi Dean recently suggested the need to embrace the *common of the commons.*[58] Here the horizon of the commons provides what Gibson-Graham's alternative and diverse economies do through multiplying positionalities and offering a defense of a new collective politics.[59] Michael Hardt has similarly argued: "We have been made so stupid that we can only recognize the world as private or public. We have become blind to the common." In response, we urgently need ways that avoid the tendency to re-create the binaries that have destroyed the commons (diversity/hegemony, private/public, individual/collective, state/social) and instead affirm the commons as the "open and autonomous production of subjectivity, social relations, and the forms of life; the self-governed continuous creation of new humanity."[60]

Placing the commons at the core of an emancipatory politics in this way challenges us to engage more broadly with the possibilities of different types of property regime, alternative systems of resource management, and other ways of making decisions about the places we produce. But, as Doreen Massey constantly reminded us, such deeply relational understandings of place and space require that we also engage differently with our responsibility to others at a distance.

Notes

1. Michel Foucault, "Of Other Spaces," *Diacritics* 16, no. 1 (1968): 22–27; Edward W. Soja, *Postmodern Geographies: The Reassertion of Space in Critical Social Theory* (London: Verso, 1989).

2. David Black, Donald Kunze, and John Pickles, eds., *Commonplaces: Essays on the Nature of Place* (Lanham, MD: University Press of America, 1989).

3. John Pickles, *A History of Spaces: Cartographic Reason, Mapping and the Geo-Coded World* (London: Routledge, 2004).

4. Slavoj Žižek, "How to Begin from the Beginning," in *The Idea of Communism*, ed. Costas Douzinas and Slavoj Žižek (New York: Verso, 2010), 212–213; Michael Hardt and Antonio Negri, *Commonwealth* (Cambridge: Harvard University Press, 2009).

5. Herb Reid and Betsy Taylor, *Recovering the Commons: Democracy, Place, and Global Justice* (Urbana: University of Illinois Press, 2010), 12.

6. Arturo Escobar, *Territories of Difference: Place, Movements, Life, "Redes"* (Durham: Duke University Press, 2008), 7.

7. For example, Doreen Massey, "Questions of Locality," *Geography: Journal of the Geographical Association* 78, no. 2 (1993): 142–149; Doreen Massey, "Making Spaces, or, Geography Is Political Too," *Soundings* 1 (Autumn 1995): 193–208.

8. Benno Werlen, *Society, Action and Space* (London: Routledge, 1993); Theodore R. Schatzki, *Social Practices: A Wittgensteinian Approach to Human Activity and the Social* (Cambridge: Cambridge University Press, 1996).

9. *Place* as a concept remains highly inflected by subjective individualist and voluntarist interpretations of specific locales invested with meaning and memory. See, for example, Anne Buttimer, "Grasping the Dynamism of the Lifeworld," *Annals of the Association of American Geographers* 66 (1976): 277–292; Edward Relph, *Place and Placelessness* (London: Pion, 1976); Yi-Fu Tuan, *Space and Place: The Perspective of Experience* (Minneapolis: University of Minnesota Press, 1977); Robert D. Sack, *Conceptions of Space in Social Thought* (London: Macmillan, 1980). For a critical phenomenological approach to space and place that resists these impulses, see John Pickles, *Phenomenology, Science and Geography: Spatiality and the Human Sciences* (Cambridge: Cambridge University Press, 1985), and John Pickles, *Geography and Humanism* (Norwich, U.K.:

Geo Books, 1987). See also Tim Cresswell, *Place: A Short Introduction* (Oxford: Wiley-Blackwell, 2004).

10. Jon Lepofsky has shown how communitarian notions of place that presuppose that communities operate locally through face-to-face contact can be politically problematic. Drawing on Jean-Luc Nancy, Lepofsky has suggested that such notions of being-with-and-in "community" and "place" need to reinvent what it means to be-with and be-in. Without such reinvention, communities and places that are already patriarchal, parochial, totalitarian, or racialized tend to reproduce those characteristics. Jon D. Lepofsky, "Strange Exchange: Using a Complementary Currency to Rearticulate Ethics, Place and Community," *Ethics, Policy & Environment* 12, no. 1 (2009): 131–142.

11. Doreen Massey, *For Space* (London: Sage, 2005), 142. See also Sallie Marston, John Paul Jones III, and Keith Woodward, "Human Geography without Scale," *Transactions of the Institute of British Geographers* 30 (2005): 416–432.

12. Massey, *For Space,* 142.

13. Eddie Webster, Rob Lambert, and Andries Bezuidenhout, *Grounding Globalization: Labour in the Age of Insecurity* (London: Wiley-Blackwell, 2008).

14. Jamie Peck, "Economic Sociologies in Space," *Economic Geography* 81, no. 2 (2004): 129–175.

15. I am indebted to Larry Grossberg and Arturo Escobar for these ideas on conjuncturalism and context, and the many discussions and seminars we have shared in teasing out their implications. See particularly Lawrence Grossberg, *Cultural Studies in the Future Tense* (Durham: Duke University Press, 2010), and Escobar, *Territories of Difference.* See also John Pickles, "The Cultural Turn and the Conjunctural Economy: Economic Geography, Anthropology, and Cultural Studies," in *The Wiley-Blackwell Companion to Economic Geography,* ed. Trevor Barnes, Jamie Peck, and Eric Sheppard (New York: Wiley-Blackwell, 2012), 537–551.

16. Lawrence Grossberg, "Does Cultural Studies Have Futures? (Or What's the Matter with New York?): Cultural Studies, Contexts and Conjunctures," *Cultural Studies* 20, no. 1 (2006): 5.

17. Jacques Derrida, "Specters of Marx: The State of the Debt, the Work of Mourning and the New International," *New Left Review* 205 (May–June 1994): 31–58.

18. The concept of *conjuncture* has played an important role in the history of Marxist thought. For Louis Althusser it was the central concept of the Marxist science of politics; Louis Althusser, *For Marx* (London: Verso. 1969); Louis Althusser, *Reading Marx* (London: Verso, 1970). Antonio Gramsci distinguished between what he called "organic movements (relatively permanent) and movements which may be termed 'conjunctural' (and which appear as occasional, immediate, almost accidental)"; Antonio Gramsci, *Selections from the Prison Notebooks* (New York: International Publishers, 1971), 177. Gramsci was thereby attempting to avoid what we now call constructivist approaches ("ideologism"), in which events are explained one-sidedly in terms of voluntarist and

individual elements, and realist or naturalist approaches ("economism"), wherein the world is presumed to be merely given. Each tends to focus one-sidedly on direct and immediate causes and overlooks the complex role of indirect effects. For cultural studies, by contrast, context itself is always "overdetermined" by contexts other than itself, which in turn are overdetermined by other contexts. This is not to say that meaning is free-floating; instead, it is deeply embedded and shaped by the multiple contexts within which it gains any stability as meaning and identity. For a history of the concept, see Juha Koivisto and Mikko Lahtinen, "Conjuncture, Politico-Historical," *Historical Materialism* 20, no. 1 (2012): 267–277.

19. Hall is quoted in Grossberg, "Does Cultural Studies Have Futures?" 4.

20. Grossberg, "Does Cultural Studies Have Futures? 1–31.

21. In *The Interpretation of Dreams* (1913) (Leiden: Brill, 1990), Freud argued that the interpretation of dream elements needed to avoid ascribing single causes to them and instead must recognize their multiple and overdetermined nature, and that there is no limit to their further overdetermination. See also Louis Althusser, "Contradiction and Overdetermination," in his *For Marx*, 87–128.

22. Lawrence Grossberg, Angela McRobbie, and Paul Gilroy, *Without Guarantees: In Honour of Stuart Hall* (London: Verso, 2000).

23. Grossberg, "Does Cultural Studies Have Futures?"

24. Douglas Reichert Powell, *Critical Regionalism: Connecting Politics and Culture in the American Landscape* (Chapel Hill: University of North Carolina Press, 2007), 1.

25. Massey, *For Space,* 142. See also Doreen Massey and Stuart Hall, "Interpreting the Crisis: Doreen Massey and Stuart Hall Discuss Ways of Understanding the Current Crisis," *Soundings* 44 (Spring 2010): 57–71.

26. Doreen Massey, *Power-Geometries and the Politics of Space-Time* (Heidelberg: University of Heidelberg Press, 1999).

27. Stuart Hall in Massey and Hall, "Interpreting the Crisis," 57.

28. J. K. Gibson-Graham, Stephen Resnick, and Richard Wolff, *Re/presenting Class: Essays in Postmodern Marxism* (Durham: Duke University Press, 2001).

29. Doreen Massey, "Questions of Locality," *Geography: Journal of the Geographical Association* 78, no. 2 (1993): 149.

30. Mikko Joronen, *The Age of Planetary Space: On Heidegger, Being, and the Metaphysics of Globalization* (Turku, Finland: University of Turku, 2010); Mikko Joronen, "The Technological Metaphysics of Planetary Space: Being in the Age of Globalization," *Environment and Planning: Society & Space* 26, no. 4 (2008): 596–610.

31. Joronen, *Age of Planetary Space,* 2.

32. Ellen Meiskins Wood, "Back to Marx," *Monthly Review* 49, no. 2 (1997): 1–9.

33. J. K. Gibson-Graham, *The End of Capitalism (As We Knew It): A Feminist Critique of Political Economy* (Oxford: Blackwell, 1996); J. K. Gibson-Graham, *A Postcapitalist Politics* (Minneapolis: University of Minnesota Press, 2006), 126

34. Pickles, *Phenomenology, Science and Geography.*

35. Carl Schmitt, *The "Nomos" of the Earth in the International Law of the "Jus Publicum Europaeum,"* trans. G. L. Ulmen (1950; repr., New York: Telos, 2003).

36. This is, of course, not to say that its effects are not more widespread or that the Euro-Atlantic *nomos* was not deeply influenced by complex forms of regional exchange and processes of transculturation.

37. Stuart Elden, "Reading Schmitt Geopolitically: *Nomos,* Territory and Großraum," *Radical Philosophy* 161 (May–June 2010): 24. For a more engaged reading of Schmitt's significance, see the 2005 special issue "World Orders: Confronting Carl Schmitt's Theory of the Nomos," *South Atlantic Quarterly,* 104, no. 2 (2005). See also Carlo Galli, *Political Spaces and Global War,* trans. Elisabeth Fay (Minneapolis: University of Minnesota Press, 2010).

38. Massey, *Power-Geometries and the Politics of Space-Time,* 29.

39. Michael Burawoy, "From Polanyi to Pollyanna: The False Optimism of Global Labor Studies," *Global Labour Journal* 1, no. 2 (2010): 306. For a critique of claims that see locality studies as localist or parochial, see Doreen Massey, "Questions of Locality," 142–149.

40. Donella Caspersz, "From Pollyanna to the Pollyanna Principle: A Response to Michael Burawoy's 'From Polanyi to Pollyanna: The False Optimism of Global Labour Studies,'" *Global Labour Journal* 1, no. 3 (2010): 393–397; Dan Clawson, "'False' Optimism: The Key to Historic Breakthroughs? A Response to Michael Burawoy's 'From Polanyi to Pollyanna: The False Optimism of Global Labour Studies,'" *Global Labour Journal* 1, no. 3 (2010): 398–400; Rob Lambert, "Unionism in One Country Is No Longer an Option: A Response to Michael Burawoy's 'From Polanyi to Pollyanna: The False Optimism of Global Labour Studies,'" *Global Labour Journal* 1, no. 3 (2010): 388–392. For his response, see Michael Burawoy, "On Uncompromising Pessimism: Response to My Critics," *Global Labour Journal* 2, no. 1 (2011): 73–77.

41. Boaventura de Sousa Santos, "The World Social Forum: Toward a Counter-Hegemonic Globalisation (Part 1)," in *World Social Forum: Challenging Empires,* ed. Jai Sen, Anita Anand, Arturo Escobar, and Peter Waterman (New Delhi: Viveka Foundation, 2004), 242.

42. See Michal Osterweil, "A Different (Kind of) Politics Is Possible: Conflict and Problem(s) at the USSF," in *The World and US Social Forums: A Better World Is Possible and Necessary,* ed. Judith Blau and Marina Karides (Leiden: Brill, 2009), 71–89; Doreen Massey, "Geographies of Responsibility," *Geografiska Annaler: Series B, Human Geography* 86, no. 1 (2004): 5–1; and Gibson-Graham, *A Postcapitalist Politics.*

43. Federico Luisetti, John Pickles, Wilson Kaiser, eds., *The Anomie of the Earth: Philosophy, Politics, and Autonomy in Europe and the Americas* (Durham: Duke University Press, 2015).

44. See also Escobar, *Territories of Difference.*

45. Yann Moulier Boutang, *Cognitive Capitalism,* trans. Ed Emery (Malden, MA: Polity Press, 2011), 3.

46. David Harvey, *Rebel Cities: From the Right to the City to the Urban Revolution* (London: Verso Books, 2012), 74.

47. Ibid., 73.

48. Ibid., 72–73.

49. Ibid. For elaboration of this point see Maribel Casas-Cortés, Sebastian Cobarrubias, and John Pickles, "Commons," in *A Companion to Urban Anthropology*, ed. Donald Nonini (New York: Wiley, 2014), 449–469.

50. Manuel Callahan, "In Defense of Conviviality and the Collective Subject," *Polis: Revista Latinamericana* 33 (2012), http://polis.revues.org/8432, accessed April 9, 2013.

51. See Reid and Taylor, *Recovering the Commons;* Kathryn Newfont, *Blue Ridge Commons: Environmental Activism and Forest History in Western North Carolina* (Athens: University of Georgia Press, 2012); Bryan T. McNeil, *Combatting Mountaintop Removal: New Directions in the Fight against Big Coal* (Urbana: University of Illinois Press, 2011); and Amanda L. Fickey, "Redefining Development: Exploring Alternative Economic Practices in Appalachia" (Ph.D. diss., University of Kentucky, 2013).

52. Jeffrey S. Juris, "Reflections on #Occupy Everywhere: Social Media, Public Space, and Emerging Logics of Aggregation," *American Ethnologist* 39, no. 2 (2012): 259–279.

53. Michael Rustin, "A Relational Society," *Soundings* 54 (August 2013): 24.

54. See Priscilla Vaz, "Solidarity Economy as a Pedagogical Praxis of Autonomy" (master's thesis, University of North Carolina at Chapel Hill, 2012), for a detailed elaboration of the solidarity economies of Brazil.

55. This is always an open political project, as Jean-Luc Nancy, *The Inoperative Community,* trans. Peter Connor et al. (Minneapolis: University of Minnesota Press, 1991), xxxix, has stressed in cautioning against seeing community and place as purely fixed as "a local," presupposing face-to-face contact: "The community that becomes *a single* thing (body, mind, fatherland, Leader . . .) necessarily loses the *in* of being-*in*-common. Or, it loses the *with* or the *together* that defines it. It yields its being-together to a being *of* togetherness. The truth of community, on the contrary, resides in the retreat of such a being"; emphases in original.

56. Gustavo Esteva, "Hope from the Margins," in *The Wealth of the Commons: A World beyond Market & State,* ed. David Bollier and Silke Helfrich (Amherst, MA: Levellers Press, 2012), www.wealthofthecommons.org/essay/hope-margins.

57. Reid and Taylor, *Recovering the Commons,* 12.

58. Jodi Dean, *The Communist Horizon* (New York: Verso, 2012), 12–16.

59. See Gibson-Graham, *A Postcapitalist Politics,* and Julie Graham, Stephen Healy, and Kenneth Byrne, "Constructing the Community Economy: Civic Professionalism and the Politics of Sustainable Regions," *Journal of Appalachian Studies* 8, no. 1 (2010): 50–61.

60. Michael Hardt, "Reclaim the Common in Communism," *Guardian,* February 3, 2011, www.guardian.co.uk/commentisfree/2011/feb/03/communism-capitalism-socialism-property. I am grateful to Dwight Billings for pointing this out. There is an

important tension in the ways in which J. K. Gibson-Graham and her colleagues and Michael Hardt elaborate their understanding of "common of the commons." For Hardt the common of the commons relates fundamentally to the abolition of private property. Gibson-Graham, Resnick, and Wolff, *Re/presenting Class,* focus their attention on distinguishing the forms and effects of the appropriation and distribution of social surplus from the various property regimes that help organize and legitimate appropriation and distribution. They view communalism as the collective or democratic appropriation and distribution of surplus by its producers—not the abolition of private property per se.

4

The Power of Place and the Place of Power

John Gaventa

This chapter explores the interaction between place and power. On the one hand, places shape power. In the preface to their book, *Transforming Places: Lessons from Appalachia*, Stephen Fisher and Barbara Smith write about "the importance of place as a source for personal identity and motivating force in local and regional struggles." Places that shape one's identity can help shape and nourish "*the power within*" people to act, to raise voices, to struggle for change. Places that shape identity also help give roots for people to gain the "*power to*"—to take action, to realize personal agency, on the basis of these identities. In that sense, place becomes fundamental to the operation of power.[1]

On the other hand, power shapes place. The "power within" and the "power to" are often constrained by another form of power, the "power over," which actors within the same place, or indeed in another place, have over others. Power affects who has a place at the decision-making table, whose voices and identities are considered important, and whose knowledge counts. When we think about how power and place interact, we need to do so not only in terms of local places, but in terms of how the local and the global interact as well.

In this chapter I would like to begin with some personal reflections on how various places in which I have lived and worked have shaped my own conceptions and experiences of power. I shall then turn to sharing an approach to power, one that has come to be called "the power cube," showing how it links place to the forms, spaces, and levels of power that may shape the boundaries of action within it. Developed with colleagues in recent years, this power-cube framework is deeply rooted in my own experiences of power in the Appalachian region some forty years ago—experiences that continue to shape my thinking. Drawing on this framework, I will offer some examples from across Appalachia, as well as from other research I have done internationally, that speak to the interaction of place and power.[2]

Places Matter: an Autobiographical Reflection

Though I have lived in many places, I have Appalachian roots. My mother comes from eastern Tennessee, a place that she left at an early age, escaping with her family the ravages of the Depression to search for new livelihoods in Florida. Florida became her home, but her Tennessee roots remained strong: family members always returned to the eastern Tennessee hills they considered home, and they continue to do so generations later.

But though these are my roots, I wasn't raised there. My childhood home was a small village in the heart of Nigeria known as Eku. When I was six weeks old, my Tennessee mother and my father, originally from Georgia but also raised in Florida (and just graduated from medical school), went to Nigeria with the dream of building a hospital in a remote part of the Niger Delta. Nigeria became my "growing-up place" for the next fifteen years, and it was their place—their home—for thirty-five years. In this small place, an ocean away, I didn't hear much about my Appalachian roots, yet I later began to realize some commonalities to both places.

In the small village in Nigeria, my favorite boyhood adventure was floating on hardwood logs down a beautiful tropical river through the jungle. The logs made great diving platforms, with monkeys above and tropical fish below. While they were part of that place, only later did I realize the significance of where those logs were going. They had been cut by a British company. They were being shipped down the river to the port, for export to the United Kingdom and other parts of the world. I realized later in life, when I began to research the effect of absentee ownership in eastern Tennessee, that I had grown up in a place that bore similarities: a place of poverty amid abundance, a beautiful place whose resources were threatened by extractive economies serving the needs of other, more powerful places.

In later years, this place in which I was raised also became the site of massive oil exploration and extraction. Indeed, the Niger Delta, one of the most diverse ecological systems in the world, continues also to be host to some of the largest oil companies in the world, whose practices threaten the traditional livelihoods of the farmers and fisher folk of villages like the one in which I was raised.

A decade ago, I had a chance to return to my boyhood place. The idyllic memories that I carried with me were now filtered through other realities. A new road and airport made getting there easier, but the local roads where I grew up seemed as rough and impassable as ever. While money is flowing, it does so unequally. The chief has a big new house, a replica of a European palace, a product of his links to the oil companies. Open flares from the natural gas keep the village lit all night, and women dry their clothes and cassavas under them, barely aware of the toxins that poison the local environment. Even as natural gas is wasted, they walk farther and farther in the overcut forest to collect firewood with which to cook for their families. This was the place in which I was raised: a place whose future is being shaped by external forces, by those with "power over." It is also now a place of resistance, as armed youth militias patrol the waters and roads, seeking to gain their power and voice over what they consider to be their own.

Though I had Appalachian roots, it was only after returning from Nigeria to Kentucky for high school and to Tennessee for university that I began to learn more about these roots. At Vanderbilt University, I got involved in the Student Health Coalition. In the summer of 1971, I joined some other students to do a small study of who owned the land and who paid the taxes in the five largest coal-producing counties of upper eastern Tennessee. The study found what many local people already knew: the majority of the land was owned and controlled by a handful of absentee companies that paid a pittance in local taxes. But armed with some facts, local residents could do something about the situation. In the fall of 1971, a dozen citizens gathered in a church basement to discuss the study and what could be done. They banded together and filed a lawsuit—and remained together to form the next year the grassroots organizing group Save Our Cumberland Mountains, which remains strong to this day.

One of the communities that I visited during that time was owned largely by a British company, ironically called the American Association. Knowing that I had a scholarship to study the following year in England, members of the community approached me and asked, "Will you find out who owns us and help tell them how bad it is?" Being naive about power at the time, I said something like "Sure, no problem, I'll give it a try."

The first year I was in graduate school in Oxford, I spent countless days going through company records in London trying to trace the ownership of this rural part of Appalachia. I found that these 80,000 acres of coal-rich land, spanning parts of Tennessee and Kentucky, were part of a global web of hundreds of companies, at the top of which sat one of Britain's wealthiest men and a onetime lord mayor of London. This particular company, holding sway over this particular place in Appalachia, represented to him only one of several hundred companies that he owned or controlled around the world.[3]

Teaming up with a British TV producer for the series *World in Action,* I worked with residents of this Appalachian valley to tell their story, through what became a documentary entitled *The Stripping of Appalachia,* aired nationally in the United Kingdom. In it the residents of the valley spoke powerfully about the effects of the company's practices and policies on their lives. The film brought the media, first the BBC, then the U.S. press, into the valley. The publicity led to calls for government investigations, but when the media went away, the result was what we had feared: violence against those people who had spoken out. Some people had their houses burned. My car was sabotaged. Community members said, "Thanks for finding out who owns us, but why don't you go back to school for a while?"[4]

The experience in that one place, a small Appalachian valley community, like my experience in a small village in Nigeria, was a powerful one. It set me on a lifelong project of trying to understand both the power of places—and the sense of community, identity, and resistance that arises from them—but also how external power, the "power over," shapes the ability of localities and local people to make their own futures.

While I was struggling to understand this interaction of place and power, I remember people in the Appalachian valley suggesting that perhaps I should visit the Highlander Center, located a couple of hours' drive away. At Highlander, I discovered the power of a different kind of place: a place where people can come together to share their experiences and develop their own knowledge and capacities to act. With this approach, over eighty years, Highlander has been a key "gathering place" for the emerging movements for labor rights, civil rights, and economic and environmental justice. Writing about this role, the historian Aldon Morris talks about the importance of what he calls "movement halfway houses," which contribute not only to the skills and tactics of social change, but also to "a vision of a future society."[5]

It was while working at Highlander that I first began to realize the important interconnections of knowledge and power. The control of knowledge serves to shape what people know about their places and communities, and thus how they act within them. The creation or recovery of knowledge about community through people's own research can become an important form of building awareness and action. It was at Highlander, for instance, that a group of communities that were affected by the floods of 1977 decided to come together to find out who really owned the land of Appalachia and do something about it. That led to a major study, *The Appalachian Land Ownership Study,* involving dozens of researchers and activists across the region. This study, like my earlier experiences, pointed to the importance of the land to the culture and livelihoods of those who lived on it. But it also pointed to the power of the ownership of land to shape and control the futures of these rural places.[6]

In the mid-1990s, after almost twenty years at Highlander, I moved to the Institute of Development Studies (IDS), based at the University of Sussex. IDS is a center for research and education on development issues around the world. For me, it was an exciting opportunity to link my work in rural Tennessee and Appalachia with my earlier international background. Over the next fifteen years, I was involved in many projects that looked at how citizens mobilize around the world, including work with a research team, Power, Participation and Social Change, and an international network known as the Development Research Centre on Citizenship, Participation and Accountability. It was here that I began to understand much more about the way that global forces affect local places. It was also here that I began to see commonalities among communities across the world that, while struggling in different places on different issues, face similar processes of mobilizing for change and challenging power relations.[7]

From 2011 to 2014 I was on leave from IDS to serve for a few years as director of the Coady International Institute, based at St. Francis Xavier University (StFX) in Nova Scotia, Canada. Coady itself is the product of a place-based movement of the 1920s and 1930s, known as the Antigonish movement, similar in many ways to Highlander. Led by Dr. Moses Coady and Father Jimmy Tompkins, the Antigonish movement used adult education approaches to support community organization and collective action of communities across this rural region. Though Highlander's primary approach was to help people gain the power to challenge the power "over" their communities held by larger structures, the Antigonish movement put more focus on what people could do for themselves, using their own assets. From here grew a large movement of cooperatives, credit unions, and education that gradually spread to other parts of the world. In response, the Coady International Institute was formed in 1959 and continues today to be an educational center for local leaders and development workers across the world who are seeking to improve their communities. The Coady itself is a place that exemplifies linking the local and the global: though it grew from local needs and actions, its influence has been worldwide: over 6,000 graduates from 130 countries have now taken part in its educational programs.[8]

I have taken the liberty of reflecting somewhat autobiographically because place matters. These places where I have lived and worked have shaped who I am as a scholar and as an activist, what I think about and what I work on. These places in my own life journey also illustrate the interactions of place with power. Whether in rural Nigeria or rural Appalachia, I have experienced the power of locality to shape my own identity, but I have also experienced the external power that could shape the futures of such places. Whether at Highlander, IDS, or the Coady Institute, I have seen the importance of places that support the process of building knowledge to counter dominant power, and the ways in which people develop their own "power within" to think and act for themselves. While working with local communities around the world, I have come to see their commonalities across place, and their interactions with external global forces.

All these experiences, in different places, have caused me to think a great deal about the interrelationships of place and power: about the power of place but also the place of power in understanding communities. While acknowledging the importance of place, I want to pose a challenge: How do we locate place in an increasingly global and complex world of power? What forms of power affect people's places? What are the spaces for participation within them? It is to that intellectual journey that I now turn.

Examining Power and Place

In 1961 Robert Dahl famously asked about New Haven, Connecticut, "Who governs?" His book was one of the best-known in a genre of work on community power in the United States at the time, launching a large debate on who had power, and indeed how one understood power in American democracy, especially at the local level. Power in this approach could be found very simply by examining "who participates, who gains and who loses, and who prevails in decision-making," especially at the community level, where power might be most observable.[9]

This view of power was challenged in 1974 by Steven Lukes in his perhaps even more well-known book, *Power: A Radical View* (followed by his expanded version in 2004). Critiquing the argument that power could be studied by observing who prevails in decision-making arenas, Lukes argued that power must be understood not only in terms of who participates, but also in terms of who does not. Power, he argued, had three faces: the public face that Dahl, Polsby, and others had studied; a hidden face, which served to keep issues off the agenda of decision-making arenas; and an even more insidious "third face," through which the relatively powerless came to internalize and accept their own condition, and thus might not be aware of or act on their interests in any observable way.[10]

As a student of Lukes at Oxford, I was influenced by the debates between him and Peter Bachrach on the faces of power. These ideas made a great deal of sense in relation to what I had experienced in the small coal-mining valley in the heart of the Appalachian region discussed earlier. My attempt to use these ideas to understand my own encounter with power in one place led to the book *Power and Powerlessness: Quiescence and Rebellion in an Appalachian Valley*, which was originally my doctoral thesis.[11]

Since that time, however, my views have expanded. While the three faces of power elaborated by Lukes continue to be important, in the contemporary era they must also be understood in relationship to other aspects of power, which were not considered explicitly in his earlier work. Though many of the earlier debates on power focused at the community level, changing patterns of globalization have changed the territorial or spatial relations of power, meaning that power increasingly must be understood not only at the local, the national, or the global level, but also in the interrelationships between those levels. As Ulrich Beck writes in his book *Power in a Global Age*, globalization "has introduced a new space and framework for acting: politics is no longer subject to the same boundaries as before, and is no longer tied solely to state actors and institutions, the result being that additional players, new roles, new resources, unfamiliar rules and new contradictions and conflicts appear on the scene. In the old game, each playing piece made one move only. This is no longer true of the new nameless game for power and domination."[12]

It was in this context that, while working at IDS, I and others began to search for approaches that would help examine the interrelationships of the forms of power that we were encountering in different political spaces and places. Building on my previous work, I began to argue that Lukes's three "faces" or forms of power must be understood in relation to how spaces for engagement are created, and the levels of power (from local to global) in which they occur. The forms, spaces, and levels are separate but interrelated dimensions of power, each of which has at least three components within it. We realized that these dimensions could be visually linked together into a "power cube," analogous to a Rubik's Cube. By using this framework, I argued, we could better begin to understand the multiple dimensions of power in a global context. Moreover, the approach could be a tool for reflection by activists and practitioners to map the types of power that we sought to challenge, and to look at the strategies and entry points for doing so. While some thought the cube image risked being a bit too static in its portrayal of power, for many practitioners the approach seemed to have some resonance—and the approach has now been used and elaborated by many in very different settings.[13]

In discussing each dimension of the cube, I will elaborate it in terms of what I have learned in my work within Appalachia as well as elsewhere.

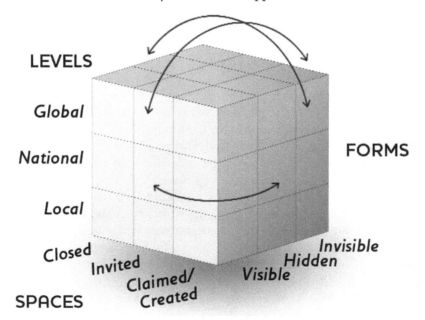

The power cube, from John Gaventa, "Finding the Spaces for Change: A Power Analysis," *IDS Bulletin* 37, no. 6 (2006): 25; see www.powercube.net.

Forms of Power

The forms of power affect who has a place at the tables of power. Within a given place, some people's voices, identities, issues, and agendas will get more visible attention than others'. Within a place, there are forms of power that mean that certain people have control and others do not. We need to understand those forms.

VISIBLE POWER

The first form of power is what we call *visible power,* in which contests over interests are assumed to be visible in public spaces, which are presumed to be relatively open. This view is based on a pluralist view of American democracy, which assumes that if citizens have an issue, then they can organize and take action. They can go to public meetings, run for election, file a lawsuit, and their voices will be heard. If they take action, the system will respond. So, therefore, if you want to find out who has power, you need to see what issues have appeared on the public agenda, and who won and who lost, with the assumption that those who prevailed are those with power.

But that understanding of power and democracy didn't quite match what I saw in the Appalachian valley. I went through all the courthouse records in both the eastern Tennessee side of the county and the eastern Kentucky side, over fifty years, and never once did I see issues associated with the company's control on the public agenda. Though violations of democratic rights, enormous inequalities in wealth, poor housing, and appalling environmental conditions were to be found everywhere, there was little visible conflict or action for change.

HIDDEN POWER

What I began to learn, of course, is that my textbook understanding of democracy was inadequate to understanding this reality. Power does not have visible forms only. Power isn't just about who wins and who loses at the table; power is about keeping certain issues, certain voices, and certain identities off that table in the first place.

Political scientists write about this hidden power as the "mobilization of bias": a prevailing set of rules, procedures, values, and symbols that will mobilize certain issues and certain actors into the system, and other issues and other actors out of the system. Within the Appalachian valley, the biases against speaking out were many. Some were based on force: the threats of losing a job, threats and realities of violence, loss of housing or welfare benefits. Others were subtler: distance from the seats of power, lack of resources to attend the meetings, lack of confidence to speak from one's own knowledge. As the book *Power and Powerlessness* details, taken together over ninety years, such barriers to participation soon become accepted, so that nonparticipation rather than public engagement becomes the status quo.[14]

INVISIBLE POWER

This is why Lukes's work made a lot of sense to me. He had argued that the most insidious use of power isn't just keeping issues off the table, it's keeping people from thinking they have an issue at all. *Invisible power,* the third form of power, is the internalization of powerlessness so that people who experience it, the victims of an unjust status quo, come to believe in its legitimacy. In such a situation, visible conflict or public engagement is preempted because people may not see a need to act at all or, just as effectively, may not believe in their own capacity to do anything about the status quo.

In the Appalachian valley, we saw many examples. One person, talking about the coal camps days, said, "We worked for a song, but we sang it ourselves." Without alternatives, people accepted the situation. Over time, numerous Appalachian stereotypes—laziness, apathy, ignorance—could all serve, if internalized, as forms of powerlessness that served to protect the legitimacy of the status quo.

This kind of power even served to distinguish the language about place. I remember talking to the farmers there about the huge conflicts between farmers over land: they would fight intensely over the encroachment of fences, animals, and so on. When I asked about the encroachment of muck from strip-mined land on their crops, however, they would say, "Oh, we can't do anything about that land, it's not private land: that's company land." "Company" had been placed in another category as something you couldn't fight over. It had been accepted as part of the status quo. One might romanticize that place: as a place of identity, of culture, and of beauty, and, yes, it was all those things, but also it was a place where all the forms of power existed. As a result, the deep issues of inequality that affected people's everyday lives rarely appeared as public grievances through the established institutional channels.

Of course, over the years in Appalachia, there's been a huge amount of work to challenge this system of power. Groups like Appalshop and others have recaptured and shared a different version of Appalachian culture. Groups like Highlander and others have helped people build their own awareness of issues, and of their capacity to act on them. Groups like SOCM (State Wide Organizing for Community eMpowerment), KFTC (Kentuckians For The Commonwealth), and many others have worked to bring hidden issues into the public arena. Indeed, a vast scholarship now documents the forms of resistance, as well as the forms of power and control, that have shaped the region's history. For understanding the interactions of power and place, such work is critical: any place contains within it multiple forms of power, which will shape how that place is experienced, preserved, and changed. But it also contains "spaces" of resistance, through which people exercise their own voice, identity, and agency.

The Spaces of Participation

Within any given place, there may be multiple spaces in which people act and participate. The notion of "space" is widely used across the literatures on power, policy, democracy, and citizen action. Some writers refer to "political spaces"; other works focus on "policy spaces"; others examine "democratic spaces," in which citizens can engage to claim citizenship and affect governance processes. From the power-cube lens, which takes a concern with citizen action and participation as its starting point, "spaces" are seen as "opportunities, moments and channels where people can act to potentially affect policies, discourses, decisions and relationships that affect their lives and interests."[15]

Within a given geographical place, there can be many different types of spaces that affect the nature of people's participation. In fact, who has power depends on whose space they are acting in. We can think, for instance, about a village woman in the most rural part of an African village not having much power in the World Bank's decision-making space. But if you bring the head of the World Bank to her village, put him down in her community, and surround him with the highly organized village women, he might also feel pretty powerless in that space. So power isn't inherent in a person. Power is related to the spaces in which people operate. The power cube distinguishes between three kinds of spaces for participation.

The first is what we call the *closed* or "*uninvited spaces*" of participation: spaces where bureaucrats, experts, elected representatives, and others make decisions with little consultation with or involvement of citizens. There are still many such places in Appalachia, and of course elsewhere, where decisions are made behind closed doors that affect the future of those communities. Whether it's in banks, legislatures, or corporate boardrooms, power remains unaccountable and often opaque. To counter these forms of power, around the world we see many calls for greater forms of transparency and public accountability through initiatives such as the Open Government Initiative, or the Publish What You Pay initiative, which calls for transparency of mining companies to make public the funds they pay to governments.[16]

Increasingly around the world, as people have struggled to claim voice, we see another kind of space emerging, what we call "*invited participation.*" As efforts are made to widen participation, new spaces are created in which authorities invite people to participate through various forms of public hearings, local consultations, or even more regularized forms, such as popular participation on governing bodies and committees. Within the Appalachian region, the politics of place has been filled with such invited participation. Public consultation and public hearings have become an accepted part of the American regulatory process. Endless hours have been spent as citizens attend public hearings to testify, for instance, on the potential environmental impact of a mine, often to feel as if their voices and efforts were ignored.

While such invited spaces may look more participatory, in fact they may be shaped by the same forms of power discussed earlier, which affect what issues arise, who participates, and with what effect. In invited spaces, people participate by "invitation," not by "right." If people are invited to the table to participate and then speak truth to power, what happens to the next invitation? They may not be invited back. The concept of invited space reminds us that those who create the space also will probably be the ones to have power within it.

While much of the work on public participation has focused on how citizens engage in such invited spaces, there are also what we call "*claimed spaces*" in any community or place, the spaces where people come together on their own terms. These are the spaces where people can speak their minds, voice their concerns with their own vernaculars, without having to disguise them from those who sit in power. These spaces are often informal: on the street corner, at the local bar or pub, at the barbershop. They can also be more formalized forms of collective action and popular acts of resistance expressed by citizens' groups or social movements. Recent work within Appalachia (such as that by Fisher and Smith, and other essays in this volume) has documented the importance of such claimed spaces and resistance movements for the protection of places and identities. In the Appalachian valley that I studied, a land trust has quietly bought up land to create a new kind of claimed space. A community center offers a space where people can meet and converse freely, a space absent historically. Such claimed spaces, whether small and informal or large and more visible, are critical to people's ability to express their voices and identities in their own terms.[17]

In my work internationally on how people mobilize to claim power, I have found that the most successful and sustained movements happen when people are able to move across spaces and combine strategies that engage with each of them. In the Philippines, for instance, a land reform movement over several decades was able, ultimately, to redistribute half of the rural land from the large landowners to small farmers. In Turkey, a women's movement was able to rewrite the constitution to give a stronger expression of women's rights. In India, a rural movement focused on the right to information resulted in one of the strongest right-to-information policies in the world. In none of these did change happen only through engaging in one kind of space. Big changes happened when people were able to work across all three. They were able to build people's movements from people's own claimed spaces. When they were invited to the table, having developed new skills and awareness in their own spaces, they were able to engage from a position of strength. They also always found people on the inside, champions of change in the "closed spaces," who were trying to make these spaces more open and bring about change from the inside out as well as the outside in.[18]

There may be lessons in these international examples for the Appalachian region: Though the region is full of examples of popular resistance, are we creating the coalitions that work across all three spaces of participation? Are we linking the people who are building their own spaces with those who are trying to occupy the invited spaces and do the lobbying and the hard work at the negotiating table that is needed? Are we finding the people who are still behind closed doors who want to help and building alliances with them? Our work internationally suggests that real change happens not only when change efforts recognize and challenge the three forms of power that I have discussed, but also when they mobilize around and span the three spaces of participation that exist in any place.

The Levels of Power

The third dimension of the power cube refers to the levels of power. Though in 1961 Robert Dahl asked, "Who governs?" in relation to New Haven, today, some fifty years later, scholars are asking similar questions at a global level.

Indeed, many argue that globalization is taken to express the expanding scale on which power is organized and exercised, posing the critical question, "Where does power reside?" For many, the study of power can no longer be focused only on a particular place. For instance, as David Held and Anthony McGrew point out, "The exclusive link between territory and political power has been broken. The contemporary era has witnessed layers of governance spreading within and across boundaries." Theirs is part of a growing literature on global governance that warns us of the dangers of focusing only on the "local," or the "national" in a globalizing world. Governance has become "multi-layered," ranging from the subnational, to the national to the supranational. It encompasses a range of sites from the very local to the regional to the global. Feminist scholars have added that these levels must also include the household and the importance of intimate relations of power as well.[19]

For those concerned with citizen action and the politics of place, such changes are significant. Many think that such action must begin locally, as it is in the arenas of everyday life in which people are able to resist power and to construct their own voice. On the other hand, globalization creates multiple levels or sites of control, many of which are outside the place of one's immediate concern. With multiple sites of decision making also come more spaces and opportunities for engagement. To protect a place, or raise an issue within it, one can mobilize in other places. Thus, just as globalization contributes to a separation of power from territory, so does it open up broader possibilities for action by relatively powerless groups, not only at the supranational level, but also through interaction at different levels. Those seeking to act on a local place-based injustice may choose not to confront those perceived to be responsible at the local level, but may go to other levels of power to exercise their voice and express their demands.[20]

In another study arising from my international work, colleagues and I explored movements and forms of citizen action that have sought to work across these levels, from the local to the national to the global. There are many examples, ranging from struggles over land and agriculture to education to occupational and public health. The case studies point both to new forms of citizen action that are spanning the local to the global and to the challenges of doing so. We found in these studies that linking the local and the global can be liberating but also that global movements can easily re-create the very forms of power across levels that they seek to challenge. Even within progressive movements, global and national actors are often assumed to be more important, and capture the most resources and set the agendas for change, than those working at the local level. And yet for change to happen and to be sustained, it needs to be effective across all levels, from the local to the regional, the national, and the global.[21]

Within the Appalachian region, we face similar challenges. Appalachia is part of a global system: its land and resources are linked to large multinational corporations, its workers compete with others in the global economy, its media and culture are shaped by the flow of global images and ideas. How then can we bring about change effectively in this place, without also linking with groups in similar places, and those who work at different levels of a global system of power? While local and regional "place" are important, to focus on them exclusively is to isolate ourselves within a much larger system of power. As Reid and Taylor challenge us to do, we need to expand the sense of the commons within a globalized world.[22]

Just as we have found in other places across the world, however, for local groups to link vertically to those working at the national or international level is often fraught with frustrations. I can remember while I was at the Highlander Center, often getting telephone calls from national campaigning organizations looking for local groups that could join their campaigns—but often on their terms. There was little attempt to define the issue together, to build effective representation and mutually accountable ways of working across the levels of power. As local place-based groups attempted to join with others at national or international levels, they often found that they had little voice in these larger efforts for change.

We can learn from other models of internationally effective movements and campaigns for change that do link local actors and places with other local groups in other places, who then come together to amplify their voices up the levels of power and decision making. In one example, Marjorie Mayo and I looked at the Global Campaign for the Right to Education, one of the oldest and largest global civil society–led campaigns around. Though we expected in this study to find examples of internal hierarchies of power within the movement, we found the coalition had been relatively effective in mobilizing across the levels of power. Several factors were particularly important: the organizers recognized the simultaneous importance of the local and the international levels; care was taken to frame global issues in a way that included local perspectives; efforts were made to build effective citizen representation across levels, as well as to try to avoid competition over scarce funding resources. Such lessons are important for place-based organizing in this region. While deepening the work in our own place, how do we not only work across spaces and across forms of power, but also build coalitions of localities across the decision-making levels as well in a more democratic and equal way?[23]

Locating Place in a Complex Web of Power

As we have seen, place matters. Place helps shape identities and provide fields of action. Without place-based meaning and agency, other forms of identity and action will remain without roots, difficult to sustain and with little effect.

And yet as we have also seen, places are embedded in a complex web of power, consisting of multiple forms, spaces, and levels. The power-cube approach suggests that to bring about change in one dimension of power may only serve to misalign power in another part of the cube. The most transformative movements for change are the ones that are able to link across all the dimensions of the cube: that are able to challenge hidden and invisible power, while effectively engaging with the visible issues as well; that are strengthening people's own claimed spaces, while also raising their voices in the "invited" spaces and opening the doors of "closed spaces"; that are working across the levels of power, from the very local to the global.

To engage with the various dimensions of power simultaneously, how-ever, is a challenge for any one group in any one place. It requires learning to work across places, spaces, levels, and forms. It requires building coalitions and joining forces with others in other places, in new forms of solidarity and action. While Appalachia has strong traditions of action and resistance within the region, I believe our biggest challenge is to learn to build hori-zontal and vertical solidarity with others in similar places. And as we learn how to build from the roots of our place to interact with other people who are also learning how to gain voice in their places, we can gradually work together to change global power across spaces, forms, and levels in thou-sands of places across the world.

Notes

This chapter is based on a lecture given at the University of Kentucky, March 1, 2012. Thanks to the Appalachian Center for assistance in transcribing and to Juliet Merrifield and Dee Scholey for editing assistance.

   1. Stephen Fisher and Barbara Smith, eds., *Transforming Places: Lessons from*

Appalachia (Urbana: University of Illinois Press, 2012), vii. This paper draws on earlier writing on power, including John Gaventa, "Finding the Spaces for Change: A Power Analysis," *IDS Bulletin* 37, no. 6 (2006): 23–33. The ideas of "power to," "power within," and "power over" are developed there, as well as in Jo Rowlands, *Questioning Empowerment: Working with Women in Honduras* (Oxford, U.K.: Oxfam Publishing, 1997), Lisa VeneKlasen and Valerie Miller, *A New Weave of People, Power and Politics: The Action Guide for Advocacy and Citizen Participation* (Oklahoma City: World Neighbors, 2002), and Raji Hunjan and Jethro Pettit, *Power: A Practical Analysis for Facilitating Social Change* (Fife, Scotland: Carnegie U.K. Trust, 2011).

2. For further elaboration and for a number of references on this approach, see www.powercube.net; Gaventa, "Finding the Spaces for Change"; John Gaventa and Bruno Martorano, "Inequality, Power and Participation—Revisiting the Links," *IDS Bulletin* 47, no. 5 (2016), 11–30.

3. John Gaventa, *Power and Powerlessness: Quiescence and Rebellion in an Appalachian Valley* (Urbana: University of Illinois Press, 1980).

4. *The Stripping of Appalachia,* in *World in Action* (London: Granada Television, 1972).

5. Aldon Morris, *The Origins of the Civil Rights Movement* (New York: Free Press, 1984).

6. Appalachian Land Ownership Task Force, *Who Owns Appalachia? Landownership and Its Impact* (Lexington: University of Kentucky Press, 1983); Shaunna Scott, "Revisiting the Appalachian Land Ownership Study: An Oral Historical Account," *Appalachian Journal* 325, no. 2 (2008): 236–252.

7. Institute of Developmental Studies, www.ids.ac.uk/team/participation-power-and-social-change; Development Research Centre, Citizenship, Participation and Accountability, www.drc-citizenship.org.

8. For further information on the Coady International Institute, see http://coady.stfx.ca/.

9. This section draws heavily from early writings on the power-cube approach, including Gaventa, *Finding the Spaces for Change,* and John Gaventa, "Levels, Spaces and Forms of Power: Analysing Opportunities for Change," in *Power in World Politics,* ed. Felix Berenskoetter and Michael J. Williams (London: Routledge, 2007), 204–224; Robert Dahl, *Who Governs? Democracy and Power in an American City* (New Haven: Yale University Press, 1961); Nelson W. Polsby, *Community Power and Political Theory* (New Haven: Yale University Press, 1963), 55.

10. Stephen Lukes, *Power: A Radical View* (London: Macmillan, 1974; 2nd ed., Basingstoke: Palgrave Macmillan, 2004); Peter Bachrach and Morton Baratz, "The Two Faces of Power," *American Political Science Review* 56, no. 4 (1962): 947–952.

11. Gaventa, *Power and Powerlessness.*

12. Ulrich Beck, *Power in the Global Age: A New Global Political Economy,* trans. Kathleen Cross (Cambridge, U.K.: Polity Press, 2005), 3–4.

13. Gaventa, *Finding the Spaces for Change;* see www. powercube.net.

14. Elmer Eric Schattsneider, *The Semi-Sovereign People: A Realist's View of Democracy in America* (Austin, TX: Holt, Rinehart and Winston, 1960); Gaventa, *Power and Powerlessness.*

15. See, for example, Andrea Cornwall and Vera Schatten Coelho, eds., *Spaces for Change: The Politics of Citizen Participation in New Democratic Arenas* (London: Zed Books, 2007); Gaventa, *Finding the Spaces for Change,* 26.

16. For further information on this initiative, see www.publishwhatyoupay.org/.

17. See, for example, Fisher and Smith, *Transforming Places.*

18. Further information on these cases may be found in John Gaventa and Rosemary McGee, eds., *Citizen Action and National Policy Reform: Making Change Happen* (London: Zed Books, 2010).

19. David Held and Anthony McGrew, eds., *The Global Transformations Reader: An Introduction to the Globalization Debate* (Cambridge, U.K.: Polity Press, 2003), 11; Robert O. Keohane and Joseph F. Nye Jr., eds., *Governance in a Globalizing World* (Cambridge, U.K.: Visions of Governance in the 21st Century, 2000); Naila Kabeer, *Reversed Realities: Gender Hierarchies in Development Thought* (London: Verso, 1994); VeneKlasen and Miller, *A New Weave of People, Power and Politics.*

20. See, for instance, Margaret E. Keck and Kathryn Sikkink, *Activists beyond Borders: Advocacy Networks in International Politics* (Ithaca: Cornell University Press, 1998); Sidney Tarrow, *The New Transnational Activism* (Cambridge: Cambridge University Press, 2005).

21. John Gaventa and Rajesh Tandon, eds., *Globalising Citizens: New Dynamics of Inclusion and Exclusion* (London: Zed Books, 2010).

22. Herbert Reid and Betsy Taylor, *Recovering the Commons: Democracy, Place, and Global Justice* (Urbana: University of Illinois Press, 2010).

23. John Gaventa and Marjorie Mayo, *Spanning the Spaces of Citizenship through Transnational Coalitions: The Case of the Global Campaign for Education,* IDS Working Paper no. 327 (Brighton, U.K.: Institute of Development Studies, 2009).

16.
go high up
climb to the very top
look out
remnants of
majesty remain
here where soldiers stand
watching their gods die
what will be given
in return for shelter
an end to hunger
sanctuary
look from the mountaintops
an army of broken promises
land invaded then left
as though there were no other way
to claim belonging

       —bell hooks

5

"There Are No Gay People Here"

Expanding the Boundaries of Queer Youth Visibility in the Rural United States

Mary L. Gray

In 2002 I joined representatives of the Berea chapter of Parents and Friends of Lesbians and Gays (PFLAG) and students from Berea College, one of the oldest evangelical Christian colleges in the United States, to visit Berea's Kentucky State House representative, Lonnie Napier. Napier won his district seat in a special runoff election in 1984 and had held it ever since. His district includes the college town of Berea, an economic engine in the district, as well as less flush neighboring cities, such as Paint Lick, Waco, and Napier's hometown of Lancaster, Kentucky. When the House was not in session, Napier could be found around town working as an auctioneer or running his clothing store and real estate business in Lancaster. Standing in front of Napier was a Church of Christ pastor and several young people from Berea College. All the young people were queer-identifying in one way or another. We came to Napier to talk about the importance of fairness to lesbian, gay, bisexual, and transgender people in his district. Astonishingly, after the students described discrimination experienced at local jobs and the pastor passionately described his son's fear of returning to Kentucky as a gay dad with two newly adopted children, Napier looked at us and said, "Well, there are no gay people here, there are no gay people in my district, so I do not need to worry about this." Mind you, he was talking with a father who was, at the time, the cochair of PFLAG, and young people, most born and raised within thirty miles of Napier's birthplace, who identify as queer.

The cognitive dissonance of the exchange with Representative Napier didn't really make sense to me then. In many ways, the moment represented a much more complicated puzzle that would require another year of work to piece together. What seemed important then, perhaps even more so today, was figuring out how to reckon with Napier's statement and understand how he might see his rural community as the last place he would find real gay people. I did not want to simply toss aside his comments as dismissive politics or assume that he was in deep denial of the truth in front of him, though surely those are both parts of the puzzle. My goal (the "higher calling" of anthropology, if you will) was to get at the logics of what he was saying. What would drive this person to say these people aren't here when they're standing right in front of him? In many ways, he was saying, well, I don't have to worry about these politics because they're not my own. But it resonated with the broader conversation of why it is so hard to do advocacy and conceptualize queer gender and sexual difference in places outside cities.

The politics of place, gender, class, race—sociocultural dynamics that shape how we are seen by others, our experience of the world, and how we move through it—intersect. While intersectionality as a politics of multivalence has made its way from global feminisms to queer studies (Eng and Hom 1998; Masequesmay and Metzger 2009), it has been less attentive to articulations of class and location (for exceptions see Henderson 2013; Tongson 2011; and Mason 2015). Drawing on the lived experiences of LGBT and questioning youth navigating both rural communities and mass-mediated images of what I call "the good gay life," I argue that popular representations of rural queer life permeate popular culture and political organizing for not only Lonnie Napier but also national LGBT advocacy organizations. This is not to say that representations of the good gay life are summarily defining, or that they determine how people ultimately see themselves or others. Rather, I argue, these popular representations set the terms for imagining what queer life is like in both rural and non-metropolitan places. Though digital media can disrupt mainstream narratives—indeed, I will show moments that they do—I build on Halberstam's use of the term *metronormative* (2005) to consider how positioning urban settings as necessary to the flourishing of LGBT life and politics does more than just anchor LGBT identities. Yes, metronormative sensibilities seep into our everyday understandings of LGBT identity, prompting us to imagine: Who are LGBT people? How different are LGBT people from their peers? What should I wear if I'm trying to date someone who's LGBT-identifying? But metronormative values also prompt us to assume where and how LGBT people live and thrive, organizing the political work and agenda setting that count as "good LGBT advocacy" in the United States. Metronormative logics set in motion assumptions about LGBT people's "typical" genders, class backgrounds, and ethnic ties. They outline the political possibilities of those places where an "army of lovers" ("Queers Read This" 1990) with class mobility and capital can independently manifest queer "counter-publics" (Berlant and Freeman 1993; Warner 1992, 1993).

This chapter looks closely at the popular representation of the good gay life found in the widely available television drama *Queer as Folk*. I use close readings of the program to understand how this text might privilege particular dreams of queer critical mass, pink dollars, and safe spaces while simultaneously framing rural queer life as always already lacking. In reworking what can be done in rural communities, explored through the ethnographic study of young people living in rural Kentucky, I offer rural LGBT-identifying people's experiences as a compelling example of how to reimagine queer living through strategies of familiarity, coalition, and boundary crossing. I argue that what I call "boundary publics"—iterative, ephemeral experiences of belonging that circulate across the outskirts and through the center(s) of a more recognized and validated public sphere—press us to consider what youth need to constitute queer living in rural communities. As I argue elsewhere, experiences of boundary publics can transform the superstores, churches, and other de facto public spaces of the rural United States (Gray 2009, 137). While vibrant critiques of Jürgen Habermas's public sphere, most notably from Fraser and Warner, offer generative frameworks for subaltern counter-publics, they implicitly reinforce a reliance on material wealth to imagine public dialogue (Fraser 1990; Warner 1992, 2005; Berlant and Freeman 1993). Boundary publics are not theorized as concrete places that rely on material wealth to control safe spaces for dialogue. Rather, they offer moments in which we glimpse a complex web of relations that links multiple identities that also vie for recognition and attention. I draw on the analytic power of boundary publics to help us reorient to how enmeshed "online" and "offline" experiences are for young people negotiating their identities in a digital era, making an interdisciplinary analysis that considers space and place more necessary now than ever before.

Interrogating Queer Living

Bridging the gap between Lonnie Napier's statement and the people standing in front of him begins, for me, with an interdisciplinary inquiry anchored in anthropology as praxis (Freire 1986, 36). Anthropology, as I practice it, is the business of talking with people to understand how they see the world. It aims to transform what we ask about the world by exploring how others see it. In looking for other vantage points, anthropology asks us to consider: What do we take for granted? What are the different sets of assumptions and life conditions that organize people's experience of the world?

Queer anthropology, as a subfield, has rarely explored the experiences of being rural and queer, except for the lives of those who ran screaming from their small towns and moved to large cities. If you asked those folks, rural communities are awful, awful places. But if you talk to people who live in rural communities and small towns, particularly those who do not have the means to leave, you get a more complicated story.

I spent nineteen months roaming around Kentucky and its borders, working in several different communities at once. It was incredibly tiring. It took a toll on my car. But, eventually, several communities became home bases for me. Most of the participants I formally interviewed—thirty-four people who became my primary theorists—were between fourteen and twenty-four; the majority were seventeen. These were young people who, for the most part, did not plan to leave their towns. Many of them would be the first to say that they don't have much choice when it comes to staying where they are. These youth offer a distinct narrative of what queer publics look like. They give us new material to consider: What kind of publicness, what I call queer visibility, can we imagine and, in imagining it, make happen? If we imagine this visibility in rural places, what are the politics that go with it? What are the actions you have to take to make queer spaces and identities possible in rural communities?

THE GOOD GAY LIFE, INC.: ARTIFACTS FOR A COLLECTIVE GRAMMAR OF QUEER EXPERIENCE

Rather than presume that identity is (only) a matter of reflection and self-discovery, I approach queer experience as a social practice that demands shared grammars and instructional materials. As a queer feminist scholar interested in the anthropology of media, I am particularly keen to understand how people come to a queer sense of self and the language that people use to describe and claim their identities. Several decades ago, the communication and media studies scholars George Gerbner and Larry Gross developed "cultivation theory" to understand the power of persistent media exposure, from sources like television, to shape viewers' perceptions of the world (Gerbner and Gross 1976). Gross and later researchers, such as the sociologist Suzanna Walters, built on this theory to suggest that mass-mediated representations of gays and lesbians had a force in making an "invisible minority" widely seen but, arguably, one-dimensional and opaque beyond the coarsest of stereotypes (Gross 2001; Walters 2001). But the post–network TV landscape of the 2000s meant there were less coherent, more diverse and multifaceted representations of gay and lesbian people bundled with each new cable channel (Turow 1997). Online resources, produced by and for these young people might further push the repertoires of LGBT representations.

Paul Dourish and Genevieve Bell (2007), two technology scholars, argue that new technologies make a difference through not only new content but also, literally, their capacity to create space. Space is a physical experience as well as a site of compilation. Our lived experiences accumulate in built environments. Our everyday interactions construct us. New technologies can, then, shape and destabilize our sense of where we imagine the centers and margins of living take place. For example, Gay Cities, one of the first mobile applications for LGBT people, strangely, did not list Berea. The absence of Berea from the app asserted that "there are no gay people" in the city of Berea. There was no obvious reason for omitting Berea from Gay Cities any more than there was a good reason for Napier to dismiss the very real presence of the queer-identifying people before him. Gay Cities, like Napier, didn't consider LGBT people in Richmond, Kentucky. It didn't list Lexington, Kentucky, either. As one might suspect, mobile access carries with it the possibility *and* impossibility of representation. Digital media circulate and reinforce where queerness happens and its "imagined audiences" (boyd 2008a). It's not a matter of waiting for Berea or Richmond to qualify for the list. Rather, cultivation theory suggests that we unpack media content to flesh out the priorities embedded in them. Who is presumed to belong in those representations? Where and how were those priorities scripted? What do young rural people do with digital media, and how is it in dialogue with popular representations and pop culture? How do they use the possibilities of visual media to transform or retell their stories? Rather than take for granted that digital and social mobile media make LGBT lives better, we can consider the ongoing tug-of-war of who counts and where LGBT people are imagined to prosper as it plays out and is produced through media. When those tussles hit the ground in rural communities, they must contend with the material conditions that are also part of the grammar and resources for queer living.

As readers may know, rural Kentucky works with inequalities that are markedly different from those of its urban cousins. To be clear, urban settings also weather distinct dimensions of inequality. More to the point here is to say that neither is "more homophobic" or "less gender-oppressive" than the other. They are different in their manifestations of systemic, interlocking oppressions, neither better nor worse than their counterparts. One might say, in the spirit of Kenneth Burke (1969), "equipment for living" is hard won in rural communities. As is true for young people everywhere in our hyper-surveilled world, there is little autonomy available, and schools are not viable access points for young people seeking information about LGBT sexualities and genders. Even though every county public school receives federally and state-subsidized broadband, it comes with default content blockers and monitoring software that make calling up websites with the words *gay* or *lesbian* in them fraught enterprises. The broadband speeds of uploading and downloading content are much closer to the dial-up modem rates of the 1990s than anything that we recognize as the "high-speed internet" (see Talbot et al. 2017). Imagine getting on YouTube and relying on it for It Gets Better, as a way of finding support or solace, and having it click-click-click. And cell service? Forget about it.

Place making through technology becomes just as much about negotiating a lack of technology as it does about the possibilities available. Yes, digital media helped create a local sense of belonging. That's primarily what young people are doing with technologies. But young people do not use technologies just as escape routes. They create narratives about their lives that they do not see elsewhere. Their "queer identity work"—threading together popular culture, local resources, and peers—helped me understand why thinking about identities as collective action becomes important (Gray 2009). For communication studies, often enamored with the possibility of "new" media for human connection, most recently social media, what kind of difference do media make? If we want to expand how we imagine and enrich people's lives vis-à-vis digital media, how will we move beyond consumerist notions of the good gay life? How does media access, in some places and in some contexts, reinforce a sense of the urban as the center, as the place to be? How might we deploy digital media as a permeable boundary rather than a fixed focal point that reproduces the centers of normative gay life?

QUEER AS FOLK: DISMANTLING THE GOOD GAY LIFE

Queer as Folk debuted in December 2000 in the United States on the premium cable network Showtime. The show was based on the British series created by Russell T. Davies (of the same title, launched in 1999) chronicling the lives of three gay men living in Manchester's gay village around Canal Street. The American series, set in Pittsburgh, was the first hour-long drama on American television to portray the lives of gay men and women. Touching on coming out, same-sex marriage, gay adoption, artificial insemination, HIV/AIDS, cruising—*Queer as Folk* quickly became the number one show on the Showtime roster, featuring groundbreaking scenes, beginning with the first episode, which contained the first simulated sex scene between two men shown on American television. Within a week of the Season 1 DVD box set arriving on the shelves of chain electronics and bookstores in 2002, most of the young people with whom I worked had made their way through at least three episodes of the season. For the most part, nobody could afford premium cable access. Even if their families could afford it, the regional cable providers didn't deliver the premium channels. At the time of my research, the majority of households where I spent my time simply couldn't get Showtime if they had wanted it. The DVDs made the perfect organizing tool for a house party. People gathered to binge-watch the first season's episodes after their late shifts at local fast-food chains or in the early morning after parents left for work.

Queer as Folk offers a quintessential snapshot of the good gay life in the popular imagination of the early 2000s. Episode 1 of Season 1 delivers, from its opening scenes, a vibrant queer world predicated on the liberatory possibility of controlling one's access to queer bodies and the pleasures of being surrounded by the family we choose and endless options for queer consumption (Weston 1997). A voiceover from another key character, competing with club music for viewers' attention, introduces the program's lead characters. Brian Kinney, a white, brooding bar owner and entrepreneur, and Justin Taylor, a white, blond-haired suburban teen runaway, meet in a moment drenched in the motifs of the good gay life: nightclubs, innuendos, and people signaling their sexual desires and identities out in the open crowd the scene. Brian approaches Justin, assessing what this young man, so close to his eighteenth birthday, has to offer; Justin, in turn, names local bars that might confer legitimacy and sexual prowess on the newcomer. The moment closes with music pumping, steam swirling in the streets, and tires burning as Brian and Justin drive off together with seemingly little care for anyone or anything outside Brian's Jeep Wrangler.

The encounter depicted in this scene puts three key elements of the good gay life on display. I would argue that these elements are the organizing principles of gay and lesbian representation found in most contemporary popular media, from film and television to novels and narrative nonfiction. These elements anchor the narratives that we use to orient to "what you have to do, where you have to be" to have the good gay life. The first element is the presence of a critical mass of LGBT-identifying people. This element presumes that fully accepting oneself relies on the recognition not only of one's own sense of queerness but also validation through the acknowledgment of others. The second element of the good gay life is access to disposable income. To own queerness, one must have the means to accumulate the look, feel, and experience of living in a gay world. And, relatedly, a third element of the good gay life is the availability of safe space—gayborhoods and other counter-publics, where one and one's peers own the streets—even if it is property in the less desirable real estate market of Pittsburgh, *Queer as Folk*'s fictional backdrop.

In Brian Kinney's world, you can barhop and, as is played out in later seasons, do legislative work along the way. Kinney's wealth underwrites the best parties for cruising and fund-raisers for electoral politics. But even if someone like Justin doesn't have money in his own pockets, his proximity to Brian's largesse and queer community spaces makes reaching for the good gay life a pleasurable, smooth ride. The good gay life promises that geography can deliver the privilege of sexual and gender freedom. Gay safe havens are exclusively yours (ours), in that we're here, we're queer, get used to it. Even in episodes when *Queer as Folk*'s writers fracture viewers' sense of security through story lines of gay club bombings and hate crimes leveled against beloved characters, the acts of violence are presented as anathematic aberrations that, together, we can eradicate, if we come out, en masse, and apply collective will and money to the problem of hate.

These three elements—critical mass, money, and safe spaces of our own—define what I argue are the politics of visibility. What makes it possible for us to be out, loud, and proud? For the most part, we operate with an unexamined sense that visibility and political power hinge on these other resources. There is no denying that there is great pleasure in "owning the streets" and feeling the deep comfort of seeing oneself surrounded by others "like me." Yet we do little to consider the privilege of such approaches to organizing. LGBT advocacy, like popular representations of the good gay life, operates with the assumption that if LGBT people have access to our own communities, money, and locations, our everyday lives will be better for it. The representation of the good gay life presumes this is how we create visibility. More important, it suggests that this is the only respectable route to political change.

RETHINKING THE GOOD GAY LIFE FROM THE LENS OF RURAL QUEER STUDIES

Popular media such as *Queer as Folk* may circulate images of the good gay life, but national organizing campaigns for lesbian, gay, bi, and trans advocacy position critical mass, disposable capital, and LGBTQ-controlled spaces as *the only* way for organizing and identity formation to make progress. But for many small towns and rural communities these conditions are far from universal. Heteronormativity produces more allies than LGBT-identifying people. It is difficult to have a critical mass of LGBT-identifying people in a town of five thousand, at least on a par with the teaming streets of *Queer as Folk*'s Pittsburgh. In a perfect world, we're all queer-identifying. Until that day arrives, smaller towns will have better odds organizing a critical mass of visible LGBT allies. There is rarely enough money for families to afford the thirty-dollars-a-year memberships in most national chapter-based LGBT nonprofits. And spaces are often multipurpose, juggling a church potluck one afternoon and a community meeting the next. Moreover, in places where it's rare to meet strangers, maintaining one's legibility as a local—being "so and so's" son or daughter—is the identity that unlocks material stability when times are tough. Familiarity, not anonymity, is the prized currency in places with deep interdependencies holding the safety net together. In most rural communities, with their limited tax bases and anemic public infrastructure, churches and family networks are the de facto public services, offering job boards, health-care services, housing, and shelter to local residents. Lastly, rural LGBT community members can't assume access to their own permanent spaces. Though representations of nightlife in *Queer as Folk* celebrate a rich tradition of bars and bookstores that played key roles in the gay liberation movements of the mid- and late twentieth century, rural places offer different possibilities for queer assembly. For many complicated reasons, beyond the idea that the local community members would come out with clubs and pitchforks, rural queer landscapes don't lend themselves to gayborhoods. That said, there are other ways in which public performances that scream queer circulate in rural towns and are as vibrant and effective, particularly for the young people I was working with, for creating moments of social recognition as any gay bar I've frequented. We know sociologically that these moments of acknowledgment—having somebody else recognize who we are—are key to our sense of identity. These moments are entirely possible in rural places, but they are done differently.

Queering the Country

Borrowing the notion of "equipment for living" (Burke 1969), I ask what are the tenets and materials that LGBT and questioning young people living in the rural United States use to make the most of their queer lives? What are they using if they do not have access to a critical mass of queer folks, disposable income for queer action, or safe spaces that they can call their own? How do rural LGBT communities navigate their needs? As I will detail below, rural communities offer a rich set of tools for queer organizing. First, they use their identities as locals to recruit straight allies. While certainly a well-established strategy for LGBT organizing, it plays a particularly pivotal and, arguably, different role in rural communities. In some cases, the elderly parents of those LGBT people who have returned to care for their aging family members are the new allies. In other cases, new alliances are formed when queer couples put their children in local schools and work alongside straight, cis parents at sporting events and PTAs. These new allies play a critical and robust role as brokers of familiarity in rural communities. Second, whether it's sharing a car to get to the closest city or money to buy the latest LGBT-themed DVD or book, many of the young people I worked with pooled resources to consume what was often presented as the staples of queer life. Most were incredibly conscious of the need to dress right or understand the most relevant popular culture references when they went to larger cities, such as Nashville or Louisville, to attend an affirming church service or go to a gay bar. Popular culture and mass media stylize what it means to be LGBT-identifying. Whether one can afford this aesthetic or not, it is still part of the grammar we call on to speak to each other. And, finally, young people knew how to occupy spaces that were not entirely their own, but that still gave them room to walk that fine line between being familiar— "you know me, I'm so and so's son or daughter"—and also being fabulously queer. Bear in mind, when rural young people lay claim to LGBT identities or questioning heteronormativity, they're not just marking themselves as different. Our representations of the good gay life perpetuate a story that queerness is a "city thing." Rural young people must carefully deploy queerness while keeping their identities as locals in the balance. Of course, if we look at the latest U.S. census, we see gay- and lesbian-identifying couples in every single county. But, like Lonnie Napier, we can quickly fall back on those urban scenes of *Queer as Folk* and forget that we're everywhere. By establishing a queer presence in their hometowns, especially among immediate and extended families, rural queer youth radically remake where queerness can live. That to me is the most profound political challenge to Lonnie Napier's denial of queer difference. Let me turn now to the specifics of rural young people's public assertions of queer difference through boundary publics. What do queer boundary publics look like? What kind of visibility do they offer, and what are the political possibilities that go with them?

THE HIGHLAND PRIDE PICNIC

I met members of the Eastern Kentucky Highland Pride group as they finalized details of their first public community event, a Pride potluck picnic. They decided to host the event at a popular regional state park's picnic shelter to make it easier to find for those traveling from other counties. Several members expressed concern that area residents, using the park for their own family gatherings, might be caught off-guard by "a gay thing" happening in the park. They went back and forth about where they could place the group's rainbow flag, to signal that they were having this event and identify their picnic shelter to people visiting from out of town. The group's quick consensus that a rainbow flag could effectively communicate an LGBT event is significant. While the iconic flag might be lost on some people driving by or persuade a family setting up a barbecue to pick a picnic shelter farther away from the potluck ruckus and dance music, certainly peers looking for the Highland Pride event would get it and know to join them. The iconography and grammar of the rainbow flag, ubiquitous in LGBT organizing and popular media, made it a convenient resource for marketing and demarcating the Pride event. They could attach it to the rafters of a state picnic shelter and create a local and concrete boundary public, at least for their afternoon in the park. Perhaps, ironically, they talked about another group they wanted to subtly signal: the men who used the park to cruise for sex. Several of them imagined that someone cruising the park for anonymous sex might welcome the opportunity to go someplace else rather than be associated with an explicitly LGBT-marked gathering. There was no strong hostility or shaming of anyone who might be in the park for sex rather than community—only lighthearted teasing of the male Highland Pride members most likely to run into an ex-boyfriend if they didn't scare people away with the rainbow flag. The group's members carefully considered the needs of as many community members as possible before draping the rainbow flag over a wooden beam in the center of the shelter. The gesture was both tenderhearted and pragmatic, as they wanted to avoid any conflict that might make securing the picnic shelter harder the next time they wanted to hold an event. Unlike the queer-owned counter-publics of city gay bars and bookstores, the picnic shelter could become their space for a twenty-five-dollar fee, on the condition that they navigate it as shared space that, ultimately, was not theirs to own. They could not control it to the exclusion of others, and they didn't presume otherwise. They wanted to occupy it for a set amount of time, have some hot dishes, and go home. And, to the delight of their fellow Pride members and friends, that's what they did.

BLURRING ONLINE-OFFLINE VISIBILITY

Though the Highland Pride picnic illustrates how to use physical structures to balance legibility as a local with the desire to amass queer visibility and own queer spaces, online environments could also be reworked as boundary publics. Social media like Facebook and Twitter weren't yet popular among the people I met in my research for simple reasons. Facebook was still restricted to college students with .edu email addresses, and Twitter didn't make much sense without a steady cell phone signal and an affordable smartphone service plan, two things hard to find in the mountainous southeastern Appalachian range. Few rural youth I met had easy access to a secure computer or media literacy skills to create elaborate Myspace sites.

At the same time, free, simple-to-use web-page hosting services, such as GeoCities, and regional chats and discussion lists on commercial services, like PlanetOut, blurred the distinction between online and offline community spaces. Young people used web-based digital media to transform the stories about what it means to be queer and rural, generating new online narratives about staying put rather than escaping to New York or San Francisco. And they were very much using these resources to connect with each other locally. Every young person I met shared this narrative of going online for the first time and scouring resource lists and groups for evidence of someone else in their zip code or town. They creatively used digital media not to tunnel out but, rather, to bring together a critical mass of LGBT people in their own backyards. Working within the constraints and modest means that defined most people's lives, these youth cobbled together digital environments and the most readily available offline spaces: local churches and chain stores, such as Walmart.

SKATE PARK PUNK

An evangelical Christian church built a skate park and punk music venue in its cavernous performance hall during my second summer of fieldwork. As the group's charismatic youth pastors explained to me, they wanted to create a space that would be cool and welcoming to area youth, rather than "churchy." What the pastors didn't seem to know (or readily acknowledge to me) was that the skate park became a thriving "queercore" punk music concert venue within a matter of months after its opening. One of the more popular bands regularly selling out its shows was the local favorite, Jarvis Avenue. They drew an eclectic, queer-identifying audience, typically dressed from head to toe in black, wearing goth-style makeup and clothes and adorned in metal rainbow pride rings safety-pinned to their black leather jackets.

People came from across state lines for Jarvis Ave concerts at this skate park. The band advertised its shows through a simple list of fans who had signed up for email announcements at previous performances. When the band members wrote and recorded new songs, they burned them to CDs and sold copies after the show. But they also emailed announcements and links to MP3 files of their songs, archived on their band's GeoCities website. The lead singer wrote very queer-specific lyrics about girl-on-girl love and surviving a broken heart, sung with the intensity and grit typical of a punk ballad. Jarvis Ave sold its CDs for a few dollars more than the cost of the blank CD-RW discs the drummer bought for the band in bulk at the regional Walmart, four miles from his house. But the band happily emailed links to the MP3 files to whoever joined the email list. The band's GeoCities website served as the perfect boundary public, in that it entailed moving online and offline—circulating Jarvis Ave and its queer sensibilities and space making through the digital distribution of its songs. If local youth could not afford to attend the concerts (the cover charge was often between five and seven dollars) or buy a CD (another five dollars), they could still participate in the localness of the queercore scene by sharing songs with friends who could afford the costs of the concerts or time away from their own part-time jobs.

In many ways, the church and youth supporting Jarvis Ave's music under-wrote the expenses of keeping the band afloat as a boundary public and resource for queer identity work.

WALMART DRAG AS A BOUNDARY PUBLIC

While Jarvis Ave had a loyal following and ambitious evangelical pastors to boost its visibility as a queer boundary public, other youth used the cos-metic counters, clothing racks, and fluorescent lights flooding the aisles of a regional Walmart to suspend the heteronormativity of their local landscapes. Why Walmart? Walmart, it turns out, is the quintessential boundary public (though, since completing my research, I've learned from readers that Sears and Fry's are just as likely to serve this function). For the most part, other than churches, large chain retailers operate as de facto public town squares. After Walmart and its box store brethren gutted the competitive viability of local businesses struggling to weather the economic climate of the late 1990s and early 2000s, they quickly filled the void by becoming the place everyone gathered. In these areas, Walmart was one of the only places open twenty-four hours a day. So, if you want to hang out with LGBT-identifying friends at one o'clock in the morning, particularly in so-called dry counties, which ban the sale of alcohol, the options are to head to Walmart or drive to the nearest gay bar, at least an hour away. Local LGBT youth could readily create a sense of queer public space by going to Walmart if they knew how to occupy the space as a boundary public.

It is important to note the cultural cues that helped make Walmart a viable location for queer visibility and safe space. At the time I met the young people using Walmart as a boundary public, the store had just announced that it would extend domestic partnership benefits to its employees. Local youth talked about this as a kind of affirmation that allayed some of their concerns about meeting at the store. One can certainly question Walmart's motives for offering domestic partnership benefits and see it simply as a marketing ploy. At the same time, the policy did get taken up as a tacit sig-nal of queer support. "Safe space" is, arguably, always a more imagined than a tangible reality. LGBT people work with the hope that some modicum of control or privilege will be enough to generate safe conditions for gather-ing. Walmart's policies offered the suggestion of queer affirmation that could make it a viable boundary public with almost no capital investment required (not to mention easy access to wigs, fuzzy jackets, and sample makeup).

The other factor that determined Walmart's viability as a habitable boundary public was the presence of friends working at the store, typically part-time on an evening shift. Youth were able to add drag at the regional Walmart to their usual rotation of "things to do when bored" because several of them had friends who worked there. They checked in with their friends to make sure that they had local support for their antics. Put another way, they localized the national chain, making it something familiar through their connections to neighbors, family, and friends, to make Walmart a safe space. They know they will not be tossed out because of Walmart's logics that recognize them as "guests" through their consumer status. But, more important, they know that when trusted friends and family are working, they can appeal to them, through their shared identities as locals, to help them hold the space as a queer boundary public a bit longer than they might on their own. These youth walk the razor-thin line between the heteronormative public space of a family discount store and a queer subaltern counter-public. They taunt and tease each other through the aisles of the store. Taking photos of each other in drag and posting them to friends turned out to be as important as the experience of drag itself. Only a few young people at any one time would dress up and stomp through the store like models on a runway. They all took part in chronicling the outing and circulating the photos through emails and their obscure group website. Because these were the days before Google's success as a search engine, it was practically impossible to find their buried website unless you knew the exact URL. The website and email distribution lists made it possible for them to circulate their visibility to a broader network of friends so that they could vicariously participate in this experience of a queer public. These youth bring queerness home. These are not pictures of Christopher Street or the Castro. In bringing queer home, boundary publics and digitally mediated representations of them create new venues for experiences of belonging.

TRANS YOUTH BLOGS: NARRATING RURAL QUEER EXPERIENCE

My last example of a boundary public that builds alliances to address the need for recognition and critical mass considers the material costs of aspiring to a "good life" not readily available in rural communities; it also grapples with the limits of controlling capital for space making that is, perhaps, the most pivotal case of blurring online and offline publicness. I am referring to the trans youth blogs that became, arguably, a genre between 2001 and 2003. The mechanics of web rings made it easy for bloggers to interlace their sites through hyperlink icons and facilitate readers' hopscotching across connected blog sites. Web rings broadened trans-identifying, genderqueer, and gender-questioning young people's sense of community. AJ, a teen who transitioned from an out lesbian to a transman, used his blog to describe what he called his "journey from female to male identifying." He shifted, several times in the course of our conversations, on the issues of whether or how he would identify as trans. When I met him, he was adamant that he was a transman and that it was a very important part of his sense of self to identify as such. Over the nearly year and a half that we spent together, AJ changed his position, and his identity as a man became most salient to him. He kept an incredibly detailed website about himself, posting updates and pictures of his body as it was transformed while he was taking testosterone. He called this section of his blog "the gallery of T effects." He also kept pictures of his surgeries as he had them done and a complete list of the health resources that he used.

Most of AJ's material and emotional support came from his mom. He saw a rebroadcast of a 1984 documentary on *Discovery Health* called *What Sex Am I?* when he was sixteen and identifying as a lesbian. As the first-person interviews progressed, the narratives resonated for him and he thought, "Ah, that's what's going on." He recorded the program on his VCR, and when his mom came home from work, he asked her to watch it with him. They watched it in silence until she finally asked, "Do you feel like this is what's going on?" He said yes and broke down sobbing. She matter-of-factly said, "Okay, well, it looks like we need to do whatever they're doing on that video." That evening they went back through the video together and wrote down every term and procedure listed by the medical expert on the video, working through "what does it take to be the trans person my child thinks is a part of who he is?"

I asked AJ's mom, a woman unaware of the PFLAG chapter just a few counties over in Berea, "Where did this well of support come from?" She said, without much thought to the matter, "I'm a religious person, and God don't make trash." That was it. It was that simple. For her it was certainly imaginable that there was more that she could do to make AJ's trans life possible in their hometown, and she was going to do everything that should could.

The tension and ambivalence between a popular media text that defined, in very clear terms, what is expected of AJ to achieve trans visibility and what it means to be trans for AJ, play out across AJ's blog as an instantiation of a queer boundary public.

One of the resources that he needed the most and that he could not get locally was mental health care. The barrier to so much of his transition at certain points was not the support of his family; it was certainly finances, to some degree, but that had everything to do with the crisis of unavailable health-care services in rural states. He couldn't access one of the key components of transitioning because of the nation's failure to provide adequate health care to rural areas. Keeping the gallery of T effects was, for AJ, about making his trans identity possible where he lives and modeling that possibility of alliance and support for other young people. The first two pages of the blog's guest book are filled with entries from his family saying, "Way to go AJ!" This is where he can hear affirmation that was, often, muted at the kitchen table, particularly in conversations with his father. This was not what he heard from his family at gatherings after church. In those cases, there was silence about his transition. In those moments, for him, being able to go to that guest book was a way of hearing the affirmation he was less likely to hear in his day-to-day interactions with his family, still awkward and unsure of how to address AJ. Although AJ drove, monthly, to a larger city with a medical school to attend different support groups, his guest book played a pivotal role as a boundary public able to echo affirmation but also give his family a way to chime in more loudly than they knew how to do in their offline lives.

Young people gathering around the Highland Pride picnic, Jarvis Ave concerts, drag in Walmart, or a blog's guest book push the boundaries of what it means to be queerly present in rural areas. These youth use strategies of social recognition that include but also challenge being out, loud, and proud. They do not describe their experiences of queering the boundaries of their local belonging in terms of a deficit or loss. They don't lament that they can't be more queer where they are because they make sense of their LGBT identities in relation to other priorities regarding their social identity as familiar locals. As is clear by now, reliance on boundary publics highlights what a (white, middle-class, cis) privilege it is to sidestep the need to juggle multiple social identities, like race, ethnicity, and class, in our everyday lives.

We all put multiple visibility strategies in play to constitute our queerness. These examples of queer world-making should "count" as much as (perhaps more than?) the activities on display in mainstream representations of the good gay life. Diminishing rural queer lives and creating hierarchies of who's doing queerness right miss an opportunity to learn strategies for building out queerness in places where we will have more non-LBGT allies than an army of lovers, few local wealthy donor circles, and the need to share space in coalition with others.

We have hit a wall in LGBT organizing, beyond major coastal metropoles, in the past ten years. My home state of California is a great example. On November 4, 2008, California voters approved the statewide ballot measure Proposition 8, barring the right of same-sex couples to marry. The measure made marriage equality illegal in California. When LGBT rights advocacy organizations worked to get out the "No on 8" campaign, they avoided the conservative Central Valley region of the state. The area was written off as destined to vote against LGBT people no matter what campaigning took place. As organizers, we have lost our capacity to stay in the deep discomfort and heat of engaging with those who don't already agree with us. While it is an immeasurable pleasure to be in complete agreement with those around us and to see ourselves in others, it is also an entitlement that few have the privilege to claim 24/7. We need strategies for addressing and drawing in people beyond those who agree or identify with us to expand justice. Boundary publics offer an analytic tool for thinking through any set of conditions where people negotiate their space and place in the world. It doesn't presume that people come together as equals, but it also doesn't presume that a stable counter-public exists, either. What can we do in places that call on us to contend with power that contains us and how our power undercuts others? The rural young people I met for my research do navigate these realities every day. They can tell us how to do it better to constitute something more expansive than the good gay life. We need their expertise, now more than ever.

References

Berlant, Lauren, and Elizabeth Freeman. 1993. "Queer Nationality." In *Fear of a Queer Planet: Queer Politics and Social Theory,* edited by Michael Warner, 193–229. Minneapolis: University of Minnesota Press.

boyd, danah. 2008a. "Taken Out of Context: American Teen Sociality in Networked Publics." Ph.D. diss., University of California, Berkeley.

———. 2008b. "Why Youth (Heart) Social Network Sites: The Role of Networked Publics in Teenage Social Life." In *Youth, Identity, and Digital Media,* edited by David Buckingham, 119–142. Cambridge: MIT Press. https://papers.ssrn.com/abstract=1518924.

Burke, Kenneth. 1969. *A Grammar of Motives* (1945; reprint). Berkeley: University of California Press.

DiMaggio, Paul, and Eszter Hargittai. 2001. "From the 'Digital Divide' to 'Digital

Inequality': Studying Internet Use as Penetration Increases." Princeton Center for Arts and Cultural Policy Studies, Working Paper 15. https://pdfs.semantic-scholar.org/4843/610b79d670136e3cdd12311f91f5cc98d2ee.pdf.

Dourish, Paul, and Genevieve Bell. 2007. "The Infrastructure of Experience and the Experience of Infrastructure: Meaning and Structure in Everyday Encounters with Space." *Environment and Planning B: Planning and Design* 34.3: 414–430. doi:10.1068/b32035t.

Eng, David L., and Alice Y. Hom. 1998. *Q & A: Queer in Asian America*. Philadelphia: Temple University Press.

Fraser, Nancy. 1990. "Rethinking the Public Sphere: A Contribution to the Critique of Actually Existing Democracy." *Social Text,* no. 25/26: 56–80. doi:10.2307/466240.

Freire, Paulo. 1986. *Pedagogy of the Oppressed*. Translated by Myra Bergman Ramos. New York: Continuum.

Gerbner, George, and Larry Gross. 1976. "Living with Television: The Violence Profile." *Journal of Communication* 26.2: 172–194. doi:10.1111/j.1460-2466.1976.tb01397.x.

Gray, Mary L. 2009. *Out in the Country: Youth, Media, and Queer Visibility in Rural America*. New York: New York University Press.

Gross, Larry. 2001. *Up from Invisibility: Lesbians, Gay Men, and the Media in America*. New York: Columbia University Press.

Halberstam, Judith [Jack]. 2005. *In a Queer Time and Place: Transgender Bodies, Subcultural Lives*. New York: New York University Press.

Henderson, Lisa. 2013. *Love and Money: Queers, Class, and Cultural Production*. New York: New York University Press.

Johnson, E. Patrick, and Mae G. Henderson, eds. 2005. *Black Queer Studies: A Critical Anthology*. Durham, NC: Duke University Press.

Masequesmay, Gina, and Sean Metzger. 2009. *Embodying Asian/American Sexualities*. Lanham, MD: Lexington Books.

Mason, Carol. 2015. *Oklahomo: Lessons in Unqueering America*. Albany: State University of New York Press.

"Queers Read This." 1990. www.actupny.org/documents/QueersReadThis.pdf.

Talbot, David, Waide Warner, Susan Crawford, and Jacob White. 2017. "Citizens Take Charge: Concord, Massachusetts, Builds a Fiber Network." Municipal Fiber Initiative, February 28. Digital Access to Scholarship at Harvard. https://dash.harvard.edu/handle/1/30201055.

Tongson, Karen. 2011. *Relocations: Queer Suburban Imaginaries*. New York: New York University Press.

Turow, Joseph. 1997. *Breaking Up America: Advertisers and the New Media World*. Chicago: University of Chicago Press.

Walters, Suzanna Danuta. 2001. *All the Rage: The Story of Gay Visibility in America*. Chicago: University of Chicago Press.

Warner, Michael. 2005. *Publics and Counterpublics*. New York: Zone Books.

———. 1993. *Fear of a Queer Planet: Queer Politics and Social Theory*. Minneapolis: University of Minnesota Press.

———. 1992. "The Mass Public and the Mass Subject." In *Habermas and the Public Sphere*, edited by Craig J. Calhoun. Cambridge: MIT Press.

Weston, Kath. 1997. *Families We Choose: Lesbians, Gays, Kinship*. New York: Columbia University Press.

40.
on hallowed ground
I cast the circle
that there may be
haven for the lost
refuge and sanctuary
turning to the hills
I place feet on steady ground
letting earth hold me
in praise of air
I lift my hands
to the heavens
call down grace for blessings
for anointed being
turning toward water
I let go remembered sins
cleanse and purify
burning sage
I bring fire to warm
and illuminate
all around this body
light moves
a communion of gathered
spirits

                    —bell hooks

6

Gathering Wild Greens

Foodways Lessons from Appalachia's Past

Elizabeth S. D. Engelhardt

> I guess, if there wasn't anything to eat, I guess I could go into the woods and not starve by gathering greens for food. There's branch lettuce and crow's-foot and bear grass and creases and speckled dock. Of course, there's poke sallet, but I don't like it. And there's sochani, which you take the young leaves and parboil, then wash and fry in grease. . . . But now I'm putting up angelica for next winter. It's mighty good to eat.
> —Martha Lossiah Ross, Buncombe County, North Carolina

The wild greens listed by Martha Ross still grow in the forests of Appalachia. People in the mountains have long gathered, prepared, and fed and medicated themselves with such plants. For the most part, wild greens have never been successfully commercialized or domesticated. The few companies that tried were hard-pressed to explain why Americans with canned tomatoes, corn, seafood, meats, fruits, and even spinach in their shopping carts did not pick up other canned greens to round out their meals. Since this food, unlike others, has resisted transcending its place in order to join other national food trends, perhaps one should conclude it is unimportant. I disagree. Wild greens, one of the most humble foodways of Appalachia, are, I contend, powerful symbols of the complicated connections between people and places then and now. I suggest we move them from the margins to the center of discussion.[1]

What follows is a historical story of competing strategies of knowing and speaking at a local level centered on the beginning of the twentieth century. The lessons learned from that era's story expand outward into the present day. To move so far across time and space, this chapter first examines the challenges of looking at greens and dislodging stereotypes that make them hard to see. The case study is a disease that swept through early-century mill towns—and the competing solutions, including gathering wild greens, offered to cure it. I suggest an analytical shift might be required to understand the wisdom in gathering wild greens. Finally, I propose that a similar analytical shift might be a useful approach to a very different crisis here at the beginning of the twenty-first century: that of knowledge in the humanities.

I wrote about greens in *A Mess of Greens: Southern Gender and Southern Food*—but only from the side. There I suggested that even garden greens are difficult to face head-on because they are difficult to find in traditional academic archives. Greens rarely made it into early cookbooks; just as today one is hard-pressed to find scrambled eggs in cookbooks because cooking them is considered a basic skill, for instance, recipes for greens were similarly omitted from cookbooks then. Greens other than collards (and, rarely, mustard and turnip) continue to be absent from catalogs celebrating southern food, because such lists privilege aspirational eating, special occasion or popular food trends. (Collards themselves have been viewed with suspicion. In Flannery O'Connor's "A Stroke of Good Fortune," they threaten to reveal the fragile middle-class prosperity of a formerly poor character.) Not surprisingly, wild greens are still more elusive. Recipes for spring tonics and herbal medicines can be carefully guarded family secrets, and edible wild plants vary tremendously by locality, making them difficult to catalog comprehensively. But *Place Matters* gives me a chance to return and expand on the meanings and consequence of Appalachia's wild foods and the places that hold them.[2]

A mystery unfolded in the United States South around the turn of the twentieth century. During that era, massive industrialization in and on the edges of the mountains transformed lives. The turn of the century held a perfect storm of challenges and innovations—the naming of Appalachia, the post-Reconstruction reinvigoration of the idea of the South, and massive economic transformation of mountain food systems. In the first decades of the twentieth century, subsistence farms across Appalachia were in serious transition. Whether they ever were sites of easy self-support was debatable, but by 1900, more and more farm expenses needed to be paid for in cash.

With agricultural prices swinging wildly, barter economies and neighborhood support were insufficient for farms to avoid sinking into debt. Businesspeople representing extractive industries such as logging and mining were buying land and mineral rights out from under residents, who were sometimes willing and sometimes did not give their full consent. More and more families were facing pressures to become tenant farmers or sharecroppers as they lost or failed to acquire lands of their own. For many, then, the lure of mill life was powerful and rational. Escaping a cycle of farming that seemed to spiral ever downward, finding a way into cash economies that seemed increasingly inescapable, even representing last-ditch efforts to keep family land by paying store debts, families from around the region were drawn into mill work. A massive public relations campaign sent recruiters through the mountains, promising new, modern lives of ease for workers. Mill work, even the harsh southern form of it, promised pleasures. Emerging consumer culture could be powerfully attractive. Chewing gum, Cokes, candy, movies, books, electricity, toilets, cookstoves, window glass and screens, new dresses, items from the newly arriving mail-order catalogs, restaurants, even just paychecks, all enticed potential workers.[3]

Mills, fed by the ready influx of workers, grew rapidly in the early part of the century. For instance, in 1899, North Carolina already had 177 mills; by 1909 that number was up to 281. South Carolina boasted 80 and 147 in the same time period, and, compared to North Carolina's, South Carolina's mills tended to be larger facilities. The money was similarly impressive: mills in North Carolina grew from yearly profits of $28.4 to $72.7 million in that decade. In North Carolina thirty thousand mill jobs existed in 1900; there were forty-seven thousand by 1910. Another forty-five thousand mill workers labored in South Carolina by the later date. One scholar has calculated that by 1905 in South Carolina at least "one of every six white persons lived in a mill village." The villages varied widely in quality of life, but the common denominator was that many new workers were drawn in from high up in the mountains and surrounding valleys and found themselves in very new environments.[4]

Despite the promises of prosperity, a new disease simultaneously made headlines across the southern states. It especially seemed to target the mills and factories on the fringes of the Appalachian Mountains. Although it was not the only illness sweeping the south—hookworm, tuberculosis, pneumonia, malaria, smallpox, and the following decade's major influenza epidemic all affected many of the region's citizens—it was the most mysterious.

Family after family had at least one member who was said to have "broken down"—in the mills, in the mines, in monocultural agriculture fields. These were the images: sallow complexions, lazy demeanors, distended bellies, stunted height, and glazed expressions. Sometimes described as the "mill type," other times as "white trash" or the "typical southern Negro," victims peopled Erskine Caldwell's *Tobacco Road,* Lewis Hine's photo essays of textile workers, and Appalachia's mountain communities. Given the region's political insecurities in the post-Reconstruction era, it was especially galling that the disease seemed to target the South, where the vast majority of victims resided and deaths occurred. From this historical distance it is almost impossible to know how many people in photographs and descriptions were victims of which diseases. Yet we can conclude a hungry, tired, and ill version of the South existed alongside the visions of the prosperous one.[5]

The mystery disease remains hard to see unless we dislodge persistent ideas of southern abundance. That romantic and nostalgic vision strongly influences our sense of southern foodways. We can list the features: groaning tables; smiling hostesses; sites of racial reconciliation; comfort food made from scratch; traditions guaranteed unchanged from a long-vanished past; food swimming in butter or fried indulgences; and homemade jellies, jams, layered and legendary cakes, pies, and candies. It purports to be a singular cuisine. We repeatedly romanticize southern food as quintessentially nourishing, hearty, and comforting.[6]

Of course, such myths are not entirely untrue. But they overlook many other truths. Kitchens were public, often exploitative workspaces for many women. Restaurants were not equally accessible to everyone, which led to the Civil Rights–era sit-ins to fight Jim Crow segregation. Not all foods were homemade and, in fact, corporate foods invented by Southerners were given great loyalty. Many, such as Duke's Mayonnaise, Coca-Cola and most of the major soda brands, MoonPies and other candy bars, propped up workers through painfully long shifts. Sugary Jell-O salads and salty, fatty, processed-ingredient recipes hawked by 1950s cookbooks may well have contributed to today's regionwide health consequences such as diabetes and obesity but were often welcome relief for families struggling with precious little time or money. Southern food contains multiple cuisines that did not begin on the plantation table, but the ways we have separated foods of the slave quarters from ones on poor whites' tables have traditionally been vexed. We overprivilege cookbooks and the celebration cooking they contain (think prelapsarian Paula Deen and butter and *Southern Living*'s indulgent cakes).

If nothing else, it is worth remembering that a major portion of the southern food story is one of decidedly unromantic, painful loss, lack, and absence. Only by acknowledging the hungry South can we tease out why the greens matter and how the solution they represent can be medically wrong but culturally, socially, and politically true.[7]

Pellagra and the Southern Table

The disease was pellagra. Described as the disease of four-Ds—dermatitis, diarrhea, dementia, and death—pellagra made many of its sufferers suicidal or dangerous to others. Looking sunburned, feeling fatigued, moving with a pained and jerky gait, and unable to keep down food, early-stage pellagrins were often mistakenly labeled lazy or indolent or misdiagnosed with colds or rheumatism. Only when skin, especially on faces, peeled and hardened, leaving visible butterfly-shaped lesions and marking them much like the victims of leprosy, was pellagra undeniable. Sometimes called "the butterfly caste," sufferers of pellagra faced comparisons to leprosy victims—and similar quarantining. Fear of the disease, pellagraphobia, led friends and family (not to mention southern states' political apparatuses) to shun victims; their being turned out of homes and villages and often locked behind the doors of poorly funded institutions raised the death rate of the disease even higher. Doctors could not predict which victims would develop acute cases that led quickly to death and which would experience chronic, yearly outbreaks that debilitated but did not kill. Nor could doctors around 1900 explain why certain months saw spikes in pellagra cases, why the South seemed so vulnerable to the disease, and what role the increasingly typical workers' diets of three Ms—meat, meal, and molasses—played.[8]

After ruling out insect or infectious causes, researchers turned to the diet of victims, mapping the race, class, geographic location, gender, and age distribution of pellagrins against the available food. The resulting maps and surveys suggested wide distance between actual eating habits and theoretically available food on shelves. Especially for new industrial workers, researchers glimpsed the effects of long hours and company housing on the ability of people to supplement their diets with anything fresh or varied. They documented the sharp downturn in many families' food during winter, when gardens lay fallow and wild food could not be gathered, which, in turn, allowed researchers to understand why so many got sicker or died in early spring as meager rations completely ran out.[9]

Women, especially those of childbearing age, were much more likely to have undiagnosed but serious cases of pellagra (one study concluded working women were ten times more likely than working men to contract the disease). And pellagra devastated children in the mills, also an unexpected finding. Yet both groups were likely to eat last and less in households with limited means. African Americans had extraordinary rates of pellagra (although the researchers' focus on mill communities limited their data, given how predominantly white their study subjects were). Because of racial, age, and gender hierarchies, as researchers homed in on diversity in diet, they could see why communities that appeared to offer a diverse range of foods and sufficient calories still had members falling victim.[10]

If a Southerner in the early twentieth century ate his or her cultivated and wild greens, had fresh eggs, milk, fish, and meat regularly (which meant being close to a farm healthy enough to support its animals, as starving cows do not deliver sufficient milk, for instance), and varied their intake of fresh and canned goods and beans along with cornbread, molasses, and cured pork, they would not contract pellagra. They needed to be aware that the corn from the store was less likely to come from local farms and instead was more likely to have fewer nutrients because of greater processing and longer travel time; thus, even more than before, corn needed supplementation with other foods. Similarly, store-bought pork after the turn of the century was frequently imported and more likely to be fatback rather than their parents' staple of bacon. Curing pellagra in a society took education on how foods worked together to provide a necessary range of vitamins, calories, and nutrients. It required enough economic stability and security to weather setbacks—the temporary loss of a family member's income, the death of a cow or loss of a crop, unexpected health or housing expenses, or other personal emergency. Curing pellagra benefited from a community's ability to grow or import a range of healthy foods and its agricultural diversity rather than being in the grip of monoculture. Individuals needed either time to prepare diverse foods or sufficiently high-quality equipment and convenient ingredients to cook good food quickly. Societies that cured pellagra dislodged their internal racism and sexism enough to focus on feeding adequate amounts to the most vulnerable as well as the most privileged—so that everyone in the household or community had a sufficient share of a range of foods.[11]

In experiments to induce the disease by withholding foods, researchers eventually concluded that pellagra comes from a deficiency of a specific nutrient. Though the exact vitamin, niacin, would not be identified until decades later (and, indeed, though vitamins in general were poorly understood until the midpoint of the century), effective, if temporary, treatments were developed that involved supplementing diets with niacin-rich foods such as canned salmon, nutritional yeast, and canned tomatoes. Pellagra was really put to rest in the post–World War II era with enriched flours and other staples. But at the turn of the century, the "official" treatment basically came down to consistently adding more variety to a person's diet. That was fine, as far as it went, but in the early century pinning the cure on purchasing (either by individuals or by employers, state governments, or private philanthropic donation) supplemental food was tenuous. Economic downturns, miscommunication and mistrust of top-down or perceived outsider prescriptions, and labor disputes time and again stopped the flow of niacin-rich foods and numbers of pellagra victims rose.[12]

Take a Walk, Gather Wild Greens

Local solutions, especially to counter illnesses at the end of long, lean winters, did not require the exchange of money, company and general stores, new medical research, or outside charity. Many pellagra victims and families worried about the disease turned back to those community solutions. The solutions were simple: go for walks; see what was growing in the forest, along the road, in the overlooked spaces; gather wild greens; make tonics or messes of greens to relieve the sameness of pantries, especially those depleted over winter.

We have tantalizing glimpses of the practice in oral histories, family memories, and fictional portraits of the time. You have to search a bit to find records of spring tonics written down—lists of ingredients, proportions, and directions for preparation and use. Nonetheless, scholars such as Fred Sauceman agree foraging is a long-established hallmark of eating across the South, that "Southerners have pickled watermelon rinds, made wine out of corn cobs, stewed mudbugs, killed spring lettuce with vinegar and bacon grease, and sautéed dandelion greens, thereby creating America's most diverse indigenous cuisine." And foraging is the heart of pellagra's local solution. Appalachians have been some of the most dedicated foragers— their prey encompassing everything from crawdads to possums to poke and reflected even in names disparaging the habits from sang diggers to molly moochers. Early spring in Appalachia sends folks out for poke, cress or branch lettuce, dock, ramps, and more.[13]

A few locally produced community cookbooks, interviews, and archives document how wild foods were prepared. Asked about poke, Mrs. Elvie Corn told John Parris, "There's different ways of fixing poke. . . . I've never seen any written recipes for it. I learned how to fix it from my mother and my grandmother. But all of it has got to be cooked." She has gone out for poke ever since being "kneehigh to a duck." Branch lettuce, although "it's mighty good," is also "hard to come by. Not like poke. Grows only in the winding hollows where the water comes warm from the earth, or in and near the edge of a branch where the soil is dark and damp." She warns, "You won't find it on just any spring." Rosie Powell, from Rosman, North Carolina, offered a recipe for Wilted Branch Lettuce and Ramps to her community's fund-raising cookbook. She directed, "Gather branch lettuce (wild lettuce) and clean good. Chop lettuce and ramps together; toss to mix. Fry bacon or fatback; remove meat from pan and crumble over lettuce and ramps. Heat meat drippings to sizzling hot. Pour over lettuce. Eat immediately before it has chance to get cold. Good with meats or any other vegetable. Especially good with hot corn bread." North Georgia's Foxfire team focused on spring tonics in one of their volumes. Recipes collected from their oral history interviews claim "there is almost nothing better after a long winter . . . than a mess of dandelion, lamb's quarter, or cress." "Potherbs," "garden sass," and "sallet" "gathered while young and tender" all stood in for medicine "before the days of vitamin pills and supermarkets." The diversity of the plants and preparations collectively affirm the belief that blood strengthening would occur through the use of teas and tonics. Insofar as these recipes relieved the damaging monotony of the restricted meat, meal, and molasses diet, they did no harm and in fact helped overall health. But as a cure for pellagra, they fail.[14]

Wild greens taken at the first sign of spring—the Appalachian spring tonic, most often cited as a cure for winter weakness such as that experienced by pellagra victims—cannot actually cure the disease by themselves. The herbs and plants gathered are not especially rich in niacin. Must they then be dismissed as misguided folklore? As harmful anecdote?

Before turning away from this bit of food history, let me propose a shift in the terms of analysis. In other words, concluding that greens fail on a medical level may not necessarily mean they fail on all grounds. I am suggesting that what gathering the greens represents, how they were consumed, and what follows from them could, in fact, "cure" a societal problem like pellagra. Gathering wild greens challenges and indicts parts of the new social structures of the mills, the limits of researchers' processed food supplements, and the general reliance on cash exchanges. What pellagrins symbolize is countered by what gathering wild greens symbolizes. But parsing the message requires turning not to nutritional science but instead to the humanities—in this case, a closer reading of the community solution.

For the solution did not call for wild greens only. It directs one to *gather* wild greens. That active verb makes all the difference. Wild greens are food—delicious, varied, nutritious, but not sufficient. Gathering wild greens is a practice of Appalachian foodways—gathering suggests attention to place, devotion of time, and care of community, and in this way gathering "cures" the social problem of pellagra. If food is a material object, foodways are the processes, practices, cultural negotiations, and social meanings on, around, and constitutive of the promise of the foods. The solution is not the greens themselves; rather, it is the gathering of the greens. Fictional and historical narratives in which consequences of not gathering greens are explored make visible why the verb matters.

Time, Consumption, and Gathering Wisdom

When in 1929 a violent strike broke out in Gastonia, North Carolina, on the edges of the Blue Ridge Mountains, years of illness and malnutrition within hardworking families came to the surface. Food for families, health care, and an economic safety net all were demands of the strike, which was notable for the participation (and assassination) of women, a surge in pellagra during its worst moments, involvement of the radical Left, brutal violence and a corrupt justice system that sanctioned it, and a proliferation of novels and songs produced about it. Most famous was the ballad "Mill Mother's Lament," by Ella May Wiggins, who lost at least one of her four children who died to pellagra. The novels include Mary Heaton Vorse's *Strike!* (1930), Olive Tilford Dargan's *Call Home the Heart* (1932), Grace Lumpkin's *To Make My Bread* (1932), Myra Page's *Gathering Storm* (1932), Sherwood Anderson's *Beyond Desire* (1932), and William Rollins Jr.'s *The Shadow Before* (1935). Almost all featured characters were suffering from pellagra. Dargan calls it mother sickness; all position it as one of the greatest challenges faced by working families leading up to the strikes.[15]

Lumpkin's *To Make My Bread* focuses on the McClure family, especially John and Bonnie, brother and sister. Bonnie, loosely based on Wiggins, is assassinated; before that her mother, Ella, contracts and dies from pellagra.

The novel wrestles with why a family would leave the mountains to face such tragedies in the mills—and Lumpkin poignantly describes hunger in both locations. By the end of the novel, not only have Bonnie and Ella died, but also two other family members have passed away, another brother survives but only by rejecting his family, and John stands alone to face the strikes. Dargan's *Call Home the Heart* focuses on Ishma, who tries to pull her family out of poverty by following the latest agricultural extension advice and education; she wants to wean the family from their overdependence on the general store. Years of crop failures and difficult pregnancies, however, cause Ishma to leave her husband (and true love), Brit, in the mountains to work down in the mills. Fearful of crushing Brit's dreams, Ishma sees this as a compassionate choice. Though Ishma is reunited with Brit by the end of the novel, in between she becomes involved in union and strike work, nursing, and an intellectual community. Her heart leads her home to the mountains as she finds the mill owners' and labor organizers' solutions equally naive in their reliance on outside donations.

The novelists depart from the historical record in at least one crucial detail. Historically, pellagrins were generally institutionalized when their disease flared. But in the novels, the pellagrin as a family member or neighbor was not removed from the community. They stayed at home and they died at home, but not before serving as critics of the structures that led to their illness. Novels highlighted conflicting theories and feelings of despair about the practices of who ate, when, and in what quantities—decisions that had everything to do with how race, class, gender, and age were distributed in the people at any given table. These fictional pellagrins function as tragic reminders of food that did not nourish. Pellagrins embody the problems of rigid, standardized factory time and the brutal conflation of consumption with consumerism that starves the physical body. Made more visible by the contrast, gathering greens is revealed as a process of nurturing, unstructured time, and sustaining food practices.[16]

Taking a walk to gather wild greens, by its very nature, resists rigid standardization. How do you gather greens? Can you schedule it by perfectly predicting how long it will take? Can you walk in a straight line to a specific place every time? Of course not. You have to follow a wandering stream for branch lettuce. You need to peek under the forest's carpet for the first sprouts of ramps. You have to see if this year the same patch of ground has been fertile for dock and sorrels. You simply may have to walk until you stumble across this year's bounty. More than that, you have to think about the season or nature's time, what has sprouted and what remains to come, how the year's rain, sun, and passing has resulted in new patches or lost bunches.

Today, watches can be had for pennies. Learning to tell time is a developmental marker in children. Our cell phones, computers, ovens, even our cars blink the time at us. But time is not natural or preordained. We made a conscious decision as a society to standardize time around the globe, to value a mechanical division of the day, and to give priority to hours over seasons, cycles, or moon phases. That decision happened in fits and starts, but it was formalized in the United States in the late nineteenth century, as railroads, science, and communication technologies all played roles. Also, and significantly, factories shaped our present-day definitions of time. Families had clocks. But they were routinely stopped to mark death. They were set to an agreed-on local time, not to mean standard time, and minutes could be more like suggestions than absolute imperatives. The first encounter mill workers often had with strictly standardized time was the mill recruiter who entered their farms, villages, and homes, wearing a watch prominently across his chest. Time profoundly affected their new lives, food, and health. Mill time, and the watch that represented it, was, whether subtly or overtly, a symbol of ownership. It symbolized a lack of freedom in mill life. It made going out to gather greens a profoundly subversive choice.[17]

In Lumpkin's *To Make My Bread,* one of first things the family acquires upon moving to the mill town is an alarm clock and the lessons they need to read it. Yet Lumpkin explicitly claims that time is the one thing workers do not control. In fact, efficiency experts coming into the mill and installing "hank clocks" on each machine spur the strike. Clocks usher in the stretch-out system, which makes fewer workers produce more goods for less pay. Even the name, stretch-out, evokes mills' absolute control of time. Time could be stretched, internationalized, corporatized, standardized, manipulated, and withheld; but it could not nourish. Lest this seem too far from pellagra, in the novels discussions of clocks nestle up to discussions of pellagra. In Lumpkin's novel, Emma, right before contracting pellagra herself, combines the criticism of hours in daylight with a brutal assessment of the monoculture surrounding the mills. Not only is she unable to get the garden planted before darkness falls, but she knows Granpap needs every single inch of land possible for cotton in order to break even—failure to balance the two demands ultimately leads to the death of both. One of the most intriguing studies performed by researchers at the time showed that two otherwise identical mill villages differed on pellagra because only one had access to a single vegetable farm and a single slaughterhouse—and the time during daylight for residents to purchase from them. In a tight radius, the main characters, changes in methods of work, painful realities of lack of food, and violent consequences all collide. Time should provide rest or restoration, health or energy—but none of Lumpkin's working characters have enough of it.[18]

Dargan's pellagrins are eloquent about what researchers were slow to learn: how pellagra also targeted women through consumerism and cultural misunderstanding. In the mill village, Ishma meets Mame Wallace, an "advanced 'case'" of pellagra. A conversation between Ishma, her mentor, Derry Unthank, and the pellagrin maps out the disease's complications. Unthank asks Wallace, "Just starved yourself into bed, eh, Mrs. Wallace? Forgot what I told you two years ago?" When Wallace replies, "Don't be too hard on me, doctor. There's so many of us." Unthank adds, "And of course when the biscuits won't go round, mother will hunt up that piece of day-before-yesterday's cornbread and be perfectly satisfied with it." Wallace acknowledges that truth, but claims she quickly started preferring it: "I got so I'd ruther have it. I'd just ruther have it, doctor. . . . I'd always bake a big pone for supper an' give the children milk with it." Dargan is at pains, through Unthank in this case, not to demonize the cornbread itself. At issue is the balance in diet, as well as the gender disparity that causes the rest of the family to benefit from what range Wallace can muster, but which punishes her as a result. Unthank says, "That was fine, but mother didn't take any milk, and there was always enough of the pone left over for her to nibble a bit for breakfast and dinner next day." More than that, Wallace reveals that she subsists on cornbread and cold water. She says a neighbor "let me go over to her house ever' day an' get some cold water out of her 'frigerator to drink with it. That made it good. She kept a bottle o' water just for me, knowin' I liked it with my bread. It was better 'n milk that got as warm as dishwater in the coolest place I could find." Here the pellagrin herself moves the disease beyond nutritional neglect and into cultural terrain, as differences in taste (preferring anything cold over something nutritious) and prevailing gender roles (wanting to sacrifice for her children) all lead to Wallace's case. Pellagra (symbolic and actual) is so evocative and painful because it is never simple.[19]

For Dargan, the problem is consumerism itself. A second pellagrin, Cindy, deliberately sacrifices herself for things. Cindy is very sick when Ishma goes to her, but she refuses to take a break from her shifts. She has a long list of reasons:

"Stop work?" cried Cindy, amazed. "Why, I'm payin' on a sewin'-machine, a 'frigerator, an' a bed-room set! I've wanted a sewin'-machine since I was twelve years old, an' I'm gettin' it now. An' I had to have a 'frigerator. A mountain person can't drink the water down here in the summer time without coolin' it off. Can't do it an' live. I had to have a bed too. Up in the mountains it didn't make any difference if I slept on a pallet, I could *sleep*. But down here I come out o' the mill feelin' like a squeezed dish-rag, an' if I don't get my sleep I'm done fer. I had to have a bed I could rest on. Then I had to buy two more fer the boys. I couldn't take the best, an' leave my younguns to the cobs."

Cindy, in many ways, *is* her sewing machine, refrigerator, furniture, and mattresses. In other words, not only are consumer goods increasingly available, but also definitions of self shift to incorporate the goods; status is defined by purchasing material objects. Cindy is caught in the gruesome change—she believes that only through objects can she have an identity in the mill village, yet acquiring the objects kills her physical body.[20]

Lumpkin's characters dream of fresh foods and mountain paths, but Dargan's novel stands alone in that her main character leaves before the deaths, before the ballad singers are shot, before the women marching for their children are gunned down. Ishma walks home to Brit and the farm he held onto for her; Ishma calls him "the last farmer in history, safe on his rock ledge with its fertile spots and patches, feeding his family out of his hand." In their reconciliation, she remembers a song sung by Granny Starkweather, the last true nurturer and greens gatherer of her family. From the Grange (an earlier political organization dedicated to uniting workers, especially agricultural ones), the ditty celebrates the virtues of the simple plough. Though Ishma is not certain that the plough will be enough to save her people, and though Dargan's message gets muddled between faith in technology versus Soviet-style collective farming, Ishma makes a plan that relies on a new relationship between people, place, and food. Her plan deliberately turns away from money and consumerism. Ishma says, "I wasn't thinking about making money. I was thinking about a lot of little kids that I'd like to bring up here in the summer—every summer. I'd like to give them plenty to eat and turn them loose on the mountain to get strong. . . . We could build bark shelters for them, or use your old tobacco sheds, since you're not going to worry with tobacco any more. It will take a lot of milk and eggs." She wants to expand the farm so that "some of the mothers can come up and help me with the hens and cows. And I know men that the mills have scrapped who'd be made over by one summer up here." One imagines the pellagrins surrounded by greens, walking, meandering, moseying, and gathering with no regard to time, selves defined not by refrigerators but by community and health.[21]

In the novels, as in the oral histories and cookbooks, the suggestion, then, is to take a walk to gather greens. Greens resist domestication (much to many valiant experimenters' chagrin, as they report failed attempts to profit from wild plants transplanted to efficient garden beds). They have little market value. The seeds are not patented. Companies are largely unsuccessful at canning them. You have to plan to eat flexibly and with a palate open to variety—because you do not know exactly what will be ripe during any given walk. You are out of view, off the grid, as it were. And you have to reclaim some control of your own time, your own self.

So it is not the food per se. It is the foodways: the process, the local knowledge, and the set of priorities. Dargan offers two ideal meals to illustrate the point. The first comes when Ishma goes out for a walk and happens across cymlings (small pumpkins) along a fence line. She decides in the midst of hard times for the family to create and cook a supremely local meal in the mountains. She cooks the cymlings with molasses and herbs and adds dried apple turnovers to round out the meal. It is practically a textbook example of how to avoid pellagra, even with few financial resources. The second meal is even more symbolic. It is a good place to end, because it is clearly not an actual meal—but is instead the spirit of the wild greens I am urging be added to today's intellectual tables. When a teacher tries to show Ishma's sister how to set a table, "Ishma thought that the set-out must have been a very drab affair." Instead, she makes her own ideal table setting, "as was in her heart" in the woods: "With a stick she would trace an oval on a bit of mossy ground and mark the line carefully with tiny fernleaves. Her service set would be of galax. Flattened, the leaves were plates, and she could have them in any size; but she could twist them and pin them with their own stems into cups, bowls, dishes of whatever kind she wished." Ishma makes "food" out of "wild-flower petals and the tender rosy and red-hued baby oaks and maples that had pushed a few inches above the ground." When a rabbit and bird eat at her table while she watches, Ishma never plays the game again, believing she experienced perfection. The desire to merge nature and local food with modern life foreshadows Ishma's final plans to counter pellagra and the haunting figures of pellagrins in literature. It illustrates how the symbolic gathering of wild greens counters the specter of pellagra and an unhealthy allegiance to a national and transnational version of consumerism.[22]

Gathering Wild Greens in the Modern Classroom

The active wisdom held in the Appalachian community cure for pellagra specifically and health more broadly might not be confined to individual or group physical health. We might compose a long list of institutions in today's world that put pressure on the ability of communities to thrive. Further, we might find many of those institutions are, like the mills discussed here, flawed less in conception but more in practice. These structures, in other words, could be reclaimed, revised, improved, and collaborated with in order to help the largest possible number of participants grow and prosper. I want to focus here on one: higher education.

I firmly believe the U.S. higher education systems—the network, histories, and future promise of our public and private universities, colleges, community colleges, and continuing education institutions—constitute one of the best ideas we have created as a society. And I further believe that one of its best characteristics is the responsibility embedded that we always strive to make it better—more inclusive, more responsive, more rigorous, and more compassionate. So I offer the following questions in the spirit of reflection, accountability, and critical hopefulness.

How might the wisdom in gathering greens in Appalachia guide those of us engaged in university education today? Parallel metaphors support the thought experiment: it is hardly new to compare the U.S. education system to a factory or mill. Nineteenth-century education reformers set out explicitly to train future factory workers in revolutionary school "systems" at the same time textile mills expanded across the U.S. South. In the present day, a quick glance at the rhetoric about higher education shows modern equivalents to standardizing time, extreme quantifying of human labor, and subsuming individuals into profit-only systems. Pellagra-vulnerable mills had watches, stretch-outs, and conflation of individuals into goods, profits, and paychecks. Education today has standardized testing, business models judging success, entrepreneurial partnerships for school supplies, branding, and discussions of students as customers. Metaphors for education have shifted in revealing ways: students are often called customers and their education a product delivered. We talk about badges and levels even in qualitative and humanities-based fields. Outcomes are measured by assessments that work best when broken down into single vectors.[23]

What if we try viewing the humanities as the practice and process, as the gathering of greens rather than the greens themselves? I urge us to ask ourselves what our metaphorical walk for greens is as we interact in classrooms today. What is still in the woods? What knowledge has refused to be domesticated in the university garden? What do we need to slow down, wander, and gather? How do we need to collaborate in order to succeed? More specifically, what do Appalachia's forests, streams, pockets of wisdom still hold that will nourish and guide us if we set the table and see what happens? I do not live in Appalachia today, despite having grown up in North Carolina's mountains and being shaped by Appalachian communities. I write from Chapel Hill, North Carolina, having recently moved from Austin, Texas, two places short on mountains but long on the potential to be national leaders on these issues. And I write in conversation with you, reading this book today—from whatever location on or off college campuses, in places large and small, near and far—certain that you too have wisdom to offer on this walk. What is in our local places and how does wandering in and through *them* matter? What happens if we walk not in a line with strict hierarchies but instead as a group, together? I do not have definitive answers, but the gathering of wild greens encourages the process, the poetry, the intuition, the ecological, and the walk. In times of hopelessness, with budget slashing and social contract devaluing, we could perform a similar shift. Let's not just eat greens or acquire a diploma. Let's go together on a walk as we gather knowledge, learning, and curiosity just as we might gather wild greens, learning old lessons and new about sustaining ourselves and our students across time and place.

Notes

Portions of this chapter appeared earlier in *A Mess of Greens: Southern Gender and Southern Food* (University of Georgia Press, 2011) and are reprinted here with permission.

1. John Parris, *Mountain Cooking* (Asheville, NC: Asheville Citizen-Times Publishing Co., 1978), 110. For examples of companies trying to profit from canning wild greens, see Elizabeth Engelhardt, *A Mess of Greens: Southern Gender and Southern Food* (Athens: University of Georgia Press, 2011). Allen's and Betty Ann's, two regional canned goods companies, experimented with creecy greens and other mixed greens selections with only local success. Neither company's greens are in production today.

2. Flannery O'Connor, "A Stroke of Good Fortune," in *The Complete Stories* (1946; repr., New York: Farrar, Straus and Giroux, 1986), 95–107. My own family tells of a famous salve that was lost in the unexpected death of the only person who knew how to make it; at the time, it was recognized as valuable to both the family and the community.

3. Albert E. Cowdrey, *This Land, This South: An Environmental History* (Lexington: University Press of Kentucky, 1983), 103–107. Nan Enstad, *Ladies of Labor, Girls of Adventure: Working Women, Popular Culture, and Labor Politics at the Turn of the Twentieth Century* (New York: Columbia University Press, 1999), 17–19. Kathy Peiss, *Cheap Amusements: Working Women and Leisure in Turn-of-the-Century New York* (Philadelphia: Temple University Press, 1986), 5–7.

4. Edward H. Beardsley, *A History of Neglect: Health Care for Blacks and Mill Workers in the Twentieth-Century South* (Knoxville: University of Tennessee Press, 1987), 43. David L. Carlton, *Mill and Town in South Carolina, 1880–1920* (Baton Rouge: Louisiana State University Press, 1982), 7.

5. Elizabeth W. Etheridge, *The Butterfly Caste: A Social History of Pellagra in the South* (Westport, CT: Greenwood, 1972). Alan M. Kraut, *Goldberger's War: The Life and Work of a Public Health Crusader* (New York: Hill and Wang, 2003). Harry M. Marks, "Epidemiologists Explain Pellagra: Gender, Race, and Political Economy in the Work of Edgar Sydenstricker," *Journal of the History of Medicine* 58 (January 2003): 34–55. Erskine Caldwell, *Tobacco Road* (New York: Grosset and Dunlap, 1932). Lewis W. Hine, *Lewis Hine: Photographs of Child Labor in the New South,* ed. John R. Kemp (Jackson: University Press of Mississippi, 1986).

6. See, for instance, the stable of southern cooks on the Food Network, any issue of *Southern Living,* the yearly food issue of *Garden and Gun,* and numerous blogs (for which there is a dedicated conference, Food Media South, hosted by the Southern Foodways Alliance, on whose board I serve). See, www.foodnetwork.com/chefs/index.html, http://gardenandgun.com/food, www.southernliving.com/food/, and www.southernfoodways.org/events/2017-food-media-south/. For a thoughtful take on how these romantic ideas took hold, see Marcie Cohen Ferris, *The Edible South: The Power of Food and the Making of an American Region* (Chapel Hill: University of North Carolina Press, 2014).

7. Rebecca Sharpless, *Cooking in Other Women's Kitchens: Domestic Workers in the South, 1865–1960* (Chapel Hill: University of North Carolina Press, 2010). On restaurants and segregation, see Angela Jill Cooley, *To Live and Dine in Dixie: The Evolution of Urban Food Culture in the Jim Crow South* (Athens: University of Georgia Press, 2015). Jessica B. Harris, "African American Foodways," in *The New Encyclopedia of Southern Culture,* vol. 7, *Foodways,* ed. John T. Edge and Charles Reagan Wilson (Chapel Hill: University of North Carolina Press, 2007), 15–18. Elizabeth Leland, "A Sip of Relief," *Our State Magazine,* www.ourstate.com/dope-wagon/). On the regional prevalence of diabetes and obesity, see, for instance, www.cdc.gov/obesity/data/prevalence-maps.html. For a counterargument, see Julie Guthman, *Weighing In: Obesity, Food Justice, and the Limits of Capitalism* (Berkeley: University of California Press, 2011). Frederick Douglass

Opie, *Hog and Hominy: Soul Food from Africa to America* (New York: Columbia University Press, 2008). Psyche A. Williams Forson, *Building Houses Out of Chicken Legs: Black Women, Food, and Power* (Chapel Hill: University of North Carolina Press, 2006).

8. Etheridge, *Butterfly Caste,* 7–8. Kraut, *Goldberger's War,* 164–167. Interestingly, female victims were more likely to drown themselves; male ones were more likely to hurt others (Etheridge, *Butterfly Caste,* 38).

9. In addition, one did not have to work in the mills to be affected by them. Pressures to limit acreage devoted to gardens in order to produce more cotton to be processed in those factories changed the diets of farmers in the region, for instance. The influx of workers to the mills meant more reliance on cash purchases for everyone, thus cutting down on what had previously been thriving barter systems for food exchange. See Etheridge, *Butterfly Caste,* and Kraut, *Goldberger's War.*

10. Jacquelyn Dowd Hall et al., *Like a Family: The Making of a Southern Cotton Mill World* (New York: W. W. Norton, 1987), 150–151. Racist assumptions that African Americans would be "naturally" immune to diseases like pellagra interfered with research and treatment as well. See, for instance, Beardsley, *History of Neglect.*

11. John T. Edge and Joe Gray Taylor, "Southern Foodways," in Edge and Wilson, *Foodways,* 6. Frederick Douglass Opie, "Molasses-Colored Glasses: WPA and Sundry Sources on Molasses and Southern Foodways," *Southern Cultures* 14, no. 1 (2008): 84–85.

12. Much like the later, more famous Tuskegee syphilis experiments, Goldberger's experiments involving withheld food were conducted on vulnerable populations—in the pellagra experiments, prisoners. They have been criticized for racism and exploitation (Kraut, *Goldberger's War,* 121–124). Harvey Levenstein, *Revolution at the Table: The Transformation of the American Diet* (Berkeley: University of California Press, 2003), 147–160. On programs to enrich flour, see Etheridge, *Butterfly Caste,* 214.

13. Fred Sauceman, "Social Class and Food," in Edge and Wilson, *Foodways,* 104. Mary Hufford, "Molly Mooching on Bradley Mountain: The Aesthetic Ecology of Appalachian Morels," *Gastronomica* 6, no. 2 (Spring 2006): 49–56. Amelie Rives Troubetzkoy, *Tanis, the Sang-Digger* (New York: Town Topics, 1893). Indeed, I carried my mulberry bucket all through spring when I lived in Atlanta and walked to graduate classes; I chewed on sassafras root on hikes in the woods as I worked in West Virginia; and I am always on the lookout for black raspberries or abandoned apple orchards on trips home to the North Carolina mountains. Foraging has a downside, however, if people do not respect property rights, hunger solutions for the most vulnerable in a community, and long-term plant life cycles in order for all to thrive.

14. Elvie Corn's memories are in Parris, *Mountain Cooking,* 161–162. Rosie Powell is quoted in Eastatoe Community Club, *Our Country Recipes* (Rosman, NC, 1992), n.p., where she also gives a more modern recipe, one that incorporates processed food. (Cracker Barrel cheddar was introduced in 1954; see www.crackerbarrelcheese.com/ our-brand-story/.) Her recipe for "Poke casserole" calls for "2c parboiled poke, drained, 1/2c margarine, melted, 6 eggs, beaten, 1T flour, 1 large container cottage cheese, 1 stick

Cracker Barrel sharp cheddar cheese, 1 pkg. grated Cheddar cheese." She writes, "Mix all ingredients, adding poke last. Put in greased casserole dish. Bake in a 350° oven for 1 hour. Let stand 20 minutes before serving." Eliot Wigginton, ed., *Foxfire 2* (Garden City, NY: Anchor Books, 1973), 47–94. See also John van Willigen and Anne van Willigen, *Food and Everyday Life on Kentucky Family Farms, 1920–1950* (Lexington: University Press of Kentucky, 2006).

    15. Vorse, *Strike!* (New York: H. Liveright, 1930). Fielding Burke [pseud. of Olive Dargan], *Call Home the Heart* (1932; repr., Old Westbury, NY: Feminist Press, 1983). Lumpkin, *To Make My Bread* (1932; repr., Urbana: University of Illinois Press, 1995). Page, *Gathering Storm* (New York: International, 1932). Anderson, *Beyond Desire* (New York: Liveright, 1932). Rollins, *The Shadow Before* (London: V. Gollancz, 1935). For a discussion of pellagra in the strike novels, see Kathy Cantley Ackerman, *The Heart of Revolution: The Radical Life and Novels of Olive Dargan* (Knoxville: University of Tennessee Press, 2004), 67–75. Note that Dargan calls pellagra "mother sickness" in her sequel, *A Stone Came Rolling* (New York: Longmans, Green, 1935).

    16. Linda R. Monk, "A Plague of Cornbread," *Gravy* 34 (Winter 2009): 2–4.

    17. The classic argument about time by the economic historian E. P. Thompson is reviewed and applied to the South in Aaron Marrs, "Railroads and Time Consciousness in the Antebellum South," *Enterprise and Society* 9, no. 3 (2008): 433–456. Michael O'Malley, a cultural studies scholar, extends the argument to observe that time zones, easily available watches, synchronized time, and factory clocks "established new patterns for self-discipline, social order, and the organization of knowledge," which, in turn, led to, "on the one hand, outright resistance to clock time, or the desire to control it, and on the other a peculiar concern with internalizing clock authority and finding one's niche in the new framework of standardized time"—both of which could be seen in the strike novels. O'Malley, *Keeping Watch: A History of American Time* (New York: Viking, 1990), ix, 152.

    18. Lumpkin, *To Make My Bread*, 199–202, 235–246, 329. Lenoir Chambers, "Stop-Watches Led to Textile Strikes," *New York Times*, April 7, 1929, E1:6. Etheridge, *Butterfly Caste*, 127.

    19. Dargan, *Call Home the Heart*, 200–201.

    20. Ibid., 213–214; emphasis in original. Patricia Yaeger, *Dirt and Desire: Reconstructing Southern Women's Writing, 1930–1990* (Chicago: University of Chicago Press, 2000), 210. Yaeger also points out, as some of the mill novelists already had, that this new identity was supported by the New South's system of white privilege. African American mill town residents were few, and their ability to acquire consumer goods was lessened by their lower wages. Grace Hale would add that their too easy purchases were likely to trigger the violence of Jim Crow lynch mobs, as the goods soon were thought to distinguish white from black. Grace Elizabeth Hale, *Making Whiteness: The Culture of Segregation in the South, 1890–1940* (New York: Pantheon, 1998), 168–179.

    21. Dargan, *Call Home the Heart*, 429–430.

22. Ibid., 7–12.

23. See, for instance, the *Chronicle of Higher Education,* Gates Foundation policy papers, and any number of reports on productivity, innovation, and entrepreneurship in education. In particular, see Christopher Newfield, *Ivy and Industry: Business and the Making of the American University, 1880–1980* (Durham: Duke University Press, 2003), and *Unmaking the Public University: The Forty-Year Assault on the Middle Class* (Cambridge: Harvard University Press, 2008), for summaries of these arguments and history.

18.
when trees die
all small hearts break
little living creatures
happy and safe
uprooted
now in need of finding
new places
when home
cracks and breaks and falls
all life becomes danger
how to find
another place
where all is not
yet barren

—bell hooks

7

Buckwild Mad Men

Necropolitics and Masculinity in Appalachia

Carol Mason

> Dying's the best/Of all the arts men learn in a dead place.
> —James Wright, "At the Executed Murderer's Grave" (1958)

In 1927 the poet James Wright was born on the Buckeye side of the Ohio River in Martins Ferry, about four miles north of Wheeling, West Virginia. Contrary to historians' characterization of Wheeling in the first half of the century as the lively premiere city of the state, Wright saw the Ohio–West Virginia border as a "dead place" in which men learn the art of dying. More than a cynical expression of someone who suffered alcoholism and depression, Wright's celebrated poetry was influenced by world travel and study of Germany and South America, in particular. Yet so much of what he wrote explored the ravages of postindustrial Appalachia and the aesthetics of dying there.

Wright's phrasing invites the question: What are these "arts men learn in a dead place"? Are they the social aspects of actually relinquishing life, the social graces involved in saying good-bye to the world? Or the social conventions of bereavement, including proper funeral attire and visitations with food and flowers? Or the aesthetics of presentation and preservation—the mortician's makeup, the clergy's bedside manner, the cadence of eulogies, the meter of elegies, the design of a memorial, a bucolic burial plot, or the masonry of the headstone? On the contrary, for Wright, those arts included the less obvious slow-death sport of football. In "Autumn Begins in Martins Ferry, Ohio," he recognizes that youthful boys on the gridiron are "suicidally beautiful" long before Americans began to question the fatal harm in tackling.[1] Becoming a man on the Ohio–West Virginia border meant, for Wright, not just adopting a fatalism of certain death in the future but also recognizing in the present the processes by which we are always already good as dead, even at a young age. For Wright, masculinity was constructed through the ongoing act and art of dying in postindustrial Appalachia.

In the era of globalization, however, "dead places" are not confined to the wastelands of erstwhile industrial zones, or even war zones. Now such zones are exponentially expanded. The zones of resource extraction, for example, are no longer confined to mines or field wells. Today the effect of mountaintop removal coal mining and hydraulic fracturing for natural gas is not confined to places of industry, or to workers' bodies. Unlike deep mining or strip-mining, mountaintop removal involves the devastation of whole ecosystems. Unlike drilling, "fracking" for natural gas results in earthquakes felt miles away, and in reproductive health hazards that alter lives not yet lived. These are industrial zones beyond the geographic scope that a twentieth-century citizen such as Wright knew. Likewise, war zones have become borderless, amorphous, and perpetual in the twenty-first century as America deployed preemptive strikes and declared war not against any country with geographical boundaries but against "terror" unbound by any spatial demarcation. Thus, the dead place that was Wright's twentieth-century Appalachia is not the dead place with which we contend today, even if we also live in Appalachia. The zones and the politics of death have changed. So, too, must we change our understanding of what men learn, how men act, and how they construct their manhood in the "dead places" of late capitalism and globalization, including Appalachia.

This chapter therefore examines the depiction of masculinity in two early twenty-first-century representations of Appalachia: the short-lived comedic reality show *Buckwild,* which aired on MTV in 2013, and Rebecca Scott's scholarly study titled *Removing Mountains: Extracting Nature and Identity in the Appalachian Coalfields* and published by the University of Minnesota Press in 2010. I will look at them both as offering portraits of men contending with their vanishing ways of life—depictions that I do not condone but examine as cultural productions of masculinity worthy of our acknowledgment and critique. I analyze these representations of masculinity as depictions that shape our ideas of men; it is not my intention to provide an ethnography or sociology of the lived experience of particular people. I will also propose necropolitics, first described by the Kenyan scholar Achille Mbembe in 2003, as a useful framework for theorizing the dead places of the twenty-first century, such as the coal war fields of a globalized economy. In this way, the chapter takes "place" as a matrix of meanings that includes racial and gendered politics of space, which is always already configured according to class, and the social existences and identities that emerge from those configured areas. More specifically, Mbembe's theories help illuminate the spatialization of Appalachian work spaces and domestic spaces—coal-mining sites, dispossessed and reclaimed land that constitutes those sites, homes of miners, and the miners themselves, whose bodies are not just sites on which tyrannical corporate power lays a heavy load. Those bodies are, like the Earth itself, inextricably saturated and mutated by the substances and social forces of the industry and the discourses that justify it.

Buckwild

As always, recent images of Appalachia perform the cultural work of articulating national anxieties. A show such as *Buckwild,* which was filmed in Sissonville and Charleston, West Virginia, and canceled after two seasons, served up hillbilly stereotypes to provide viewers with an escapist and voyeuristic adventure in rural settings. Copying the formula for the very popular show *Jersey Shore,* MTV produced *Buckwild* to showcase youthful foolishness, physical buffoonery, and sexual tension featuring typical reality show characters and conflicts mashed up with stereotypical hillbilly personae. The result entails reckless young partiers who disavow modern amenities like the Internet and cell phones and revel in forms of entertainment more rustic than urban clubbing, such as riding all-terrain vehicles in the mud and tubing on the river. Appalled by the first episodes, West Virginia Senator Joe Manchin appealed to the MTV producers to cease the show, recognizing it as both an exploitation of young people who were paid for outlandish behavior and as a belittling of the state and its people.[2] But *Buckwild* was more than "class porn" and the continuation of demeaning people living in the mountain South. As we can see by comparing it with a couple of its contemporaries, *Buckwild* reflected concerns not confined to a region—namely, anxieties about class mobility, white privilege, and the dissolving boundaries between men and women. Most significantly, *Buckwild* shared with other shows the theme of presenting precarious societies whose ways of life are always portrayed as already dying. In what follows, I examine two episodic dramas in particular—*Downton Abbey* and, especially, *Mad Men*—to reveal how *Buckwild* shares this common theme of not only precarious societies but also of doomed men in particular.

Existing comparisons between *Buckwild* and *Downton Abbey* recognize a standard narrative of the implausibility of class mobility playing out in both shows.[3] Despite their starkly different settings—*Downton Abbey* taking place in Yorkshire, England, between 1912 and 1922 and *Buckwild* taking place in Charleston and Sissonville, West Virginia, a full century later, in 2012—the shows suggest that you cannot rise above the ranks in which you were born. "Whether you're living on welfare in a broken-down trailer, are a servant in a great English house, or own the house and employ the servants, you're pretty much stuck where you are. It's tough to change position on the social and economic ladder."[4] For the working class in Yorkshire, the social structure disallows any real movement up, despite the encroaching modernization that portends an evening out of class privilege that looks something like equality (especially for the ladies in the show). For the working class in Sissonville, it would seem, it is their own degenerate foolishness that keeps them in the ruins of modern life. *Buckwild* features a core cast of six young unemployed people mudding, drinking, and "bucking" around in settings that highlight dilapidation.

The scripted plots of each show, moreover, suggest a preoccupation with dispossession. The family in *Downton Abbey* is in the throes of possibly losing the grand estate after which the show is named. With this plot, the show maps onto the early twentieth century the anxiety of losing one's house that is very particular to the early twenty-first century. *Downton Abbey* showcases the anxiety of losing real estate, a theme that no doubt resonates with an American audience still reeling from the subprime mortgage housing crisis of 2008. In a reverse image of this anxiety, *Buckwild* reflects a nostalgia for not having to live up to bourgeois norms of home ownership—a nostalgia for a childlike, wildlike time when house and yard are mere locales for romping that is designed to tear things up. *Buckwild* gives us a good laugh by showing us a place and time where destruction is a regular part of life. Like *Downton Abbey*, which is promoted as offering "a spot-on portrait of a vanishing way of life," *Buckwild* offers a portrait of a way of life that is, according to long-standing depictions of Appalachia, a relic of bygone irresponsible behaviors.[5]

Representing a vanishing way of life is also a key theme for the enormously popular AMC drama *Mad Men*. The main character, Don Draper, represents an unabashed white male privilege that is on its way out, vanishing with the onset of the 1960s, that time of sexual revolution and racial unrest. Don is so recognizable to us today because he exemplifies a standard discourse of masculinity in popular culture known as the bro code. The bro code proudly proclaims a fraternity of male bonding that trumps any connections with females; in other words, it's "bros before 'hos." Don and his colleagues are womanizers, objectifying any female who crosses their path. They ruthlessly harass Peggy Olsen, for example, on her first day of work, commenting on every aspect of her physicality and presentation of self. A Catholic woman in 1960, Peggy has no recourse but to endure the harassment and see it as part of the job owing to the supposed fact that boys will be boys and she is in the realm of mad men.

In this way, the sexual politics of *Mad Men* and *Buckwild* are remarkably similar, and they hark back to a Darwinian natural sex selection in which the survival of the race depends on women's ability to choose competent mates.[6] Both shows essentialize men and women as beings so different that heterosexual compatibility and a happy ending to stories of sexual cruising or romantic courtship are nigh impossible.[7] To remedy this seemingly unobtainable happy ending, popular culture divides male characters into good and bad men, and it is the job of the woman to choose wisely.[8] In a twenty-first-century version of nineteenth-century natural sex selection, women must determine which of the men is not a cad, not the bro who is bent on avoiding commitment, denying emotional attachment, and exploiting women. In *Mad Men*, we see this choice for almost every female character—especially Peggy, who is taught literally from day one on the job at Sterling Cooper that she needs to be sexually available to the men in the office.[9] The women of *Mad Men* must choose which type of man will best serve their needs.

It is likewise in *Buckwild*. Even though the women exemplify what Angela McRobbie calls a new femininity that includes being as sexually aggressive as young men, ultimately they all want to secure a good man. For example, in episode twelve, Ashley and Kate confront Tyler, whose only redeeming quality (says Ashley) is that he is good-looking. Tyler has been denying hooking up with Kate and, in the process, cheating on Ashley. Both women join together to chastise him for not caring about either woman's feelings. And thus the show articulates the problem of who is the most honorable and therefore most ultimately desirable man.

Canceled before the producers apparently had intended, *Buckwild* never developed enough to make a crystal-clear division between good and bad men because one of its core six characters, Shain Gandee, died in the midst of production of the show's second season. Notably, he died accidentally while mudding, an activity frequently depicted on the program. Consequently, the plots did not develop. It seems certain from existing episodes, however, that Shain was scripted to play the rowdy, fun-loving good ol' boy who respected women more than the two-timing Tyler. The television character of Shain was constructed through editing as the hillbilly with a heart of gold who would be a good prize for any girl. With an accent that the producers sometimes saw fit to explicate with captions, Shain served as the sympathetic character, the underdog in his unrequited attraction for Cara, and "the audience's entrée into this foreign world" of West Virginia.[10] Even this unforeseen event of the tragedy of Shain's death fits the gendered formula that popular culture sets out for white women who, regardless of their own sexual romps, really want to secure a good husband, and for the elusive white men who refuse commitment, deny emotions, and want to be players all their lives. Both shows perpetuate an expectation of doom for such mad men: wild ways mean their days are limited. The recklessness both of Draper in his serial infidelity and his relentless smoking and drinking, and of the *Buckwild* boys, with their dangerous antics, is likely not to end up being death-defying, as Shain's tragic death demonstrates.

While these shows may seem at first glance to offer a standard homogeneous sense of fatalism, imagery from the shows designates the demises of white men in particularly twenty-first-century terms. The opening of *Mad Men,* for example, gives us the image of a man falling from a New York City skyscraper. This introduction alludes to largely censored scenes from the September 11, 2001, attacks of the World Trade towers, in which jumpers were forced to choose which type of death would end them—asphyxiation and inferno or free fall to fatal impact. Thus, the opening credits of *Mad Men* retroactively map onto the 1960s the cultural anxieties of a post–9/11 world.[11] We see a slow decline, a free-falling descent that is predicated on what Mbembe calls a "symbolics of the *top*" that, as I will explain in greater depth later, characterizes other contemporary representations of masculinity.[12]

The introductory sequence for *Buckwild* features an open coalfield with pitch-black heaps amid other surrounding green summits. Like the falling body of *Mad Men*'s introduction, this image points to the idea that characters, if not viewers, have relinquished control of the top, in both the spatial and social sense of the word. The image of the open coalfield also maps onto a reality show of reckless youth the portending problems of mountaintop removal coal mining, a late twentieth- and twenty-first-century practice. Recent scholarship, fiction, and narrative and documentary film have depicted coal mining by mountaintop removal as an irrevocable environmental devastation of human lives and ecosystems that cannot endure the toxicity and geological restructuring that results from this method of resource extraction. Indeed, many of the physical stunts designed for *Buckwild* involve industrial equipment crudely repurposed for recreation—such as backhoe skiing or an ATV-powered catapult—and thereby suggest that occupational safety is a laughable matter for people who have so little regard for their own personal safety. While *Buckwild* and *Mad Men* can be read as standard boys-will-be-boys narratives, therefore, they also reflect the particular anxieties of twenty-first-century men and pose the question of what manliness can possibly mean in landscapes marked by fatalism of near-apocalyptic proportions.

Removing Mountains

In *Removing Mountains,* Rebecca Scott takes up this question of manliness. She explores the lives of men and the role masculinity plays in Appalachian coalfields where mountaintop removal is reshaping the cultural and physical environment. She discusses three discourses of "mining masculinity": the family man, the tough guy, and the modern man. This taxonomy of men demonstrates the evolution of masculinity vis-à-vis coal, in which male identity responds to historical and technical developments in the industry.

According to Scott's analysis, the family man is characterized by earning a wage in the coalfields. His sense of masculinity is marked by the pride of providing for his wife and children, whose dependency is a necessary condition of his own claim to independence.[13] Therefore, manliness depends on gender inequalities in the workplace—men rather than women should work. It also, explains Scott, depends on racial inequalities in ways that always render manliness as a property of whiteness. The coal miner is always a man and always "symbolically white because the racially segmented labor market has historically reserved the family wage as a privilege of white men, which has helped ensure their status as national citizens."[14] As mountaintop removal supplanted underground mining and the quantity of high-earning jobs was radically reduced, the family man faced the problem of working in the service industry, coded as feminine, as soft work. With changes in the industry, the family man negotiates a crisis in masculinity that has heretofore been predicated on making a substantial paycheck through physical labor.

In contrast to the family man who is motivated by paternalism, the tough guy is motivated by the adrenaline rush of working in the dangerous conditions of mines. Scott's ethnography of tough guys features tales of everyday thrills and heroism involved in detonating explosions, securing underground ceilings before they have a chance to cave in, and getting out of the mine alive on a daily basis. If we can take local poetry as a reflection of how such stories are received, Crystal Good's poem "Boom Boom" attests to the sexual politics of this kind of miner masculinity.[15] Borrowing phrases that usually apply to mining situations and putting them in the context of relationships between men and women, "Boom Boom" metaphorically compares miners' treatment of the mountains with their treatment of women. Both mountains and women endure the economic exploitation of "stripping," a relinquishing of (mineral or human) "rights," scarring and resurfacing (de- then reforestation or cosmetic surgery), the "blasting" of songs of male triumph, and intoxication brought on by slurry and other "toxic messes." In the end, Good prescriptively observes that the mountain women "explode" as all these male-driven forces are detonated around them. In addition to being challenged by women who see sexism in the tough-guy romanticization of mine work, moreover, the machismo involved in enduring such truly perilous working conditions is challenged as mountaintop removal resituates miners on top of the Earth, not down in it. The jobs are far more technical than physical because draglines have replaced drills. Instead of burrowing into the ground, mountaintop removal employees operate huge earthmoving machinery or serve as security officers to make certain no one trespasses. Explosions remain, but a good part of the danger—hence the romance—of working as a coal miner has rendered those tough guys without the usual means of asserting their masculinity.

Emergent with mountaintop removal, then, is a third sort of miner masculinity, according to Scott: the modern man, who embraces the new conditions of mountaintop removal. He is a "friend of coal," a worker and a resident who denies the devastation wrought by mountaintop removal by seeing it as development. The modern man embraces the idea of mountaintop removal as "a masculine technology of control against irrational and feminine-coded Appalachian nature." He rationalizes the use of mountaintop removal by situating it in a historical context of seemingly natural economic progress. At the time when strip mining was an innovation, so too were strip malls, for example.[16] Mountaintop removal provides a flatter area when the land is "reclaimed" after coal has been extracted. Mountaintop removal is therefore conducive, ostensibly, to development heretofore unavailable to mountaineers—a flattened space where more retail or resort ventures can proliferate, adding more jobs, bringing in more wages and economic stability if not affluence. With this type of rationalization, the modern man grounds his manhood on a "technical domination of nature" that "represents an ideal of modern masculinity and is part of the everything-is-going-to-be-all-right story that coal companies repeatedly tell local residents," says Scott.[17]

This configuration of miner masculinity implicitly relies on the entrepreneurial spirit that is a hallmark of neoliberalism, and on the erasure of how the coal industry reemerged in the early 2000s. The manly domination of nature depends on the man who recognizes the flattened mountain as an opportunity instead of a catastrophic degradation of geology and ecology. Only those willing to see it as an opportunity are deserving of economic advancement. The neoliberal logic suggests that if you do not take advantage of the flat top of the mountain, you'll never get to the top, so to speak, and it is through your own fault that you may suffer poverty. Thus, individuals are judged by the same logic that revived the industry from its doldrums in the final quarter of the twentieth century; "during the [19]80's and [19]90's, coal prices flattened. Profits, if there were any, were measured in pennies per ton." But then along came "George W. Bush of Texas, the state that consumes more coal than any other in the country, together with Dick Cheney, who hails from the largest coal-producing state in the country." In May of their inaugural year in the White House, "the administration announced an 'energy plan' that openly championed coal, positioning it as America's favored source of electricity generation for decades to come. To anyone who believes that technological progress moves in a straight line, this has been a weird turn of events. It's as if a wormhole opened in the cosmos and we slid back to the 1890's." Only by denying the politically contrived "turn of events" that flew in the face of a linear narrative of economic and technological progress can an administration or an individual emerge as "a friend of coal" who believes that mountaintop removal is just part of the natural history of man dominating nature through industry and technology. Reviving big coal through mountaintop removal thus predisposed modern man to tolerate, if not embrace, "weird turn[s] of events" and, as Scott's descriptions make clear, weird living conditions, too.[18]

Scott's ethnography of the modern man examines the quality of his domestic life in a way that highlights how masculine notions of work have been reconfigured because of mountaintop removal. It also shows how the very notion of living has been reconfigured. As a resident living on reclaimed land, the modern man/friend of coal is not really living, Scott's work suggests. He is, instead, entombed in a space nearly hermetically sealed from the "instability of nature in the shadow of coal." Thus, Scott bemoans a "funeral parlor aesthetic" that has come to characterize the so-called reclaimed land devastated by mountaintop removal. In this coalfield landscape, "one type of new construction that exemplifies the look," continues Scott, "is a large new house of the design called 'New American,' built in the center of a wide, empty lawn." She describes one such house owned by one of her respondents: "His home office was off to one side of the entryway. The house was immaculate and cooled by central air. Tiled stairs led to a carpeted hallway, and I could see a perfectly clean kitchen through the hall. Large green artificial plants decorated his office. It was clear that this couple worked hard on making their house look as though no one lived there; everything was in its place, spotless, and chilled."[19] Suspicious in its cleanliness, this habitat worries Scott precisely because it looks uninhabited.

Scott's description of the modern man living entombed in his minimalist house estranged from nature merits critical analysis. In one sense, this presentation is an old one, derived from an early modern concept of alienation. Scott's preoccupation with the artificial plants and flowers signals this alienation: "The florist sells mostly artificial plants and flowers, no fresh flowers. . . . One of my interviews took place in a middle-class neighborhood in Madison, across a table decorated with a beautiful lavender flowering plant. I asked what it was, and my respondent told me he didn't know and that it was fake anyway."[20] Scott's concern with the fake flower and with the artificial plants that characterize the interior of the modern man's house is reminiscent of critiques from the turn of the last century. It is a critical discourse that goes back at least to *The Adventures of Huckleberry Finn,* in which Huck ponders the artificial fruit on the Grangerfords' table as a ridiculous symbol of what is wrong with the world. That bowl of decorative artificial fruit symbolizes the embellishments of Victorian style and norms in Twain's novel, and it solidifies the dualism of man-made culture versus god-made nature, city versus country, industry versus domesticity, urban versus rural. Scott's analysis relies on these dualisms rather than recognizing how such binaries have, in the era of globalization, been blurred.

The situation of mountaintop removal warrants a more updated set of critical tools than what Scott is using because nature and industry are not as separate as they once were. The era of globalization has given us perpetual wars, frankenfood, frankenstorms, and fracking earthquakes, among other things, that restructure our ecosystems and our bodies. Since at least the 1980s, scholars have directed us away from thinking about human bodies as unitary entities and, hence, from championing bodily integrity that is compromised by harsh labor. Instead, we are compelled to see bodies as integrated into technological and ecological systems in which boundaries between human and animal, machine and human, organic and cybernetic worlds are profoundly blurred.[21] Or we can see them as utterly dis-integrated, as porous bodies open to pollutants and toxins that make us mutants and render the dream of a wholesome human body nigh impossible.

The advantage to this thinking is that it forces us to recognize the inextricability of industry and bodies and the irreversible effects one has on the other. "We could," explains Stacy Alaimo, "say that the workers' bodies are not only the sites of the direct application of power, but permeable sites that are forever transformed by the substances and forces—asbestos, coal dust, radiation—that penetrate them."[22] This is all the more appropriate as industrial mechanization gives way to digitization. For example, black lung proliferated as a manifestation of modernization of coal extraction—the machines pulverized rock and coal in ways that human workers armed with picks and shovels could not, resulting in fine coal dust that is as bad for lungs as is smoking tobacco. Today's draglines of mountaintop removal may have reduced the pneumoconiosis and silicosis in individual men's bodies, but the "cleaner" working conditions are part of a devastation whose scale goes beyond workers' bodies. The toxins involved with mountaintop removal are not only inextricable from individual bodies; they are also irreversible from whole ecosystems, according to scientists. In 2010, for example, researchers from Duke University tested the water quality in an area in West Virginia affected by mountaintop removal.[23] Their findings confirmed long-term damage to the watershed. The study provided an unprecedented set of data that proved not only extensive water quality degradation indubitably caused by surface mining but also toxic contamination of aquatic life that was manifest in deformities in fish collected from downstream waters, they claim. Their study attests to the blurring of animal bodies and the land, and it feeds fears that such damage is permanent.

This scientific news is completely compatible with Scott's analysis.

Removing Mountains suggests that "making a living" by coal mining is an oxymoron in the midst of the irrevocable devastation that mountaintop removal wreaks on individual bodies, whole communities, and entire ecosystems. For people brought up to believe that "if it weren't for the coal industry we wouldn't be here," the choice of making a living is intimately and inextricably connected to the industry's making a killing.[24] With a different critical lens we can further explore the dead place that Big Coal seeks to put us in. We can expand Scott's critique of the modern man and the minimalist funeral parlor aesthetic that characterizes his home. In so doing we entertain the idea of life on reclaimed land as a realm of the living dead. Entombed but alive, the modern man depicted in Scott's scholarship is just like the buckwild mad men of popular culture: they are all portraits of a vanishing way of *life*. Scott's critique of the "funeral parlor aesthetic" implies that mountaintop removal has also restructured death or that it reflects a new politics of *death*.

Necropolitics in Appalachia

Necropolitics, first theorized in 2003 by Achille Mbembe, is a useful critical innovation for thinking through the politics of mountaintop removal mining. Necropolitics is the study of managing death in society for political purposes. In Mbembe's discussion of necropolitics, Foucault's concept of biopower is reread for the twenty-first century and in the context of the multifaceted war on terror. Faced with world events of the late modern era, Mbembe questions whether the notion of biopower is sufficient to account for the contemporary ways of war and politics. His examination of "wars of the globalization era" can shed light on *coal* wars of the globalization era.

For example, examining Palestine as a case study of late modern colonial occupation, Mbembe focuses on a "politics of verticality" that speaks to the conditions of fighting mountaintop removal. "The battlegrounds are not located solely at the surface of the earth" any more. "The underground as well as the airspace are transformed into conflict zones." What results is a "symbolics of the *top.*" Here Mbembe borrows the distinction Foucault makes between a symbolics of blood and the analytics of sexuality, two historically contiguous regimes of truth, in order to consider how power works today. He offers a geographic pinnacle—a summit—as a symbol of epistemological place as well as the tactical terrain by which power discerns its winners and losers. The top is a vantage point in necropolitics from which we can see how "certain bodies are marked and marketed to as live, lively and deserving of life, wherein other bodies are seen as either already dead or destined towards death: their lives are of little consequence, whereas their deaths consolidate sovereign power."[25] As true as this might be in the war zone of Palestine, it may be as much so in the coal war zone of Appalachia. Textual evidence from recent Appalachian narratives about protesting mountaintop removal mining suggests that a politics of verticality is indeed in operation.

Ann Pancake's novel *Strange as This Weather Has Been* has many characters whose trajectories can attest to the politics of verticality; Corey's story is especially instructive.[26] Corey is the ten-year-old son of Lace and Jimmy Make and brother to three siblings in a West Virginia mining town. His one goal is to obtain an all-terrain vehicle. At first this seems to be only a boy's obsession with machines, but the ATV "turns out to be central to struggles over land use and coalfield identity."[27] We later learn that getting the ATV allows Corey to go up the side of the mountain, beyond the tree line and past security, to see what is happening there and expose the truth of mountaintop removal to his family and community. True to the politics of verticality, the source of devastation from mountaintop removal is high up and cannot be readily discerned from the ground. Corey craves mobility and speed as a way to get to the top. The social aspects of this motive are clear by the end of the novel, when Corey chooses to leave his mother and his mountain state home for North Carolina with Jimmy Make, whose gendered understanding of making a living corresponds with the doomed family man persona that Scott delineates in her ethnography. The father is ashamed he cannot earn a high enough wage without an underground mining job, and he migrates to Raleigh for construction work. Pancake associates the mountain with female characters and thereby codes it feminine vis-à-vis the male characters who abandon the place. The mountain mamas stay on, refusing to give up their homes, adopting the protective ethic that studies have shown characterize women's protest of mountaintop removal.[28] Not heeding the father's advice to steer clear of the coal corporation, mother (Lace) and daughter (Bant) enter protest culture not as union maids but as maternal protectors of Mother Earth. Thus, the politics of verticality, illustrated by Corey's drive to the top, is particularly gendered in Pancake's narrative about mountaintop removal.

As two films about protesting coal companies attest, the politics of verticality in the coal war zones of today is very different from the latitudinal moves that protesters of yesteryear made. Consider Barbara Kopple's Oscar-winning 1974 documentary, *Harlan County, USA,* in which the labor community faces off with company thugs to claim a stretch of road past which no scabs will go.[29] The picket line is horizontal. The fight to keep scabs from crossing the picket line is waged on the ground. By drawing a line in the sand figuratively and by blockading the roadway literally with their bodies, the striking union workers songfully declare, "We will not be moved." In contrast, the 2013 documentary *Goodbye Gauley Mountain* features protesters of coal companies who must move.[30] Like Corey in *Strange as This Weather Has Been,* protesters in *Goodbye Gauley Mountain* have to move upward, into the timberline on the side of the mountain and into the trees themselves. Annie Sprinkle and Beth Stephens, who produced, directed, and are featured in the film, interview so-called tree huggers who camp out in trees in order to block the path of machines needed for mountaintop removal mining. Sprinkle and Stephens take a lesson in how to scale a tree with rock climbing equipment; the higher up a protester goes, the less likely she can be extracted from the mountain. Sprinkle and Stephens also interview a photographer who lends his artistic merits to protest mountaintop removal. The geophysical scope of the problem of mountaintop removal can be fathomed only with the help of satellite images or aerial photography, which are paradoxically aesthetically beautiful and morally repugnant, according to the photographer featured in the film. In these ways, *Goodbye Gauley Mountain* reveals that ascension is necessary in a coal war zone of the twenty-first century because the spatialization of the (coal) war has changed.

This change in spatialization is due to employing gargantuan earthmovers as well as high-tech tools of the late modern era. The mechanical features of the huge dragline machines have remained relatively unchanged over a century, but now operators are trained like military personnel, with simulation software, until they learn how to master the complicated, expensive equipment. Just who gets access to this coveted coal job of running the earthmover, affectionately known by the hypermasculine name of Big John, is a question eclipsed by the numbers who are passed over for the position.[31] Able to move as much as 5,000 cubic feet in one bucket, Big John replaces whole communities of workers, devastating their livelihoods and changing their social status.

Even more compelling than Mbembe's spatial analysis of necropolitical war zones, then, is how to consider the social aspects of necropolitics at work in Appalachia. Scholars of gender and sexuality use Mbembe's work to examine what he called "new and unique forms of social existence in which vast populations are subject to conditions of life conferring upon them the status of living dead."[32] Likewise, we can consider the conditions of life in the context of mountaintop removal as conferring on Appalachians a status of the living dead, a status that popular culture has taught us to recognize as zombies and other forms of the undead or monstrously living.

As Rebecca Scott's and Emily Satterwhite's recent analyses of slasher films set in Appalachia suggest, current popular culture portrays mountaineers as monsters whose sexual deviance and racial ambiguity are tied up with lapses in evolution as well as overexposure to toxic messes.[33] Derived from *Deliverance*'s banjo-picking albino boy, the weirdly white grotesques of *Wrong Turn* and *The Descent* have mutated into a horrific version of mountaineers who perpetually suffer the inadequacies of living a backward life. Shifting from the usual depiction of helpless Appalachians whom viewers are called on to pity rather than save from "the environmental and economic costs of coal,"[34] movies present Appalachians as horrific predators from whom viewers need to be saved.

In news as well as entertainment media—two genres clearly merging for the sake of ratings—mountaineers are also seen as weirdly horrifying. Media representations of miners in particular draw from and reproduce this tendency to see Appalachians as deserving of rescue but only in terms of being victims of disasters, not victims of economic injustice. *Buffalo Creek: An Act of Man,* Appalshop's documentary examining the 1972 flood that descended on a southern West Virginia community living beneath a slurry and sludge retainer, brings this irony into sharp relief.[35] *Buffalo Creek: An Act of Man* calls into question what the insurance people and mining company claimed: that the disaster was categorized as "an act of God," that is, a natural disaster and not the consequence of perilous structures and practices that allowed for a massive amount of coal runoff to be collected just above workers' homes. More commonly, as Scott aptly argues, those miners are depicted as people who proudly but grimly accept their consigned role as the sacrificial workers whose deaths allow coal to keep the lights on. Scott's discussion of news coverage of the Sago mining disaster of 2006, in which miners were trapped below after a major explosion, argued that the event became "an allegory of American national character" in which "miners were portrayed as always ready to sacrifice themselves to provide for their families and the nation."[36] But news coverage of the Upper Big Branch disaster of 2010 provided weird and grotesque details of the miners that resembled less the national allegory and more the slasher narratives found in the Cineplex.

The *New York Times* reported miners' reflections afforded by their escapes: "'Rock, dust, debris. I remember just trying to find a way out.' The mantrip that came out of the mine behind him was loaded with bodies, he said, the first group of corpses he saw that day. 'Eyes filled with dirt, mouths filled with dirt, ears filled with dirt,' said Tommy Davis, another former Upper Big Branch miner, who was sitting with Mr. Stanley, describing those corpses. 'Say I stick you in a room and pump dirt in on you while you stood there, until you can't take no more. That's what it was like.'"[37] The focus on individual bodies, and especially corpses, enacts the powers of horror in this reportage.[38] The American allegory of miners sacrificing their lives for the greater national coal-consuming good becomes strained under the weight of corpses filled with dirt. This gruesome depiction renders the national allegory of sacrifice a matter of necropolitics—of power relationships that consign some populations to the status of the living dead in order to reap benefits and profits.

Survivors of disasters such as those at Sago and Upper Big Branch, then, have to contend not only with their injuries and loss of income but also with their indelible memories of horror that shape their psyches and their lives. One Upper Big Branch survivor interviewed by the *New York Times* tattooed his arms with macabre images featuring lines from the "coal miners' prayer," an animated skeleton, and a crawling miner that "represents his personal darkness from the disaster."[39] Literally inscribing his body with images of the living dead, the miner-survivor is forced to embrace a new near-death life shaped by trauma. And thus new social existences emerge along with the sacrificial deaths that allow necropolitical companies such as coal corporations to go on. Let's reconsider both *Buckwild* and *Removing Mountains* explicitly in relation to Mbembe's notion of necropolitics to probe further the new forms of social existence that have emerged.

Shain Gandee sadly epitomizes the living dead because his image is immortalized in the existing episodes of *Buckwild,* which are available in perpetuity on the Internet despite his death. One reviewer of the show argues that Shain's death meant the death of the series because he was the only authentically interesting character. "Without a country boy—or, perhaps, without this country boy, in particular—there can be no youth-oriented, MTV series about West Virginia, and the series was cancelled. Gandee's character was the draw, the center, the interesting one."[40] But this reviewer does not acknowledge the Internet life-after-death of the series and by extension of Shain. Neither does she take into account the finale in which Shain and his cohort go to New York City, scripted as the antithesis of West Virginia and understood as the epicenter of modern America. In an episode packaged as a final tribute to Shain, a dead man, MTV proceeds along its standard course of keeping dualisms intact—namely, black and white, city and country. The white kids of West Virginia travel to cavort with African American kids of Manhattan, where—predictably—the mountaineers are again revealed to be hillbilly buffoons confounded by modern amenities, urban foodstuffs, and twenty-first-century luxuries. True to Senator Joe Manchin's misgivings, in this finale MTV continued to capitalize on American expectations that Appalachians are a retrograde, disposable population for whom backwardness and doom are a way of life. Despite a progressive narrative of racial harmony among the group of young partiers, the final show brings together two populations that neoliberal society assumes are always already dead—the urban underclass represented by African Americans and the rural poor represented by white Appalachians.

In this way *Buckwild* reflects the new social existences that the necropolitics of twenty-first-century mass incarceration have bestowed on urban blacks and Appalachian whites. As the documentary film *Up the Ridge* details, white Appalachian towns have become the sites of supermax prisons in which urban-born black prisoners are incarcerated.[41] Left economically bereft after coal companies extract natural resources and subsequently flee, citizens of towns such as Big Stone Gap, Virginia, embrace the prison-industrial complex as a means of making a living. The epitome of necro-power in the United States, mass incarceration creates what Mbembe calls death worlds that consign not just individual bodies but whole populations to living a dead-end life. As *Up the Ridge* shows, one result of a supermax economy is social conditions in prison that compel one to choose death over life—the film documents incidents of inmates committing suicide. In doing so, *Up the Ridge* powerfully supports Mbembe's claim that "under conditions of necropower, the lines between resistance and suicide, sacrifice and redemption, martyrdom and freedom are blurred."[42] In addition, the film reveals, that economy creates social conditions for the prison workers that compel them to die or kill. Thus, two populations that society sees as hopelessly doomed are pitted against each other in former mountaintop removal sites that are converted to prison industry sites. The flattened mountaintops are reclaimed as locations for the "golden gulags" that promise—but never deliver—economic advancement for townspeople.[43]

The brutalism of prison architecture on land made stark by monstrous earthmovers constitutes a living-dead aesthetics that returns us to the concerns Rebecca Scott has in *Removing Mountains*. A colossal supermax correctional facility on a bald, scarred, leveled mountaintop is as dead aesthetically as the funeral parlor look that Scott finds so disconcerting in the home of the friend of coal, that modern man whose house is spotless. But what Scott describes as funereal—immaculate, cool, and clean—also describes a look that connotes a particular trendy fashion, namely, the design elements touted as midcentury modern. As an extension of Scott's discussion, then, we can consider more thoughtfully the aesthetic choices of the "modern man" whose appreciation of minimalist interior decor and landscaping raises questions about the cultural work done by the stark, clean, straight lines of midcentury modern design that are so fashionable currently, in part because of the huge success of the show *Mad Men*. Critical essays about *Mad Men* recognize that the show perpetuates nostalgia for clean, white, straight America before the supposed fall of white male privilege brought on by the sexual revolution and new social movements. While the show "oscillates between dark suburban interiors where men feel trapped by their cloying wives" and the brightly lit, well-windowed workspaces and open-plan urban apartments where they are free to act madly, it ironically equates openness and transparency with duplicity and depravity.[44] Inspired by the AMC drama, the present-day American fixation with minimalist modern design avoids the lived-in reality of actual mid-twentieth-century American homes and nostalgically retains the most pristine of designs of the time. This desire for clean lines is coterminous with a renewed neoliberal desire for the midcentury racialized and gendered politics of space and place—both social and geographic. Segregation and disenfranchisement may be outlawed by midcentury decisions in *Brown v. Board of Education* and the 1964 Civil Rights Act. But charter education and voter registration rules have once again attempted to define places such as schools and polling places in ways that privilege white Americans. The efforts to roll back women's rights have been so persistent and blatant that the idea of a "war on women" has circulated for more than a decade. Not only do Scott's depiction of today's "modern man" and AMC's presentation of "mad men," therefore, share a white privilege dependent on economic exploitation of working-class women and people of color. They both also seem to be characterized by a fetishization of sleek, modern, design—an emptiness, openness, and *transparency* worthy of consideration.

As I previously noted, mountaintop removal mining is in one sense far more open a travesty than is underground coal mining. Lop off the top of mountain and you leave a bald, flat, toxic runway where once a curvaceous overgrown hill existed. But for all the open obviousness of mountaintop removal when seen from above, it actually is not easy to see until you get up past the timberline. This particular operation of coal mining therefore relies on a transparency that is not clear. This fundamental irony of mountaintop removal mining reflects a typical paradox of neoliberal systems of organization. Originally a practice of accounting, transparency in a fiduciary sense is achieved by requesting and providing painstaking detail of all transactions, a demand for constant surveillance of business relations.[45] As a practice of governance, transparency also increases the demand for surveillance; it relies on a constant flow of information that is tracked and assessed. The opacity of details—so-called hard facts, solid data, and concrete outcomes that can be quantified and accounted—paradoxically produces the transparency of operation. Because of this paradox, transparency is hardly democratic. Our necropolitical world offers citizens no transparency when it comes to budgets, governments, secret sites of interrogation, secret legal maneuverings to bypass international law and approve torture, and secret legal maneuverings to bypass national law and approve spying on U.S. citizens without warrants. And so the lack of transparency of the state depends on the exploitation of transparency of citizen's lives. There is no privacy left. Our lives now are splayed out in the microdocumentaries of Facebook, Twitter, Instagram, and identification cards that serve also as tracking devices. We are complicit in providing microarchives that aggregate into big data and allow for data mining, that untransparent practice that relies on the transparency of our lives. It should come as no surprise then, to learn that the baron of Massey Coal, Don Blankenship, who studied accounting at Marshall University and managed books at a Massey subsidiary in his youth, required production reports every half hour, reading them off a fax machine like a banker reading a tickertape.[46] Should the data reveal a slowdown in production, he was on the phone demanding the miners continue work even in dangerous conditions. In his constant surveillance of the operation of his mines, Blankenship relied on the transparency afforded him by the data to keep production rolling regardless of health and safety—all the while fending off the surveillance of inspectors and the effect of regulatory policies, which he thwarted with an elaborate circuitry of tip-offs, kickbacks, and buyouts. The deadly results of Blankenship's demand for transparency for himself but not for others were predictable, even expected. The death of twenty-nine people in the Upper Big Branch explosion of 2010 was something Blankenship banked on.

Today, big coal operates like big data—coal mining and data mining both rely on a paradox of transparency. For coal miners whose predictable deaths are seen as national sacrifices, for those modern men and buckwild boys whose masculinities emerge amid the presumption that their lives are always already doomed, getting to the top is an ambition that is both paramount and impossible, according to recent representations in entertainment, news, and scholarly media. Mbembe's theories recognize these spatial and social dynamics and can therefore illuminate the death worlds in which Appalachian men strive to live.

Given the sustained discourse of doomed mad men and buckwild boys that extends from popular culture to academic analysis, I have employed necropolitics as a framework by which to examine contemporary articulations of masculinity in Appalachia. I have explored the necropolitics of coal wars in terms of the tactics of ascension in a politics of verticality, looking to narratives of protesting mountaintop removal mining to see how symbolics of the top operate. I have also examined the social aspects of necropolitics, taking into account how white Appalachian and black urban populations are consigned to the realm of the living dead in reclaimed mountaintop mining spaces repurposed for supermax prisons. In so doing, I do not wish to perpetuate fatalism so often ascribed to Appalachia by giving in to death and dying. I do not want to *accept* "places" as "dead," but rather to explore, as did James Wright, *how* we live in the midst of a deadly world we cannot deny; to examine what arts men learn in their suicidal living; and to consider whether any art or action can intervene in the twenty-first-century death worlds with which we contend. With this application of Mbembe's theory of necropolitics, I hope we may better understand what *new forms of cultural creation and social existences* emerge and how they are gendered and racialized within hierarchies of class. That is to say, we may better analyze portraits of vanishing ways of *life* as they operate in the neoliberal politics of *death* in Appalachia and beyond.

Notes

1. Wright, "Autumn Begins in Martin's Ferry, Ohio," in *The Branch Will Not Break* (Middletown, CT: Wesleyan University Press, 1963), 15.

2. Alex Moaba, "'Buckwild' Controversy: West Virginia Senator Joe Manchin Demands MTV Cancel Show," *Huffington Post,* December 7, 2012.

3. David Mould, "*Buckwild* and *Downtown Abbey:* TV's Social Reality," *Montreal Review,* January 2013, www.themontrealreview.com/2009/Buckwild-and-Downton-Abbey-TVs-Social-Reality.php.

4. Ibid.

5. *Downton Abbey,* www.pbs.org/wgbh/masterpiece/downtonabbey/season1.html.

6. Alys Eve Weinbaum, *Wayward Reproductions: Genealogies of Race and Nation in Transatlantic Modern Thought* (Durham: Duke University Press, 2004).

7. Katie Milestone and Aneke Meyer, *Gender and Popular Culture* (Cambridge, U.K.: Polity Press, 2011).

8. Angela McRobbie, *The Aftermath of Feminism: Gender, Culture, and Social Change* (Los Angeles: Sage, 2009).

9. Leslie Reagan, "After the Sex, What? A Feminist Reading of Reproductive History in *Mad Men,*" in *Mad Men, Mad World: Sex, Politics, Style, and the 1960s,* ed. Lauren M. E. Goodlad, Lilya Kaganovsky, and Robert A. Rushing (Durham: Duke University Press, 2013), 92–110.

10. Alexandra Bradner, "'*Buckwild*' or '*Hollow*'? Representing West Virginia through the Incommensurable Lenses of Justice and Care" *Appalachian Studies* 19, nos. 1–2 (2013): 230.

11. Stacy Takacs, *Terrorism TV: Popular Entertainment in Post–9/11 America* (Lawrence: University Press of Kansas, 2012).

12. Achille Mbembe, "Necropolitics," trans. Libby Meintjes, *Public Culture* 15, no. 1 (2003): 29.

13. Rebecca Scott, *Removing Mountains: Extracting Nature and Identity in the Appalachian Coalfields* (Minneapolis: University of Minnesota Press, 2010), chap. 3.

14. Ibid., 71.

15. Crystal Good, "Boom Boom," in *Valley Girl* (Charleston, WV: author 2012).

16. Scott, *Removing Mountains,* 80.

17. Ibid., 85.

18. Jeff Goodell, "Blasts from the Past," *New York Times Magazine,* July 22, 2001, 32.

19. Scott, *Removing Mountains,* 202.

20. Ibid.

21. Donna Haraway, "A Cyborg Manifesto: Science, Technology, and Socialist-Feminism in the Late Twentieth Century," in Haraway, *Simians, Cyborgs, and Women: The Reinvention of Nature* (New York: Routledge, 1991), 149–181.

22. Stacy Alaimo, *Bodily Natures: Science, Environment, and the Material Self* (Bloomington: Indiana University Press, 2010), 30.

23. Ken Ward Jr., "New Study Confirms Mountaintop Removal Stream Damage," *Charleston Gazette,* December 12, 2011, www.wvgazettemail.com/News/201112120118.

24. Scott, *Removing Mountains,* 98.

25. Michelle R. Martin-Baron, "(Hyper/In)Visibility and the Military Corps(e)," in

Queer Necropolitics, ed. Jin Haritaworn, Adi Kuntsman, and Silvia Posocco (New York: Routledge, 2014), 51.

26. Ann Pancake, *Strange as This Weather Has Been: A Novel* (Berkeley, CA: Shoemaker and Hoard, 2007).

27. Scott, *Removing Mountains,* 28.

28. Shannon Elizabeth Bell and Yvonne A. Braun. "Coal, Identity, and the Gendering of Environmental Justice Activism in Central Appalachia," *Gender & Society* 24, no. 6 (2010): 794–813.

29. *Harlan County, USA,* directed by Barbara Kopple (1977; New York: Sony Pictures Home Entertainment, 2010), DVD.

30. *Goodbye Gauley Mountain: An Ecosexual Love Story,* directed by Beth Stephens and Annie Sprinkle (2013; New York: Alive Mind Cinema, 2015), DVD.

31. Scott, *Removing Mountains,* 81.

32. Mbembe, "Necropolitics," 40.

33. Scott, *Moving Mountains.* Emily Satterwhite, *Dear Appalachia: Readers, Identity, and Popular Fiction since 1878* (Lexington: University Press of Kentucky, 2012). Emily Satterwhite, "Hillbilly Horror," presentation for the Gender and Women's Studies Department, University of Kentucky, February 23, 2015.

34. Scott, *Removing Mountains,* 57.

35. *The Buffalo Creek Flood: An Act of Man,* directed by Mimi Pickering (1975; Whitesburg, KY: Appalshop, 1975), film.

36. Scott, *Removing Mountains,* 61.

37. David Segal, "The People v. the Coal Baron," *New York Times,* June 21, 2015.

38. Julia Kristeva, *The Powers of Horror,* trans. Leon S. Roudiez (New York: Columbia University Press, 1982); Carol Mason, "The Hillbilly Defense: Culturally Mediating U.S. Terror at Home and Abroad," *NWSA Journal* 17, no. 3 (2005): 39–63.

39. Segal, "The People v. the Coal Baron."

40. Bradner, "'*Buckwild*' or '*Hollow*'?" 230.

41. *Up the Ridge,* directed by Nick Szuberla and Amelia Kirby (Whitesburg, KY: Appalshop, 2006), DVD.

42. Mbembe, "Necropolitics," 40.

43. Ruth Gilmore, *Golden Gulag: Prisons, Surplus, Crisis, and Opposition in Globalizing California* (Berkeley: University of California Press, 2007). Judah Schept, "Carceral Geography in the Transitional Economy: Prison Growth in Appalachia," presentation at Sharing Work on Appalachia in Progress, October 20, 2014, Lexington, KY.

44. Goodlad et al., introduction to *Mad Men, Mad World,* 1–52; and Dianne Harris, "Mad Space," ibid., 53–72.

45. Richard Warren Perry and Bill Maurer, *Globalization under Construction: Governmentality, Law, and Identity* (Minneapolis: University of Minnesota Press, 2003).

46. Segal, "People v. Coal Baron." Tim Murphy, "The Fall of King Coal," *Mother Jones,* September 30, 2015.

56.
star of david
tree of life
double wedding band
a nine patch
such patterns
once shaped our destiny
pieces of cloth
marking a woman's life
sewn together scraps
bits and pieces
tell us life stories
pieced by hand
remnants of passion
an unfulfilled desire
sisters coming together
making peace
offering comfort
ways to warm
to open hearts

—bell hooks

8

Reclaiming Place

Making Home

bell hooks

When we move beyond sentimental notions of and identification with place, we work to uncover what is most profound in our understanding of what we mean by place. When we say "place matters," we see clearly that there is a crisis in our nation resulting from so many citizens feeling that they have no place. If we know most truly who we are, when we experience ourselves at home, it is evident that, as Ronald Rolheiser (2002) says in *Against an Infinite Horizon,* "to be at home one needs a place, a home land." He explains, "Sadly today, for many of us, there is no longer any sense of home as place, no homeland, in a world of transience, of future shock—when people, organization, knowledge, things, and places move through our lives at an ever increasing rate—where perhaps we have never been able to sink meaningful roots in any place, it is no accident that more and more of us find ourselves morally lonely and anything but steady." When we have no place to identify with, no roots to drink from, no tree trunks to guide us in clear directions, it is no accident that we can't on any given day feel sincerely that we know who we really are, what our values are, what we mean, and which of our seemingly multiple personalities is the true one. From lack of home we suffer schizophrenia, dislocation, and much loneliness, both psychologically and morally. And part of that lack of home has to do with place. Place is also a home.

Again and again I contemplate the fact if anyone had told me that at fifty-nine I would come back to Kentucky, I would have said, "No way. I would be in a little box, shipped back to mom and dad, before I would come back to Kentucky." But, in fact, that's not how it turned out. Mom and Dad were aging in Hopkinsville, Kentucky, where I'm from. I was living in New York City, but I realized that my relationship to Kentucky was deeply formed by my relationship to my parents. In my mind, Kentucky meant my parents. So that if my parents were near death, as my daddy would say—he was on his descent, he was climbing down that mountain, and he would never be going up the mountain again—I needed to come home to be close to them. This need deeply informed my decision to return to Kentucky to live because I realized if I wanted to have a place that mattered, that was Kentucky. I had to establish that place in my adulthood, independent of my parents. And of course, as you all know who read my work, I didn't go back to live in Hopkinsville. I never felt that Hopkinsville was a place for me—the severe racial apartheid I'd grown up in, all those things—but I came to give a lecture at Berea, Kentucky, and I felt immediately that Berea was a place for me that I could come and abide in. I think that, for me, talking about Kentucky and reclaiming it has so much to do with the passage of time. When I was away from Kentucky going to grad school in California, I knew that my elders were here maintaining the legacies of our lives in Kentucky: the hills, the backwoods, the small town. As they began to pass away, however, I began to see that my relationship with Kentucky was being altered. I realized especially as my parents were getting ill, and as they both died in the last few years, that if I wanted to have that intimate relationship with Kentucky—its, landscape, my people—I would have to come home and make it, because my dad and the other elders would not be there to make it for me.

I think there are multiple layers of ways we create and reclaim place that we make home. I think Barbara Kingsolver (2007) hinted at that in her much-admired book with her family, *Animal, Vegetable, Miracle: A Year of Food Life*. We reclaim identities through many ways, through genealogies of desire, and that may mean food, people, place, and smell. For me, it was the world of tobacco. The tobacco crop really dominated the region that I grew up in. Is it any accident then, that the longing with which I write about tobacco and my need to respect tobacco as a crop was rooted in girlhood? I just want the reality that everyone needs to stop smoking poisonous cigarettes to be separated from tobacco itself. That is a legacy for me that I've always held dear, that has always had meaning, and that I reclaim.

One way that we can reclaim is through the visual gaze. We reclaim through the act of making art. I encourage you to see the work of Richard

Bell. He began to make art at age thirty-five as a direct response to what he felt was the objectification of aboriginal people. His art is a contestation of how aboriginal people are constructed. I feel like much of my work in these last few years, which has focused on farming and sustainability, has been a contestation moving against the notion that black people are not interested in ecosustainability, ecofeminism, or organic anything. For me, it has been about this: let's recover that engagement that we as African American people have had and continue to have with the land, with the world of organic farming. My favorite book of last year was Elizabeth Wilkerson's 2010 book, *The Warmth of Other Suns,* which is about the mass migration from agrarian southern states to northern cities.[1] It's so deeply moving when you see how wedded to land black people were, and to growing food, and to having a very independent life.

In the foreword to my poetry book *Appalachian Elegy* (2012), I comment on the notion that if psychologists are right and there is a core identity scripted into us by the time we are five or six, then, I said, my soul is imprinted with the hills of Kentucky. In fact, my nonfiction book *Writing beyond Race* (2013) is a collection of essays in which I'm talking about the fact that the only time in my life that I felt unaware of race was when I was a girl in the Kentucky hills, and the most profound relationship of that period of my life was with the environment. There weren't really any close-by neighbors. It was not the world of white people, white supremacy, but it was the world of nature, snakes, and other animals that could possibly attack you. It was never "be wary of white people." We were always there in this natural environment that was both for us and at times against us, and you had to respect it.

We then moved from living in the hills to the city, where I began to experience racial apartheid and binary consciousness. Gone was this whole relationship to a world beyond race. Everything became deeply raced and deeply gendered. I remember an incident when my grandfather had to go to the Social Security office; it was a really, really hot day and he walked there, as we did in those days, and he got there and he didn't have the right paper. They could have given him that paper but they sent him home. They could have given him another one, but the white lady waiting on him sent this elderly black man out into the heat, out to walk miles when she could have just given him the form he needed. For me, this is one of those incidents of that aggression against black people, against elder black people, that I experienced so much growing up in Hopkinsville, Kentucky. When we entered that mainstream, racist, segregated white culture we were treated badly or were made to do things that we would never have had to do if we were white. These experiences created in me, even as a child, a bitterness toward Kentucky and toward the land.

Had there not been those years spent in exile, away from Kentucky, I would not have experienced the longing to reclaim and explore my Kentucky roots. I was able to remember the Kentucky landscape as my birthright and to see beyond the dictates of white supremacy and race. I am reminded of the South African slogan, "Our struggle is also a struggle of memory against forgetting." We can't remember just the trauma and the negativity; we also have to remember the beauty. I have likened all my writing to the cooking of a stew. There is a certain element in it that draws people in, but they don't know what the element is. I consider it the element of the Kentucky backwoods, the hills that were the ground of my being, and for me it's like adding coriander or cumin. People don't know what that spice is, but they can taste the difference. I think that's been true of my writing career since the very first book I published—there was a quality of boldness and clarity of speech and voice, and yet no one ever tried to link it to geography. In fact, I don't think people ever paid much attention to the fact that I was from Kentucky. It's as if the world that celebrated me never really wanted to deal with my origins as a Kentucky thinker and writer. I've been thinking about my home in the hills—this home that I came and reclaimed and bought. I went up there with a bunch of ecofeminists, and we burned sage and we claimed and drummed and chanted and called forth the ancestors. I felt such a sense of triumph that I could reclaim my place in the Kentucky hills after all the years of displacement.

Now we're so fortunate to have all the recent scholarship on black farmers, especially black farmers in Kentucky and black townships in Kentucky, looking at how predatory white supremacists often just burned black people's farms, or ran them off their farms because they wanted their land and a black person had it. The land my folks owned, my parents and great-grandparents, came out of legacies of slavery: a master or mistress left a little piece to their favorite slaves. That's how a lot of black people inherited land back in the day, land that was later frequently taken away when they didn't have the money for taxes. It's so great to be in a world where a lot of that story is being recovered or reimagined. A film was recently produced: *Slavery by Another Name* (Pollard 2012). It reveals the way laws were created once slavery ended to continue to enslave black people. You see the amazing resilience of black people in surviving all this. We'll never know the stories of all the world of black people who have taken care of horses, right here in Lexington, Kentucky. All the black grooms, and enslaved and servant black people who took care of horses, black males—we'll never know their story. Frank X Walker portrayed Isaac Murphy so well in his book *Isaac Murphy: I Dedicate This Ride* (2010), but we never hear about the people at the bottom. The people who communed with those horses: Who took care of them? In the same way, when people are talking about the Kentucky Derby, they're never thinking about the people who clean the horses and clean out the stables, whose lives are not million dollar lives—people whose lives are about hard labor, and hard labor for not the kind of wealth we often see as we drive by those beautiful Kentucky horse farms. We cannot survive on this planet if we cannot embrace our unity with all living things. In Buddhism, we say that all sentient beings, everything, has body and voice and breath.

When I went to Stanford as an undergraduate, leaving Kentucky at the tender age of seventeen, I was so stunned by all the things that were being said about black people. I talked with the students about this earlier: one thing about the discipline of sociology—when it began as a discipline, it was never interested in rural black people. Blackness became identified with urban cities, so when people talked about black people they were usually talking about people in the industrialized North. When I went to Stanford as an undergraduate and I heard white people talking about "no black men in the home, black men not working," all the ways they talked about black people, I didn't know any black people like that. Every home I knew in Hopkinsville, Kentucky, had men in it. They might not be bio-whatever but they were grandfathers, great-grandfathers. I felt stunned. Here I was, this naive girl from the country, with all these memories of a certain notion of blackness, being in the academy where white people were telling me a whole other version of blackness that in no way related to my experience. That, for a while, silenced me. Then I began to think. All I had ever known was rural black life and the accompanying sense of engagement with the animal world. There was never a moment in our life growing up that there weren't dogs. In fact, in our family life, there was always a kind of world of animals. One of my favorite things to do, for which I got whippings, was always a kind of "feed the pigs to hear them crunch coal" and to feed them and to clean them and to smell them and later, of course, to smoke and eat them. It was encountering the mean-spirited world of white owners of dogs who used them as weapons of terror that has caused me and many other black people to fear dogs. It has been really hard for me to try to overcome this so I can live comfortably in the hills and even in the very bourgeois neighborhood in the town that I live in. Everybody seems to have a dog, or two or three. I've written a lot of essays about sitting on the porch in Hopkinsville and seeing white people drive home with their black maids and the little dog would be in the front seat with its head out, and the black person would be scrunched down in the back seat. I think this reality has fueled much of the psycho-history of many black people who both fear and dislike dogs. We had dogs, but we never valued them over humans. We were taught to value every animal including humans, and to believe they had their place in the holistic wheel of life. The point was to respect all our places—places that matter. You certainly didn't treat a person with violence and hatred while you worshiped at the throne of your dog. For many people there are yet to be so many false constructions of who black people are that we cannot document and write enough about how our perceptions of the world define who we are. A lot of times lately I get asked, "bell hooks, your perspectives have changed, you're writing about love now, you're writing about the earth." And I tell them, "No, go back to one of my earliest books, *Sisters of the Yam* (1993)." I'm writing about love in that book, I'm writing about black people and the earth. This is one of the dangers you face when you have a diverse body of work that is talked about primarily by unenlightened white people. I'll have someone who happens upon *All about Love* (2000) and they love it and they think, "Oh, this is a good book," and "bell is changing her mind." People don't go to those books that they saw as being directly aimed at black people, like *Sisters of the Yam: Black People and Self-Recovery,* which is one of the bell hooks books that got very few reviews but was very much shaped by my sense of Kentucky and my feeling about the world that had been shaped by being in Kentucky.

I remember that part of what really drew me back into Kentucky was my feeling about the practice of loving kindness, which I felt I had grown up in, that I found was echoed in Buddhism. It made me realize that many of the values I have learned from living in Kentucky were the values I was also learning in Eastern mysticism and Eastern religion. There is a chapter in *Sisters of the Yam* that came out in the 1980s about black people and the earth. I think that was because I was coming from agrarian roots. I've always been obsessed with our relationship to the land and the healing powers of the land. I think that one of the things that happens within white supremacy is that people become much more interested in what I have to say about race and gender than they are about what I have to say about the environment or landscapes or farming. Of course, that goes along with the lack of people's interest in farming in the United States as a whole. Just recently, when I tried to negotiate the contract for my new book, I was told, "Well, we can't give you very much money because your book *Belonging: A Culture of Place,* just didn't sell that well." And, of course, I believe that *Belonging* got hardly any reviews or didn't sell because it was about Kentucky. It wasn't about race and gender and class specifically and directly; it was about land and real estate and black people's relationship to land. It tries to use Kentucky, and especially small-town Kentucky, as a starting point for all things happening in our nation as a whole. I echo what Ann Kingsolver asserts in *Tobacco Town Futures* (2011) when she talks about encounters in rural Kentucky and reminds us that globalization describes a process of spatial, social, and economic interconnectedness. For me, in Buddhism, that also becomes interdependency.

Using the local environment of Kentucky can actually offer us great ways to understand the larger environment, what we must do to build community, and what we must do to make sustainability affordable. I have been fortunate that geographers have been interested in *Belonging* and have ordered and used this work. How many books do we have by black American writers talking about our culture of place, about the environment, self-identified as ecofeminists as part of their sense of who they are? Part of what we struggle with in imperialist, white supremacist, capitalist patriarchy is a culture that wants to limit us to only one category. One thing I can say is joyful about being over fifty: you care less about how other people construct you and what categories they put you in, and more about how you feel—you can give expression to whatever passions set you on fire. What I learned from being with the Brazilian educator Paulo Freire was that, as he used to say, "we cannot enter the struggle as objects in order to later become subjects." That was a powerful declaration for me to hear as a young woman, a graduate student, because it sparked in me a tremendous awareness about the need to develop critical thinking, critical consciousness. It also resonated, for me, with the work of Ivan Van Sertima (1976), who wrote *They Came before Columbus,* about Africans in the New World before Columbus. When I heard Ivan Van Sertima speak for the first time and he said, "We have not just been colonized in our minds, we have also been colonized in our imaginations," that just opened up a new world to me. We cannot liberate ourselves as black people, as any group of oppressed and exploited people, if we cannot imagine ourselves as radically different from how our oppressors and exploiters have seen us.

If we look at my early work, much of it is about decolonizing the mind in terms of race, gender, and class; that was one of the processes by which I made myself subject. Running around in the Kentucky hills was also a process that could not be recognized until we had a full environmental movement, which began to think about the natural landscapes having an influence on our psychic landscapes. When I went to the Sundance film festival for the first time, I saw so many bad films—so many films dominated by the perspective of white patriarchal supremacy, but the one film that actually had people of color speaking was an incredible documentary on the history of the environmental justice movement: *A Fierce Green Fire* (Kitchell 2012). Of all the many films I saw there, three films a day for six days, it was the only one that had female voices, women of color among them. The film highlighted the fact that the term *environmental justice* had begun in the Deep South with black people protesting toxic waste dumps. It cut through the fiction that black people have not been concerned with environmental justice. We also saw the black and white women in solidarity with Love Canal residents. We saw so many examples of solidarity in the film; I felt deeply moved. I knew about Save the Whales, but when I actually saw footage of an ordinary human being, no celebrity, no star, putting his body between a harpoon and a whale, it was just incredibly inspiring. I love the work of Paul Hawken, and he shared how in so many places in the world, people of color are engaged in environmental movements—successful movements. We saw Wangara Maathai in Kenya (who has passed away now) attempt, as a black female, to convince black males to plant trees—to change. We saw that revolution. We saw Chico Mendes, in Brazil, changing the whole way people thought through his life and his death, about how we treat the trees, how we treat the land. It was really, really awesome.

I think we can look, on all levels—food, jobs—and see the interconnectedness, see the necessity for a humane globalization that begins with our living local. We need to understand the ways living locally allows us to connect. Living locally, living in a small town like Berea, we know when the food bank is stressed and there is no food there. We know when someone needs care. There is a lot of give-and-take in that small community. You know, I go to thrift stores. When I first came to Berea, people were like, "Oh, there are no black people here." Well, actually, if you go to the Salvation Army in Richmond, there are plenty of black people. Among them are retired and aging black women who share a whole history of their life in Berea, of their life in that part of the world. But I also find people there who are in economic distress. If you want to engage in philanthropy, you don't have to have an envelope, you don't have to have someone begging you for your money—you can engage in what I call everyday philanthropy, helping in the maintenance and stability of your community. And that is what a lot of local engagement allows.

Choosing to live in Berea, I belong to a local community that welcomes and engages me—that lets me know here is where I belong. No matter how much I write, what keeps me going, especially when you're a dissent thinker and writer, is really knowing that people engage your work. And I tell people all the time that I often contemplate the lives of all the black women writers who died without having any clue that people would one day celebrate and read their work. And I have the good fortune, practically every day of my life, to receive affirmation from the Berea community about the ways my work helps folks live right—working for justice, where they honor interconnectedness and interdependency. Above all, where we choose to love.

References

hooks, bell. 2013. *Writing beyond Race: Living Theory and Practice.* New York: Routledge.

———. 2012. *Appalachian Elegy: Poetry and Place.* Lexington: University Press of Kentucky.

———. 2009. *Belonging: A Culture of Place.* New York: Routledge.

———. 2000. *All about Love: New Visions.* New York: Morrow.

———. 1993. *Sisters of the Yam: Black Women and Self-Recovery.* Boston: South End Press.

Kingsolver, Ann E. 2011. *Tobacco Town Futures: Global Encounters in Rural Kentucky.* Long Grove, IL: Waveland Press.

Kingsolver, Barbara, with Steven Hopp and Camille Kingsolver. 2007. *Animal, Vegetable, Miracle: A Year of Food Life.* New York: HarperCollins.

Kitchell, Mark, director, writer, and producer. 2012. *A Fierce Green Fire: The Battle for a Living Planet.* New York: First Run Features.

Pollard, Sam, director. 2012. *Slavery by Another Name: The Documentary Film.* Produced by Catherine Allen and Douglas Blackmon. Arlington, VA: Public Broadcasting System.

Rolheiser, Ronald. 2002. *Against the Infinite Horizon: The Finger of God in Our Everyday Lives.* Spring Valley, NY: Crossroad Publishing Co.

Van Sertima, Ivan. 1976. *They Came before Columbus.* New York: Random House.

Walker, Frank X. 2010. *Isaac Murphy: I Dedicate This Ride.* Lexington, KY: Old Cove Press.

Wilkerson, Isabel. 2010. *The Warmth of Other Suns: The Epic Story of America's Great Migration.* New York: Random House.

Note

1. This chapter is based on a transcript of bell hooks's 2012 Place Matters lecture at the University of Kentucky.

9

Somewheres on the Track

Place, Art, and Music in Eastern Kentucky

Rich Kirby, John Haywood, and Ron Pen

The Opening Melody

Place matters. It can begin with a tune, a melody that slowly unfolds like the first shy bloom on the sunny side of a holler that soon cloaks the entire hillside in a mantle of vivid hues on a fiddle tune lovingly handed down through family like a precious heirloom quilt. The tune flows like Troublesome Creek, twisting along the contour of its banks, tripping and trilling above the rocky shoals, shadowing the ancient topography of the hills, its crooked little melodic leaps skipping in harmony with a determined sense of direction. The tune bubbles along joyously until it finally seeks its repose at the homeplace. Musically, the tune begins in the key of D major, travels through harmonic and melodic adventures, and then returns to the original tonal center, the very place that launched its journey. That melodic shape closely mirrors the profile of the mountains that gave birth to it.

"MOONLIGHT"

The tune "Moonlight" had lived among Wallace Thompson's family in Green County, Kentucky, for many and many a year. The title "Moonlight" is simultaneously evocative and ambiguous; perhaps it suggests a moment in time and place. The final section of the tune is distinguished by four clearly articulated notes that could suggest the moon peeking out from behind the clouds. Maybe the melodic figurations describe a dark evening, the silvery moon's reflection shimmering on the Green River. Thompson's own associations link the music to the memory of people he once knew: "This tune is an old tune, it's an old Scottish tune called 'Moonlight.' And I heard some of the real old fiddlers play it. Daddy played it, Gusty Wallace, while still alive.[1] My great-grandmother used to hum it to me and sing some words to it and I don't remember what they were now. But it was an old tune then, and she was old. 'Moonlight.'"[2] The term *moonlight* was an old expression in the community referring to a nighttime outdoor dance or party.[3]

It all begins with the tune, a simple dance tune that was precious cargo carried in memory across the ocean from Scotland centuries ago. The tune continued to dwell among family and community for generations until it finally ventured beyond the region. In 1932, during the golden era of old-time string band "hillbilly" music, "Uncle Henry" (Henry Warren of Taylor County) formed a group called Uncle Henry's Kentucky Mountaineers with his brother Grady Hamilton, who went by the name "Coon Hunter," and his wife, Wava Ilene, known as "Sally, the Mountain Girl." The band's third fiddler was Casey Jones of Green County. This was not *the* Casey Jones (Jonathan Luther), who grew up in the town of Cayce in Fulton County and was scalded to death in the train wreck in 1900 that was immortalized in the song named after him. Casey Jones the *fiddler* played with the Kentucky Mountaineers until 1947, at which point Wallace Thompson joined the band as its fiddler. The Mountaineers never released "Moonlight" in their recordings for Brunswick, but the tune finally emerged from the community when the noted fiddler and collector Bruce Greene visited Thompson at his home in Pierce, in Green County, and recorded it March 30, 1974. Thirty-seven years later, the tune was frozen in musical transcription published in the *Milliner-Koken Collection of American Fiddle Tunes*.[4] Other folks learned the tune directly from Greene and his dulcimer-playing friend Don Pedi,[5] and then disseminated it internationally through an informal network of old-time music festivals, jams, music camps, workshops, and square dances. Local, and yet also global.

AT THE SQUARE DANCE

The late folksinger Jean Ritchie observed: "To stand in the bottom of any of the valleys is to have the feeling of being down in the center of a great round cup. To stand on top of one of the narrow ridges is like balancing on one of the innermost petals of a gigantic rose, from which you can see all around you the other petals falling away in wide rings to the horizon."[6] These are the hills and hollers of the ancient Cumberland Mountains. Imagine that you are driving along the precariously narrow bottomland that hugs the tortuous path of the North Fork of the Kentucky River, and you finally come to the little hamlet of Blackey, its buildings strung along the road like pearls on a necklace. There you pass the front porch of C. B. Caudill's General Store, packed to the rafters with coal-mining equipage, dry goods, and fine conversation. Shortly outside the town you take Elk Creek Road up and up and up Dixon Mountain, past Low Gap Branch, beyond Elk Lick Branch and the white frame Bull Creek Old Regular Baptist Church. You have to be careful not to take one of the forks that could lead you careening down a luge run of a slope toward the little coal company town of Vicco (named after the initials of Virginia Iron Coal and Coke Company) in Perry County. Then you climb up Jent Mountain, hoping against hope that you don't meet an oncoming car. Finally, you arrive at a little open spot on Devil's Backbone where the Carcassonne School is located. It was once a community boarding school, two rooms, heated by old potbelly stoves, with a little stage up at one end. The only adornments are a picture of Jesus walking on the waters and an American flag. This is the site of the monthly square dance, where folks gather to share in the music, dance, and conversation that bind local inhabitants as a community in a shared space, a special place.

Nothing weaves the fabric of community together as well as participatory music and dance. Each dance lasts twenty minutes or so, and everyone dances with everyone else in the course of a dance, from four-year-old hoydens to superannuated ninety-year-olds, as the figures geometrically twine and intertwine in time to the driving banjo and lilting fiddle.

> Circle eight and you get straight,
> And we'll all go east on a westbound freight.
> And knock down Sal and pick up Kate,
> And we'll all join hands and circle eight.[7]

There is a cakewalk in which everyone parades around on top of numbers placed on the floor. Suddenly the musicians stop playing, and when the winning number is called out, you claim the home-baked delicacy of your choice. There are dances and more dances on into the night. You all drift back to your cars, glancing up at the brilliant Cheshire cat smile of the new moon over the mountain crests as you set off down the twisty road back home. There is a particularly insistent tune, "Moonlight," that accompanies you, bearing the accumulated memories of the evening. Place is encoded in music. Place matters.

Music that springs from the soil, music that is inextricably bound to a place and a people, has the most power to affect us. Music can travel, but it loses its potency in the transit. Spotify, iTunes, cloud technology, car radios, boom boxes, and earbuds make music portable, but they do not make music powerful when it is stripped of its context. "Moonlight" at the Carcassonne dance is charged with meaning in Appalachian Kentucky. It was inherited from an extended family over generations known for their traditional music, but in the context of twenty-first-century popular music, a recorded version of the tune echoes in a pale and distant way. It seems repetitive, it seems a little out of tune, it sounds a little archaic and irrelevant, like a lingering ghost from another time and place. Music that springs from the soil, music that is inextricably bound to a people and a place, has the greatest power to move us.

MUSIC AND MEMORY

The fiddler's art is traditionally acquired through "knee-to-knee" apprenticeship, observing the nuances of tunes and technique from experienced performers. The process of learning through oral tradition also entails storytelling that enables the entire history and context of the tune to be closely associated with its tones and rhythms. Personal anecdotes establish and confirm the relationship between people and place, connect the past to the present, and imbed these in the music itself. Afterward, sharing the tune on a porch or at a dance constitutes a communion of nonverbal communication, a moment in time outside time in which people and place are remembered anew. A tune serves like a powerful mnemonic magnet, attracting memories and meaning to it with each repetition.

Somewheres on the Track

In 2011 the University of Kentucky Appalachian Center introduced a series of eight interdisciplinary lectures titled "Place Matters" that explored an understanding of place in Appalachia. The lecture scheduled for February 17, 2012, flying under the title "Somewheres Along the Track: Place, Art, and Music in Eastern Kentucky," in the University of Kentucky's Center Theater, was anything *but* a lecture: it was a conversation (moderated by Ron Pen, who wrote the opening section of this chapter) featuring Rich Kirby and

John Haywood, illustrated with music and art created by the two participants. That conversation segued directly to a concert in the evening featuring Rich and the Po' Folk, an old-time string band from eastern Kentucky
featuring Kirby and Haywood as well as two other musicians, Brett Ratliff
and Nathan Polly. This presentation did not merely talk about art, music,
and place, it *was* art and music in a place.

The conversation was a lively one, sparkling with the spontaneity of
friends gathered on a front porch. The discussion was recorded, transcribed,
and then edited for publication, but the original voices were preserved and
privileged as originally presented. This is primarily an oral, not a literary,
document. The chapter is about music and art associated with place, but,
more important, it is a story told *by* musicians and artists who are rooted in
place. Eastern Kentucky shaped the lives of Haywood and Kirby, but there
were other important stops along the track that influenced them, including
urban life in New York City and Louisville. This is not a quaint and romanticized "local color" tale, but a compelling narrative woven of heavy metal, folk
revival, video games, coal camps, tattoo parlors, punk rock, mountain scenery,
working people, banjos, family, unexpected mentors, dancing outlaws, and
cultural politics. Now, come join Rich and John somewheres along the track.

References to the musical examples are cited in the text within brackets
in the following transcript, which documented the presentation featuring
John Haywood and Rich Kirby. For example, [Music: Been a Long Time
Traveling]. The musical examples are all available through the University
Press of Kentucky website, www.kentuckypress.com. At the time of print-
ing, photographs of many paintings by John Haywood are available on his
website (https://www.haywoodarts.com/paintings). Some examples of his
work are included in this chapter, though the color paintings are reproduced
in black and white. The image on the cover of this book is also a painting
by John Haywood.

JOHN HAYWOOD AND RICH KIRBY

> Rich Kirby: When Ann [Kingsolver] contacted us about doing this,
> we had two different reactions. One, sure, yeah, place—our work
> is all about place; that's really central to it. Then wait a minute,
> we've hardly sort of examined it in that frame before, so we've
> had a kind of internal voyage putting this together here. Going
> over things we've thought about, the work that we've done many
> times intently over the years, but sort of looking at it in a different

light: we're going to do that today. We hope that you realize this is a work in progress. There's a lot of different ways that you can approach the concept of place, and so what I think we'll do to start off is begin with a bit of personal history; how the place of eastern Kentucky has shaped our lives.

John Haywood: I grew up in southeastern Kentucky in a holler. The holler was called Alum Lick, but the little place was called Risner, which is named after my mother's side of the family. Everybody up through there was kinfolks. We even had our own post office and grocery store. I hardly remember all that, other than pictures. The post office was still in operation when I was real little, but eventually it got shut down. Growing up in the mountains, I was really into art and music. My papaw was an Old Regular Baptist where they sing the unaccompanied songs. I spent a lot of time with him because both my parents worked. He taught me a lot of things about the mountains, and I would hear him sing all the time, but I never thought much of it because I was more into all the stuff I saw on TV—rock and roll, video games, all that stuff. As an artist, I was always encouraged to leave the mountains: "an artist couldn't make it in the mountains." That's still a general perception there, that you have to go to a city. I started to go to the University of Kentucky, but I decided to go to college at Morehead State University. I spent some time there and eventually made it to Louisville, where I got a master's in art—in painting. While in Louisville, I also became an apprentice in a tattoo shop and learned how to tattoo, essentially near Fort Knox military base. I graduated from the University of Louisville and also taught some community college classes while I was there, but all the while realizing how different I was, and that I didn't quite connect to things in the city, and that there was a big part of me that was searching for something I couldn't find there in the city (where I thought for some reason I was supposed to be).

I will tell you about one painting I did while I was there, called *American Saint*. I moved to Louisville in 2001, and no sooner than I got there the terrorist attacks happened and things sort of changed. But I remember seeing this homeless black guy, his name was Cuba, and he was pushing some cans down the street and he was dancing. It seemed like a time when everybody was down and out, but here this guy was dancing behind his little shopping cart with his little radio in his hand, and his American flag and all that. There was something about him that I connected to. He reminded me for some reason of somebody from back home, so I started this series called the "Saint Series," where I took folks and gave them halos and put them into this different context. I started looking at people who had been beat down, people that we maybe don't hold in high regard in society, and started giving them sainthood because of who they were on a real level, a personal level. I eventually made my way to doing a coal-mining painting, which was a portrait of my grandfather who quit school in the sixth grade to go in the coal mines. I called that one *The Saint of Electricity*. When I painted it, there was something that sort of went off in me. In the middle of the city, that sort of became my lifeline or whatever, my identity as an artist. I began exploring my own culture more and more. Getting back into the music of my grandfather and stuff like that, and playing the banjo.

Then, eventually, with the help of a mentor of mine, I was able to move back to southeastern Kentucky. For a few years, I taught music and traveled a lot, doing art and selling artwork on the road, going to fairs and festivals, but over time those sorts of things were starting to change. It was a weird thing in the air; I guess the economy was starting to tank or whatever, so eventually I took a teaching job, but hated it. For about five months I hated this teaching job. I was teaching in a public school. These kids were cussing at me and all this stuff, and I just couldn't stand it. I thought, I used to be a tattoo artist, I used to play music, and I used to travel and sell artwork, and now I'm sitting here getting cussed at by these little kids who hate me because I'm their teacher. I took all the money I made from teaching and kept putting it back [saving it]. I live on a little farm where my rent is not much at all, so I was able to put that back and in 2011 I decided to open my own little tattoo shop and art gallery. It's not like a typical tattoo shop, it's really just a private thing with an art gallery, and we have music, a painting studio, and stuff like that in there now. That's where I'm at now, back home, and I get to experience a lot more of the community this way as well. It's amazing all the different people who are my clients and customers. I'll let Rich tell you about himself.

Rich Kirby: Well, I had different details, but some of the same trajectory. My family is from eastern Kentucky. They actually moved down to the Bluegrass before I was born, then when I was seven my parents and I actually moved to New York City, of all places. I grew up there except, blessedly, we always spent summers in Kentucky with my grandparents, so I grew up in two very different worlds. I like to think I can be an outsider anywhere. There was a lot of music in my family (particularly my grandmother, who was a remarkable traditional singer), but I took it for granted and didn't pay much attention to it. As I grew up, I got to thinking of myself more and more as a northern urban person—not totally, but when the folk music craze came out in the 1950s and '60s, I began making connections between that music and the music that I heard at home. In the 1960s you could get involved in political stuff, and one of the things you could get involved with was Appalachia, and I started making connections there, too, very much wondering what to do with my life, and it all sort of came together in one particular morning in 1969. I was in a music festival, a folk festival in upstate New York, lying in my tent, and Jean Ritchie came on singing [Music: The L&N Don't Stop Here Any More] and talking about Kentucky. I just lay there in my tent and listened to it. By the time she got done singing a little forty-five-minute set, it was perfectly clear to me that I should go back to Kentucky, which I did. I ended up in Prestonsburg, Kentucky, working on a legal action project and gradually transitioned out of that lifestyle into what my grandmother would call a vagrant—with no settled employment, but a lot of interesting experiences and deep friendships and a lot of music. I ended up working at Appalshop, which I have done for the past twenty years.

John Haywood: A preacher always told me when I was living in Louisville, he always came up to me and said, "You can take the man out of the mountains but you can never take the mountains out of the man." Ever heard that saying? It probably applies to other things, too. When I was living in Louisville and realizing how much I wanted to get back home and get more in touch with where I came from, at the same time (there's this wave of things that happen sometimes), people would come through Louisville and play mountain music. There was a lot of the rock-and-roll crowd, the punk-rock crowd that I hung around with that for some reason was finding a new connection to this kind of music. I think it's probably because it's more involved. You don't just sit and listen to it all the time. You're involved in playing it. I would go to some of these little concerts and draw pictures and do paintings of things that would happen. People were having little backyard concerts, house concerts, things like that.

There is a painting, *Banjo Girl,* that sort of illustrates my attitude to the whole thing when I was about sixteen or seventeen years old, and I'll tell you this little story. I'll start by saying this. All that pop culture that I would watch on television in the 1980s, it glorified a lot of suburban life. If you think about all those movies that came out like *Sixteen Candles, Breakfast Club,* and all that sort of thing. When you're a kid you're thinking, "Well, I don't really identify with this and maybe I don't need to be here." It makes you feel kind of inadequate being from the mountains. And still, there is really a sense of that in so many people, it's unreal. One of my first reflections I had while living in Louisville was that I wanted to do a portrait of myself (it was probably for an assignment at the University of Louisville). I wanted to paint myself as that sixteen- or seventeen-year-old. I called that painting *I Don't Want Nary Part of No Hillbilly Band.*

One day I was sitting on the hood of my car about three o'clock in the morning, in downtown Prestonsburg, Kentucky. Who knows what I was playing? Out of nowhere, there appeared an old man across the street from me and he said, "Hey, you, come here!" I was like, "Me?" I was the only person there, so actually I hollered at a couple of my buddies because I thought, "Oh, no, this guy is pissed off, he's going to take my guitar, he's going to break it or something." So he invites me into this house, and I was just going in, and when we go in, we meet his son, who he calls from the bedroom. He says, "Hey, Poochie, come here a minute." Poochie walks into the room, and Poochie is the guy I put into that same painting. Poochie comes in and he's got on a "wifebeater" and some really short shorts and he talks like Elvis.

John Haywood,
Banjo Girl. Courtesy
of John Haywood.

He's like, "Heya, hey." The old man, holding the door, he was like, "Yeah, I got this feller off the street, he was out there playing guitar and I thought he might like to come and jam with you some there, Poochie." I sat down on the weight bench that was there in the living room and listened to Poochie play the guitar. He pulls out a guitar and he plays some rockabilly, country, Elvis kind of stuff and I thought, okay, I'll play along. I did for a bit or two, and the old guy said, "Buddy, you want a beer?" And I'm like, "Well, yeah." I'm sixteen years old; if a fella offers you a beer at that time, then yeah, take it. So he says, "Hey, Hoochie, bring this boy a beer." A lady came out of the kitchen, I guess her name was Hoochie, and she gave me a beer. Before I know it, the room is full of other guys. They just show up out of nowhere. One guy with a little Casio keyboard, one of those little tiny ones, like a kid would play, on this big keyboard stand. He started playing it. A dude showed up with a banjo, another dude showed up with a bass, and it was kind of like this weird surreal experience to have at three in the morning. They were so country, I was like, wait a minute (here I am with my long hair and I'm into metal, at the time); I gave them every excuse in the world why I couldn't be in their band. I was like, "I don't even live in Floyd County." I said, "I live in Knott County." They would say, "That's all right, that's not too awful far, we'll come see you." I was like, "No, no you can't come to my house." That was just my mind-set, growing up, toward that music. It was old-fashioned; it was something the old folks did. If we ever played that music, it was to make fun of the old folks. We would sit in the cellar and sing stupid versions of "Dark as a Dungeon," make up a dirty version of it even, just because we'd get a big kick out of it. Rich?

Rich Kirby: Well, I didn't have rockabilly in my growing up. I was firmly pointed toward classical music, which I firmly resisted. My grandmother was a tremendous anchor in my life, musically as well as many other ways; she was an old Baptist singer. [Music: Been a Long Time Traveling] [Music: Our Cheerful Voices Let Us Raise] I got to realize how good she was, and how important she was. I started making home recordings of her, and that eventually led into a whole association with June Appal Recordings, which a bunch of us got started at Appalshop in the early 1970s. That

John Haywood, *I Saw the Light.* Courtesy of John Haywood.

came around full circle when I was able to release a recording of her singing. For me, and for John as well, the music is kind of a way back into something we had been eased out of: a place, if you will, as well as many other things. There are so many ways you can look at place. It is a place, it is a terrain of imagination, it's an area of culture, what some people just call "way," it's just the way some people are. I guess one way to look at that is just to begin by thinking of the physical place, the fact that there are actually hills, mountains, in eastern Kentucky and what that does for the people who live there.

John Haywood: Rich was talking about the physical mountains; it does have a way with you. Being in Louisville, away from the mountain, I always felt exposed for some reason, like people could see what I was doing. I want to talk about being in the mountains and being an artist for a minute. The mountains being around, it's like this visual stimulus, and in a painting, when you're an artist, not only does the mountain produce sometimes the characters that I paint, but also it gives me a lot of stuff to play with. The actual mountains themselves make great backdrops in paintings. You can always throw those mountains in there and give people something else to look at. And the colors: in terms of being an artist, I have a certain palette I always use, which is sort of a mountain palette. It's a group of colors that make me think of eastern Kentucky. With those same colors, I can get paintings that are mellow and sort of brown that reflect that wintertime in the mountains as well as when I put more springy things into a painting—all with the same color palette. The mountains also give me stuff to work with, in the background, formal elements. What I mean by that is, if you study art as I did, you learn about abstract art. You learn how to simplify things, break them down, how to get people to look at certain things—formal aspects, meaning color, shapes, line, and textures. The mountains give me all kinds of interesting stuff to borrow, like a mountain in the background, the color of the sky, all that stuff that I'm intentionally placing there for you to look at. Using stuff like the angle of a chute, or the houses back on the hill, to give your eye something to play with. Even when doing an interior space, like in the painting I did called *Cold Frosty Morn.* It was about my papaw; if you've ever been young and worked with a bunch of old men, you know that feeling. My papaw was in the sixth grade when he started working in the mines. I was thirteen and worked for Lancer Van Company and worked up on strip jobs with a lot of older guys, so I kind of understood what it felt like to be the young guy working among some of these older, seasoned folks. Also, in the interior of a lot of the homes of old folks around home, they keep their walls covered in pictures. For me, as an artist, it's just another thing that I can add into the painting to give you something to look at and at the same time sort of tell the story. For the lighting, I try to think about these old dark houses; there are so many houses in eastern Kentucky yet that aren't up to code, that do have a dimly lit lightbulb in the living room. That's a physical interpretation of it in terms of painting.

John Haywood,
Cold Frosty Morn.
Courtesy of John
Haywood.

Rich Kirby: I say this with a little bit of hesitancy because I have
  absolutely no idea what I'm talking about, only a feeling. But
  it's an unshakeable feeling that the physical landscape of the
  mountains has its effect on the music. I've never been able to
  put a handle on this any more than maybe a quote from Letcher
  County banjo player Lee Sexton, who once said, "When you
  look out over these hills, it just makes you, it just looks kindly
  lonesome, don't it?" That word *lonesome* is one that comes up
  again and again that people use to describe a certain feeling,
  and you can hear it in tunes. [Music: Sugar in the Gourd] One
  thing that happens to people like us is that we have choices. My
  grandmother really probably didn't think about whether she had
  the choice about what kind of music she was going to be involved
  in, it was just so much of a part of her that you couldn't think of
  her without it. But someone in my life, or in John's, being pulled
  in so many different cultural directions, both of us—and many
  other people—have made this conscious choice to come back
  to this place, whatever you mean by that term. There again, that
  amorphous concept of place is at the center of what we do and
  how we do it, and I wish I were better at explaining that.
John Haywood: What's interesting is when you're from eastern
  Kentucky and you tell people you're from there, you can see it
  in their eyes. They're painting their own little picture of where it

is you come from, and they're like, "Oh, you mean Richmond,
I've been to Eastern," or, "I've been to Berea" and we're like, "uh,
no, we mean *eastern* Kentucky, like Hazard." Most people are
like, "Oh, yeah Dukes of Hazzard!" or whatever. It's interesting
when you realize that being from an area, there is so much of it
that you see and experience that other people really don't know
about. You hear about strip-mining culture or just strip-mining in
general; the holler I lived in was strip-mined. The downside is the
pollution, the upside is you had a great place where you could take
your four-wheelers and your four-wheel drives, and you could go
up there and build a big fire and do whatever you want. You could
get really outrageous. I've seen a guy take a hatchet and throw it
from here to that wall over there and kill a rabbit by just throwing
a hatchet. I've seen a richer city boy go up there and just destroy
a Jeep that his parents had just bought him. People don't think
of that a lot of times when they think of eastern Kentucky. I feel
fortunate to be in eastern Kentucky. I feel like God has just placed
me there for some reason or another. I feel like all my travels were
sort of all meant to be, and I was meant to come back.

Rich is going to talk about this here in a minute, but you get
a lot of people who also study the music, and the art, and the
lifestyle, and they get a certain idea of what it is supposed to be
in their minds, when many times it's not even really like that
at all. I'm really good friends with the banjo player Lee Sexton
and it's so interesting to see how, really, pop culture even shapes
somebody like him. Bluegrass, Earl Scruggs, Bill Monroe shaped
his old-timey banjo playing and so many other musicians. We
were talking about, what is mountain music today? What is the
true mountain music? We are not the authorities or anything, but
what is the true mountain music today? Is it people carrying on
this generation of Hiram Stamper and Art Stamper, Banjo Bill
and all those folks? Is it really those people carrying that stuff on?
In reality, it's not. It's more like a couple of dudes sitting in the
garage playing Skynyrd on their guitars. They may know all them
old-time songs too; everybody's got a papaw who played the
banjo or something like that, so everybody's kind of like, "Who
wants to fool with all that old music while we've got Skynyrd and
people like that?'

Rich Kirby: It raises the question of what is this music supposed to be, and who gets to decide? We are firmly going to take our hands off that question. I don't want to act at all like we're standing up here being any kind of authorities about what's right or wrong in terms of playing traditional music. We just have a lot of feelings about what we play and what we want to do ourselves. In a sense, I keep thinking about what happened once when I was playing in an elementary school with my longtime music buddy Tommy Bledsoe. We were in a fourth- or fifth-grade class in Knott County, and we asked the kids if they had anybody in their families that played. This one little kid said, "My brother plays the guitar, but he can't help it." And it's like, yeah, yeah, right.

We'd like to give you two or three examples of places where music and art have literally intersected in our work. One of them comes from a story that was told by a man named George Gibson, who is a banjo player from Knott County who has been a mentor as well as a landlord to John and a huge, huge reservoir of information and tunes and skills. He told a story and played

John Haywood, *General Morgan Plays a Stolen Fiddle.* Courtesy of John Haywood.

a tune that inspired one of John's paintings that depicts a man watching from the woods while the Confederate raider John Hunt Morgan plays the man's fiddle he has just stolen. [General Morgan Plays a Stolen Fiddle/Morgan's March]

Another one goes back to my family tradition. My grandmother grew up in the area where Morgan, Wolfe, and Breathitt counties all kind of run together, not too far from Hazel Green, and she used to talk about a man—recently, George Gibson discovered mention of him in the little newspaper that was published in Hazel Green for many years—his name was Grant Reed. My grandmother was telling me, he was the only African American she saw growing up, and he must have been an amazing man. He ran a little speakeasy; my grandmother didn't know that—"Blind Tiger" it was called, in the newspaper account. But what my grandmother would remember was Grant Reed would walk up and down the roads playing his banjo. She grew up in this Primitive Baptist family where there were no musical instruments and, Lord have mercy, no dancing whatsoever. I think it's in the water in eastern Kentucky, because she did know how to dance, but she said that when she would hear him coming down the road, she would sneak out of the house and get out of sight where she could still hear, and he would walk down the road playing his banjo and she would be on the other side of the house dancing to it. (That story inspired John to do a painting.) She remembered him playing "Darling Corey." [Music: Darling Corey]

John Haywood: Those are a couple of examples where my artwork reflects specific things about music, specific songs, historical incidents—not so much deriving things from what is present. Another good example of how I've been able to merge my art with music is album covers. I've been fortunate enough to do several album covers as well as a cover for the band I play in with Rich. I was really happy with my recording experience with Rich and the Po' Folks; we've got a couple other guys that play with us who are phenomenal musicians. One of our musicians is a guy named Nate Polly. Nathan Polly is a retired railroad worker. He grew up in the coal-mining community of Seco, Kentucky, which is a little coal camp. If you've been to eastern Kentucky through

John Haywood, *Addie Graham and Grant Reed.* Courtesy of John Haywood.

a coal camp, you might have seen row houses. He's the only one of us that can write a song, I swear, and he just has this way of singing. I remember they reviewed our CD and compared him to people like Ralph Stanley. I thought that was real great, because Nate Polly gets out and plays about once a week at this little open mic, and there are people who come just to see him. They leave when he's done; they'll stick around and as soon as Nate's done, they're gone. He's this smooth finger player. He's been playing bluegrass and old-timey music for thirty-some years, almost as long as I've been around. "When the Whistle Blew" is a song that he wrote for a play. They asked, what was the one thing the people of Seco remembered about growing up in the coal camp there, and they said, oh, it was when the whistle blew. The whistle signified so many different things—time to start, time to break, time to go home, and it also signified accidents, things like that. [Music: When the Whistle Blew]

Rich Kirby: We would like to spend a little bit of time talking about what we are hoping to do with all our art and music and all this. Without getting too far afield, we can say that we live in a place that has been abused and exploited in the past, in the present, and probably on into the future, if the truth could be known. A ripped-off land in a lot of ways, and in some cases, a ripped-off music and culture. One song that I participated in years ago that dated back to the strip-mining wars of the 1960s was "Dan

John Haywood,
*Sittin' on the
Porch*. Courtesy of
John Haywood.

the Red Nose," [Music: Dan the Red Nose] about resistance in
the mountains, as is John's painting *Ain't Gonna Get My Holler*.
Bringing that up is sort of a quick nod to the whole history of
resistance in the mountains.

Well, the whole question of people taking the culture out of a
place and turning it into a commodity, John did a painting of the
great banjo player String Bean playing in an artificial rendition of
that kind of place.

John Haywood: That painting and another one got me a little bit of
national recognition, because of the subject matters, and also
secured me a role in a movie. Like what I was saying before,
mountain music exists in so many different ways. There is this
character from West Virginia named Hasil Adkins who I really
loved because he had this ingenious approach to music. The story
goes that he heard Hank Williams when he was a kid on the

John Haywood,
*Ain't Gonna
Get My Holler.*
Courtesy of John
Haywood.

radio, and the announcer didn't necessarily say Hank Williams had a backup band, so he assumed Hank Williams was doing it all. So he decided he was going to do it all. He was able to create a drum set he could control with his feet, and play the guitar. In my travels, I've seen his influence spread all over—across the whole nation. I've played at festivals where there were so many one-man bands that were modeled after Hasil. [Music: Devonna Rock] The filmmaker, the guy who made the Hasil Adkins film, later made another movie about an iconic, crazy hillbilly named Jesco White. They called me and asked me to be in that movie, actually, and play music for Jesco while he danced.

This always brings up the terms of what we mean by *authentic.* You always hear of folklorists looking for authentic, hillbilly, stereotypical music. They use the term *hillbilly;* some people don't like that term. Where we're from, some people don't mind it—they feel like we're taking it back, that sort of thing. . . . But what's interesting about people like Jesco, and these dancing outlaw movies (they are worth seeing even if you don't like what they're about), is that they do explore some pretty touchy subjects as far as eastern Kentucky and the mountains of West Virginia. Jesco is seen as kind of a recluse. He tap-dances to rock-and-roll music all the time, but he's actually the living heir to this magnificent dance tradition that exists in the mountains. His dad was filmed by Mike Seeger and put in this movie called *Talking Feet,* I believe it was.[8] He was supposed to go on tour and go visit Europe and all that, but the night before he was supposed to leave he was murdered. He had passed all that on to Jesco.

Jesco would be the last person in the world a folklorist would go to and ask, "Can you show me this traditional mountain dancing?" He just kind of does it. There are these people who are conscious of what they're doing in terms of tradition, and there are some of these people who just do it because that is what they've done. When you meet them, you might not think this person is part of that, because as the outsider looking in, you wouldn't necessarily think that some guy that's known for causing trouble would have this treasure within him. You almost can't invite him to play; he gets really wild and busts out windows and causes a ruckus. He did it in Nashville and other places. One of the highlights of the past few years for me was that I got to be in this new movie they made of him. I think he's an amazing dancer. Being there in person, I've never seen anybody dance like this guy. He never missed a lick and he didn't stop for five hours. Even when the cameras were off, he danced and played music.

I guess we're going to close up here, and talk about a few little quick things. What I hope people take from me being so

John Haywood,
*Mal Gibson and
Simon Ward.*
Courtesy of John
Haywood.

stoked about my place is that I think it's important for people to really invest in their own culture, invest in the history of their culture. It can really take you from feeling kind of bad about it, feeling like you've been short-changed, to really be able to raise up your head about it. My parents still don't understand why I left Louisville, where I was making some pretty good money, to come back to the mountains and kind of be poor again. It's a mind-set; it's liberating. As far as my artwork, too, while growing up I had to copy styles. I had to copy Picasso, all these different sorts of artists they made you copy and taught you they were important because they were in Paris at *this* time or New York at *this* time. I began to notice, within the last few years, Latino culture and art, because, instead of trying to focus on a version of what things *should* be, they focus on their own culture, and because of this, Latino art exploded. African American art, and other folk arts, when people start to focus on their own culture and be happy and proud of their culture, then the artist part of it seems to flourish. I think we've got a problem about that in eastern Kentucky because

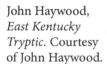

John Haywood, *East Kentucky Tryptic*. Courtesy of John Haywood.

there are still so many people who think eastern Kentucky is not worth very much. [Music: Hook and Line]

Rich Kirby: I haven't got much to add to that, except we feel pretty fortunate to be doing what we're doing, where we're doing it. It's a pretty exciting time in eastern Kentucky. There is a lot more of our kind of music going on than there was a few years ago. Our friend Beverly May likes to say that ten years ago she could count all the fiddlers in eastern Kentucky she knew on one hand, and now you can't swing a cat without hitting two or three of them. We're just glad to be part of it.

Music Examples Available at www.kentuckypress.com

Mix: Jean Ritchie/Rich and the Po' Folk, "The L&N Don't Stop Here Any More"

Addie Graham, "Been a Long Time Traveling"

Addie Graham, "Our Cheerful Voices Let Us Raise"

Bruce Greene (Manon Campbell on fiddle), "Sugar in the Gourd"

George Gibson, "General Morgan Plays a Stolen Fiddle"

George Gibson, "Morgan's March"

Addie Graham, "Darling Corey"

Rich and the Po' Folk (Nate Polly, comp.), "When the Whistle Blew"

Wry Straw (Michael Kline, comp.), "Dan the Red Nose"

Hasil Adkins (comp.), "Devonna Rock"
Rich and the Po' Folk (John Haywood on banjo), "Hook and Line"

Notes

1. Gusty Wallace (1890–1985) learned fiddle from his father, Addison Wallace, who was a well-known local musician. Gusty was born in Hart County but moved to Sulphur Well in Metcalfe County, adjoining Green County.

2. Spoken introduction by the fiddler Wallace Thompson, made on a field recording by Bruce Greene on March 30, 1974. The recording is housed at the Berea College Southern Appalachian Archives and was accessed through the Digital Library of Appalachia, http://dla.acaweb.org/cdm/singleitem/collection/berea/id/1918/rec/4.

3. Bruce Greene recalled his meeting with Wallace Thompson: "I met Wallace Thompson at a little local fiddlers' contest in Hartsville, Tennessee. He introduced himself to me, 'I'm from Pierce, Kentucky. We all call it Loafersburg, because everybody there loafs.' His father, Marvin, was a pretty good old-time fiddler, but very shy about playing for me, especially around Wallace, who was a fancy fiddler and I'm pretty sure could read music. Wallace was a close relative of Gusty Wallace, a cousin maybe. They played together quite a bit. The Wallaces and Thompsons all claimed to be direct descendants of William Wallace, the Scottish freedom fighter. They were also all Mormons. Go figure. . . . Moonlight refers to an outdoor party/dance at night, a custom among older generations in that part of Kentucky. They would say, for instance, we're having a moonlight Friday night, etc." Personal email correspondence with Bruce Greene, February 17, 2017.

4. Clare Milliner and Walt Koken, *The Milliner-Koken Collection of American Fiddle Tunes* (Kennett Square, PA: Mudthumper Music, 2011).

5. "Moonlight" was recorded by Don Pedi and Bruce Greene on *Short Time Here: Songs & Tunes from the Southern Mountains* (Marshall, NC: Walnut Mountain 904, 2004).

6. Jean Ritchie, *Singing Family of the Cumberlands* (1955; repr., Lexington: University Press of Kentucky, 1988).

7. Phil Jamison, "Dance Beat: In Search of Old-Time Patter Calls," *Old-Time Herald* 7, no. 6 (2000/2001): 11.

8. Jesco White's father, Donald Ray White (1927–1985) of Boone County, West Virginia, was featured in the documentary film *Talking Feet: Solo Southern Dance: Buck, Flatfoot and Tap,* directed by Mike Seeger (New York: Smithsonian Folkways Records, 1987).

10

Teaching Region

Dwight B. Billings, Gina Caison, David A. Davis,
Laura Hernández-Ehrisman, Philip Joseph, Kent C. Ryden,
and Emily Satterwhite

The New Critical Regionalism: Cross-Region Commonalities and Future Directions

Emily Satterwhite

The scholars in this chapter offer important thinking about the ways in which we who teach regionalism have been reconceptualizing what that might mean for the twenty-first century. Regionalist scholars from disciplinary perspectives as diverse as sociology, literature, and history are working to recognize the potential pitfalls of teaching region. Regionalism at its worst, according to Philip Joseph, has offered impoverished examples of community that students either dismiss as antimodern or else embrace as a primeval antidote to modern life. As Joseph warns us, regionalism also risks promoting a shallow kind of diversity that may allow students to feel as though they embrace inclusiveness—when in reality students of regionalism may learn only to embrace difference made familiar.

But contemporary regionalist scholars like those featured in this chapter are responding to the perils of teaching region by pushing the old models. Yes, students come to the classroom with preexisting and often questionable investments in the idea of region or in regional identities (or both). New regionalist scholars leverage those investments into an opportunity for more critical awareness of representation, economy, and inequality. Dwight Billings, for example, has students considering economic crises and industrial transformation, deindustrialization and public policy. Though he uses in part conventionally "regionalist" texts to get at these issues, he is not offering his students an apolitical Appalachia of dulcimers and quilts.

This collection of reflections on critical regionalism shares at least two additional significant principles. First, its contributors employ new geographical thinking promoted by Doreen Massey, among others, which recognizes place as a process. Laura Hernández-Ehrisman usefully refers to Doug Reichert Powell as a leading thinker in this regard. In *Critical Regionalism* Reichert Powell insists on the following more fluid notions of place and region:

- "When we talk about region, we are talking not about a stable, boundaried, autonomous place but about a cultural history."
- Region "must refer not to a specific site but to a larger network of sites."
- Rather than highlighting isolation, regionalism allows us to make "claims about how spaces and places are connected."[1]

Gina Caison's focus on Native histories, for example, enables a more dynamic long view of regionalism and place as "a process" that alerts students to a time before the South became "their 'own' region." As Kent Ryden observes, place is never as inert or uncontested as the "postcard" "fetishization" of region would have it.

Second, each of these scholars understands regionalism as central to projects of transnational and global inquiry—projects that themselves often see regionalism as an antiquated relic with nothing to offer, as Dwight Billings and Philip Joseph note. As these contributors have shown, our students can see "the global" better through the lens of region. In David Davis's words, "The emergence of globalism makes regionalism more important, not less." Davis observes that "hemispheric and global studies are actually extensions of regionalism." He points out that at a time when "globalization has lessened the significance of political boundaries" of state or nation, region is a more precise and productive unit for understanding the world. Hernández-Ehrisman helps students "uncover connections between regional conflicts and larger national and global transformations." And as Caison observes, "Any discussion of the region is already bound up with larger transnational threads." We cannot "talk about the present-day U.S. South without talking about the African, European, and indigenous peoples who contributed to the region's culture." She advocates using an indigenous studies perspective alongside a regional perspective in order to see the long scope of transnational exchange within the region. For Caison, region as a category of analysis illuminates more about transnational exchange than it occludes. Joseph teaches texts that show a local community and its subjects squarely in an interconnected nation and world.

Indeed, Dwight Billings has convinced his administration of the "complementary" nature of Appalachian studies and global citizenship studies. He has taken the currently preferred global lens and shown administrators how to see region through it. Joseph's approach shares an affinity with Billings's in this matter of employing regionalism to help students to see the interpenetration of global issues and their own backyards. For Joseph, this move promotes democratic citizenship and encourages students to become agents for change: regionalism offers "models of civic community that are both specific to place and sensitive to developments in other areas of the world."

The new critical regionalism evidenced here challenges rather than comforts students. It views place as constantly constructed and reconstructed rather than static. It presents region as interconnected, and regionalism as a way of thinking about global engagement rather than a means of self-protective isolation. As Reichert Powell argues, "Critical regionalism must be . . . a pedagogy . . . that teaches students how to draw their own regional maps connecting their experience to that of others near and far, both like and unlike themselves."[2] Critical regionalist scholars like these contributors use their classrooms to offer students a place for thinking through some of the most momentous problems of our time. Joseph notes that the Occupy movement drew "power not simply from social media and text messaging, but also from relationships and identities specific to particular geographies." Kent Ryden notes that *region* has been equated with "the sticks," "the place where nothing happens," but that "nothing could be further from the truth; region is the place where *everything* happens, right outside your classroom . . . where you can examine highly fraught cultural concepts as real, concrete things."

One additional direction that I would like to push the conversation is toward issues of regionalism and whiteness, which we have barely begun to address. Hernández-Ehrisman rightfully raises up the significance of an Austin, Texas–centered U.S. history survey for a student body that is 50 percent Latino/a. Ryden and Caison comment on the need to challenge students who would say "this region is ours and not yours." Several contributors note the ways in which white students' investments in place can be leveraged into critical thinking about hierarchy and privilege. I would like us to collectively think more about how regionalism for white students is different from regionalism for students of color—or about how it *should* be.

Doug Reichert Powell bemoans the fact that "New England Studies, Appalachian Studies, Southern Studies, Western Studies all engage in often-parallel but less-often collaborative projects." But he also highlights the work of scholars whose starting points are variously in the Pacific Northwest, the Midwest, and elsewhere (including our collaborator "Kent Ryden in New England") who "have all called for and enacted scholarship . . . that approaches the idea of region as a rich, complicated, and dynamic cultural construct rather than a static, stable geophysical entity." The reflections gathered here (from scholars specializing in New England, Appalachia, the South, the Southwest, the Midwest, and Native Americans) pick up the project Reichert Powell calls for, to emerge from "balkanized . . . self-contained, if not parochial," regionalist studies into a productive cross-regional conversation.[3]

Each author in this chapter has been asked to address these questions:

1. Why are regional studies important in your specific locale; that is, how does place matter?
2. What are your teaching objectives for your regional studies course(s)?
3. More specifically, how do you try to achieve these goals pedagogically?
4. Regionalism (like area studies) seems to be unfashionable at the moment, while transnational and hemispheric studies seem ascendant. What are regionalism's strengths and weaknesses relative to other approaches? What legitimate concerns are raised by critiques of regional studies, and which critiques of regional studies are red herrings?

Coals to Newcastle; or, Teaching the South in the South

David A. Davis

My grandmother often used the expression "like carrying coals to Newcastle." I could tell by the context that she meant something was pointless or redundant, but as a boy growing up in middle Georgia, I had no earthly idea where Newcastle was or why anyone would take coals there. Now, however, that is essentially what I do for a living.

I am a native Southerner who teaches southern studies at a southern university to mostly southern students. Perhaps that sounds a bit redundant. I am an English professor and associate director of the Spencer B. King, Jr., Center for Southern Studies at Mercer University in Macon, Georgia, which offers an undergraduate major in southern studies incorporating African American studies, English, history, journalism, geography, and religious studies. Students who have completed the program have gone to graduate programs in English and history, to medical school, law school, and journalism school, and into teaching. Our program also hosts the Lamar lectures, the most prestigious series of lectures on southern history and culture, and awards the Sidney Lanier Prize for Southern Literature, which honors significant career contribution to southern writing. We have held two NEH institutes for schoolteachers on cotton culture in the South between the Civil War and the Civil Rights movement. In addition to all these activities, we hold public lectures and a film series, and we have hosted the Southern Intellectual History Circle and other events.

Outreach is clearly an important part of our program, and we find that the Macon community provides ample interest in the South. The city of Macon is, in truth, a microcosm of southern history and culture. Once home to one of the largest Native American settlements in the Southeast, the city was settled during the period of Removal as cotton plantations moved westward. Situated on the fall line at the Ocmulgee River, the city became a busy cotton market and transportation hub in the nineteenth century. Macon declined with the end of the cotton economy and the textile industry in the middle of the twentieth century, and the city still bears obvious signs of poverty, institutionalized racism, and civic ennui, although it has been regenerated recently with the growth of a medical center, a major Air Force base in Warner Robins, and Mercer University's expansion.

Mercer's students come mostly from the South, and they reflect both the challenges of southern history and the region's changing population. Mercer was the first school in Georgia to integrate voluntarily, and we have a large percentage of African American students. We were affiliated with the Georgia Baptist Convention until 2005, so we also have a large number of students from Baptist families. Our fastest-growing demographic, however, is students from the suburban South, many of whose ancestors were not southern and some of whom are not native-born Americans and who often feel ambivalent about the South. Students of South Asian descent, who represent about 15 percent of Mercer's student body, raise an entirely different set of issues about southern identity and the Global South.

The southern studies program is important at our institution for reasons of history, location, and curriculum. Our program connects the school with the community, and it allows our students to study traditional southern identity and to develop a critical understanding of the region's past and its future.

For my part, I routinely teach courses on southern literature and southern cultural studies. My overarching goal in all my courses is to teach interpretation and critical thinking, and I find that my students' perceptions and prejudices about the South can be used in my favor. My challenge is to defamiliarize my students with their preconceptions about the South. They often come into class identifying as Southerners or as transplants and with an established set of received opinions, both positive and negative, about the region, or they come into class only because it fits their schedule, so they couldn't care less about the region, or they come into class having just pledged Kappa Alpha and prepared to duel any man who dares besmirch the honor of their native region. So I attempt to destabilize their preconceptions by introducing them to debate among writers and scholars and among themselves about issues pertaining to the region. Many students find themselves surprised to be outside an echo chamber that repeats the same opinion, and they are almost always shocked or amused to find a professor of southern studies who has an irreverent, critical, and occasionally profane attitude toward the South.

For a southern literature class, I usually begin with a theme. I'm rather dubious about the existence of canons in general and a canon of southern writing in particular, so I don't use major authors or greatest-hits approaches. Instead, I take a topic and assemble a range of texts that relate to that issue. I recently taught, for example, a course on poor white southerners in twentieth-century literature, and we read Erskine Caldwell's *God's Little Acre*, Zora Neale Hurston's *Seraph on the Sewanee*, William Faulkner's *As I Lay Dying*, Cormac McCarthy's *Suttree*, Dorothy Allison's *Bastard Out of Carolina*, and Larry Brown's *Joe*, and we screened *The Southerner* and *Searching for the Wrong-Eyed Jesus*. We focused many of our discussions on the issues of shame and pride related to poor white identity and on the spectacular display of poor whites in popular culture that continues to resonate on reality television, such as *Swamp People* or *Here Comes Honey Boo Boo*.

My cultural studies classes allow me to take this approach a step further by incorporating several disciplines into the course. I select a topic and pull together works of history, social science, cultural criticism, literature, and art to develop a mosaic understanding of the topic. So far, I have taught cultural studies classes on southern food, the southern justice system, the memory of the Civil Rights movement, and the memory of the Civil War.

I taught a course on Civil War memory to coincide with a series of lectures at Mercer on the sesquicentennial of the Civil War. We read Louis Masur's brief *The Civil War,* David Blight's *Race and Reunion,* William Faulkner's *The Unvanquished,* Charles Frazier's *Cold Mountain,* William Marvel's *Andersonville: The Last Depot,* Robert Cook's *Troubled Commemorations,* and Tony Horwitz's *Confederates in the Attic.* We visited the Andersonville National Historic Site, screened *The Birth of a Nation* and *C.S.A.: The Movie,* and attended lectures by Gary Gallagher, Fitz Brundage, and Robert Cook. In this class we discussed historical revisionism and the war's persistent legacy in popular culture and the complex associations between the war's memory and modern-day racism.

This format has a powerful influence. Students leave the course with a nuanced sense of the region, a more refined set of interpretive skills, and a less stable set of preconceptions. I am always gratified when I observe my students' preconceptions changing, although that is not my sole objective. Even if their opinions don't change, I want them to develop a critical understanding of the region, one that makes them better able to analyze the relationship between the region's past and its present and more prepared for its dynamic future.

The emergence of globalism makes regionalism more important, not less. Transnational flows of capital and population reconfigure locations, creating networks of physical and economic infrastructure, but those networks do not develop in a vacuum. They take place in the real world, in spaces that have distinctive pasts, and they affect the everyday lives of ordinary people. Truthfully, the region as a transnational unit is the most precise unit of spatial organization, not the state or the nation. Globalization has lessened the significance of political boundaries, and most people live their lives in territories bounded by familial, economic, and infrastructural relationships. They don't live on the whole Earth, but on a segment of it with which they have personal attachments.

In the past generation, the South's economy has shifted from cotton, textiles, and tobacco to service, manufacturing, industrial agriculture, and logistics, and the region's population has exploded, primarily in sprawling suburban metropolises. In response to globalization, the South has been rebranded the Sunbelt, a new region that seems to be distinct from the troubled history that preceded it. That is a clearly false premise, and the still-complicated politics of the region indicates that the South continues to wrestle with human rights. But the region's economic development is undeniable, and the processes of globalization have mostly benefited the region, at least so far.

The rise of the Sunbelt, though, has largely debunked the myth of southern exceptionalism, the notion that the South is fundamentally different from the rest of the United States because of its legacy of racial division. The nation is not a homogeneous mass, of course, and the South is still the only region ever to secede, but the South does not have a historical monopoly on either virtue or vice, and all regions are qualitatively similar. Nonetheless, it is still the case that the South plays a peculiar role in the American imagination as a site onto which poverty, weirdness, and sins of racism, lustfulness, and religious hypocrisy are projected. Though the region has certainly earned its reputation as the nation's id, it is not qualitatively better or worse than the rest of the nation.

The emergence of hemispheric studies, meanwhile, has opened a new vein of discourse about the Global South. While the South is not qualitatively different from the rest of the nation, it is the portion of the United States that participated most actively in the plantation economy that involved New World slavery. In this sense, the South has much historically in common with Cuba, Brazil, and other historically slave-based economies, so it is in some ways both part of the United States and not part of the United States. This is an indication that the region sometimes supersedes the nation and that hemispheric and global studies are actually extensions of regionalism. Teaching regionalism in the era of globalization prepares students to be more aware of and engaged with the complex international and intranational relationships that define everyday life.

Regionalism in Our Time: Teaching Garland, Hurston, and Company in the Age of Occupy Wall Street and Global English

Philip Joseph

Soon I will again teach the second half of the American literature survey for my department, and I will almost certainly include some sampling of regionalist texts, whether by Hamlin Garland or Sarah Orne Jewett or Charles Chesnutt or Willa Cather. Inclusion of these writers still feels necessary to me, but it always comes with a reminder that teaching regionalism to contemporary American students is both rewarding and treacherous. For all its potential value, teaching regionalism can sometimes make me feel like a failed educator, pushing outdated texts on students, instilling compromised values in them, and reinforcing the inadequacies of American education.

What is it about regionalism that makes it treacherous? First of all, regionalist literature offers plenty of impoverished examples of community that students either dismiss as antimodern or, worse yet, embrace as a primeval antidote to modern life. Second, and perhaps more important for me, regionalist literature can diversify a literary studies curriculum in an all-too-limited way. These texts have always reinforced a reading subject's sense of him- or herself as open to diversity and accepting of difference. Yet the question for me is whether inclusion of *regional* difference—in a nineteenth-century monthly magazine *or* in a twenty-first-century college course—can sometimes realize that value of diversity while reinforcing a reader's privilege and aversion to the unfamiliar. As many scholars have noted, regionalist texts of the nineteenth century often implied the exclusion of urban immigrants and dark-skinned residents of the United States from national citizenship. The question of regionalism's *ex*clusiveness gains its significance in the present context, for me, when we begin to think seriously about the profusion of dialect in our culture and how it relates to both disparities in English language literacy and the spread of English around the globe.

So let me first clarify: I have argued, and I continue to believe, that nineteenth- and twentieth-century American regionalism is entirely compatible with the interests and needs of twentieth-first-century American students. Our networked students live big chunks of their lives in a virtual space consisting of friends and followers situated in distant parts of the globe. By contrast, in regionalist writing, we sometimes encounter populations characterized by insularity, cultural homogeneity, rootedness, and a righteous unwillingness to adapt to modern global conditions. How, then, can regionalism possibly speak to our dislocated, hyperconnected students? What exactly does this ostensibly antiquated form still have to offer?

Though the regionalist tradition has sometimes embraced communal cohesion over individual mobility, cultural preservation more than exchange with an outside world, such a description does not, in my view, exhaust the tradition. In Hamlin Garland's work, to take one example, the intermingling of midwestern regionalism and nineteenth-century agrarian dissent leads to a form of local community in dialogue with the outside world, capable of shaping governmental decisions and of benefiting from the knowledge and experiences of external peoples. In his signature story, "Up the Coolly," the urbanized protagonist, Howard McLane, can achieve local, rural belonging only by giving the disenfranchised residents of the La Crosse valley a public voice—that is, by registering how they would represent themselves. This is a community intensely aware of its marginalization; to borrow a phrase from Michael Sandel, it is a community expressive of "democracy's discontent," angry that it has no say in how it is represented and ultimately governed.[4]

Sandel, much like the literary regionalists a century before him, reminds us that communities of proximity and presence continue to lie at the center of our democracy, and indeed at the center of our students' lives. There is nothing, in other words, *necessarily* antiquated about regionalism's emphasis on locality. The Occupy movement, for instance, drew its power not simply from social media and text messaging, but also from relationships and identities specific to particular geographies. Each instance of Occupy built on activism in distant places, not only American but foreign as well, while also gaining strength from accumulated local experience—from protesting the actions of local law enforcement, from highlighting the policies of a particular state government, or from mocking the habits of a local business elite. Approached selectively, regionalism can offer models of civic community that are both specific to place and sensitive to developments in other areas of the world. As E. J. Dionne has written, regionalism can help us "build the social, communal, ethnic, and neighborhood associations that suit these times."[5]

Citizenship—or the model of local community and belonging featured in a regionalist text—presents one set of rewards and challenges to contemporary teachers of regionalism. We encounter yet another set when we begin to think about these texts linguistically, as works that represent varieties of spoken English characteristic of regional groups. When my students embark on a book like *Their Eyes Were Watching God* (a novel that I often teach as a regionalist text), the first topic of discussion is the difficulty and resistance of the regional dialect. Far from dismissing the novel for this reason, my students are often intrigued. We concern ourselves at first with Hurston's approach to language and how we might begin to describe the nonstandard English depicted in dialogue relative to the prose of the narration.

Needless to say, regionalism of the nineteenth and early twentieth centuries participates in the explosion of what might be called dialect culture that continues into our own time. A television show like HBO's *The Wire*, for instance, thematizes the distinctive codes and speech patterns characteristic of an English-language subculture, where the type of English being spoken can sound like a challenging word puzzle to the untrained ears of the detectives who listen to it over a wiretap. Similarly, regionalism offers a set of texts in which readers confront local variants of English as they compete for prestige and status with standard written versions of the language. As a literary tradition with a foothold in the academy, regionalism offers a case study for discussing, on the one hand, the diminishment of these local variants by writers at the center of American culture and, on the other hand, the promotion of them as complex linguistic systems with grammatical and syntactical rules all their own. It invites students to think about how the standard English that they themselves have learned through formal education has been dramatically altered by the diversification of the English language, and how—despite efforts to resist this change—standard English writing has become increasingly more dependent on speech variants for its idioms and its sense of authenticity.

What exactly, then, does the explosion of dialect culture mean for populations with limited access to the norms of literacy—populations that produce the dialect in a literary representation but often do not consume it as readers? Is it fair to say that the profusion of dialect merely boosts the English literacy of those like our own majors who have learned to read and write at an early age, who have attended college, and who continue to accrue cultural capital by acquiring competency in different forms of the English language? And does it validate the oral skills of the disenfranchised at the expense of their print literacy? Less cynically, does the dialect in our culture even the playing field by attaching value to marginalized forms of English and by ensuring that speakers with limited access to linguistic norms will be listened to by the cultural elite? I would hazard to say that the answers to these questions depend, to a great extent, on the specific dialect texts that we teach and on the way that we teach them.

If regionalism raises questions, then, about the linguistic relationship between our majors and those (like the populations depicted in the texts) who have limited access to the formal English of the university, it should also make us think about the linguistic situation of our students in relation to those who don't speak English at all. The issue here has to do with regionalism's relevance to the global spread of English as the dominant world language. I want to conclude by suggesting that as a form of dialect culture, literary regionalism can tempt those in the discipline, both scholars and majors, into believing that we have sufficiently expanded our linguistic horizons—that an English curriculum can, on its own, deliver an adequate amount of linguistic diversity to the educated. While literature in "rotten English" (to use a phrase coined by the Nigerian novelist and human rights activist Ken Saro-Wiwa) encourages American students to recognize the many routes to creativity within the Anglophone world, it is also a form of literature written in the mother language of these students. My own feeling is that teachers of regionalism have a special obligation to ensure that literature in dialect does not supplant the study of foreign languages. The ability to engage with foreign-language speakers on *their* terms is a fundamental value in the humanities. Teaching in an age when foreign language departments are constantly in danger of being "discontinued," we ought to argue strongly not only for the inclusion of literature that celebrates the distinctive speech of an English-speaking regional population, but also for foreign language requirements within our majors.[6]

Teaching Region: the Austin Experience

Laura Hernández-Ehrisman

The phrase "Keep Austin Weird" has become so common it's been referred to in the *New York Times*. Austinites themselves are divided on its significance. For some, it's merely a slogan used to sell T-shirts to tourists; for others, it represents a nostalgic movement to return Austin to its era as a remote college town. For newcomers, the phrase still reflects the perception of Austin as an eccentric place of liberal nonconformity. And, inevitably, this myth of Austin informs prospective college students' understandings as well, including many of the students who come to St. Edward's University, where I teach. Once a small college that catered mainly to native central Texans, the university has grown substantially, and our students are coming from more diverse regions of the country and the world. They come for many reasons, but one big reason is to experience Austin: their expectations are based on the idea of Austin as a progressive city that embraces individual freedom.

For this reason, I decided to teach a locally themed variation of a diversity course required for all our freshmen students. The main course is called

"The American Experience," and its goal is to revisit the American historical narratives that students learned in high school in order to highlight the
stories of disempowered communities that were left out of THE American
story. While students' U.S. history education varies, many continue to come
with romanticized views of American exceptionalism, and I felt that in some
ways, these could be compared to the current celebratory accounts of Austin as a progressive space of freedom and opportunity. At times, the Weird
Austin movement disregards the fact that Austin has long been a racially
segregated city of profound economic and social inequality. The phrase
masks the real internal conflicts of Old Austin, in particular the marginalization of African American and Latinx communities.

What I was seeking in this class was a way to teach a critical regionalist variation of the U.S. history survey that uncovers connections between
regional conflicts and larger national and global transformations. In this I
am also strongly influenced by Douglas Reichert Powell's work on critical
regionalism, and the way that he defines region not as a place, but as a way
of describing relationships among places. While I was looking at region, I
was also looking for a way to ground my students' understandings of global
processes by examining and challenging the systems that make us believe
that we are living in a homogenized world. We focused on particular local
incidents, highlighted their local meanings, but then drew out the connections to various national and global transformations. As Reichert Powell
notes, the goal of critical regionalism is articulating the sense of what is
unique about a particular spot on the landscape with a critical awareness
of how that spot is part of broader configurations of history, politics, and
culture.[7]

Of course, focusing on the regional offered an opportunity to encourage more engagement with social justice movements as well. For example,
when we discuss racial segregation, it is helpful to have the opportunity to
see how these policies played out in a local context. In Austin, the line divid-
ing "white" from "black" was particularly clear—it's now an interstate that
runs through the city (all African American families were forced to move
east of this road in 1928). And great disparity in race and income remains
between East and West Austin. We took a field trip to Clarksville, the one
historically African American neighborhood that remained in West Austin,
but whose current residents are largely affluent whites. We arrived at the
close of the Sunday service at the Sweet Home Missionary Baptist Church,
attended by its still predominantly African American congregation. After

the service we watched most of the congregation get in their cars and drive out of the neighborhood. This was quite a memorable way to witness the processes of gentrification, but also a reminder that communities (in this case, a congregation) find ways to resist these processes by maintaining a presence in this historic neighborhood.

But the class does more than offer examples of "this national struggle happens here as well." Reconceptualizing this course from a local perspective meant changing the fundamental ways that the history had been organized. Many American history college textbooks remain anchored to a Turnerian narrative—there is more conflict, and multiple perspectives, but the story still follows European immigrants across the continent. If I was going to focus on the Austin experience, however, I needed to center the story in Austin from the beginning.

We also had to consider the various processes of naming and defining the political boundaries of this region, and so we focused on who drew the maps and how they changed. I began the course with the Tonkawa, and the ways that they lived in this landscape that is now called central Texas. We spent much more time than most American textbooks do with the Spanish and their conflicts with the Caddo, the Apache, and other indigenous nations, struggles that were far from settled at the end of the eighteenth century. I did not discuss the English colonies in great depth, but let them emerge as nineteenth-century immigrant narratives. Austin was discussed not as a frontier outpost awaiting Anglo-American expansion, but as a node in the networks of the Spanish, indigenous, and U.S. empires.

There are challenges to this course, however, that were difficult to surmount. Finding good local critical sources can be difficult—sometimes primary sources are hard to unearth, and some regional history is nostalgic and uncritical. I have found that using this material can be valuable, but it requires significant additional work to make these sources more interesting and accessible and to teach my students how to read them critically. Fortunately, there is now more academic study of Austin than ever before (perhaps a by-product of Austin's popularity). Ultimately it was worth it—students could engage more directly in the place where they (at least temporarily) were living, and, I hope, gain critical insight into how to connect this history to more present-oriented forms of community building.

As I prepared for this course, I also reflected on my experiences as a college freshman, far away from my home state of Texas. I thought about my longing for home, and how I gradually discovered Providence, Rhode

Island—my temporary college address—in the midst of my own homesickness. My desire to know more about the place where I was from informed my desire to know about the place where I was. I realized that when I took those college courses in American history and literature, I often felt left out—the communities I lived in, the places I called home (San Antonio and Austin), were considered late arrivals to the American story. But I also knew Latinx families who had lived in North America for over five generations, and although their stories were mentioned occasionally during the Texas Revolution and the Mexican-American War, they frequently disappeared until the Braceros of World War II and the stories of late twentieth-century Latinx immigrants. So, for these reasons, teaching a regional perspective of history also remained important to me.

Keeping Austin Weird is a movement that ties community building to the past, not the present, but it can be useful because the phrase still represents a resistance to a set of displacements connected to the larger global transformations that have had a great influence not only on Austin, but on every city. The longing for an older, weirder Austin is, at times, a critical nostalgia for a more affordable, more accessible Austin. And this struggle is not Austin's alone. Even though most of my students will leave this city, my hope is that they will carry with them more tools to understand and perhaps even challenge the social and economic transformations that are defining the places where they migrate as well.

Teaching Region: Appalachia

Dwight B. Billings

Periodically, the idea of Appalachia as a distinct region of the United States gains prominence and then recedes in public consciousness, depending on the times and the objectives of discourse. Two periods of discursive "discovery" stand out in the social construction of the region. One was during the era of rapid American industrialization and urbanization from 1865 to 1900, when—despite the extensive social change occurring in the mountain South at the time—Appalachia was imagined to be, in the oft-quoted words of an American reporter, "a strange land and a peculiar people." A source of many of the stereotypes that still persist in discussions of Appalachia today, the discourses of that era by local color writers, missionaries, scholars, journalists, and developers helped create the enduring image of Appalachia as a region apart, an isolated *other* in the heart of America. The idea of Appalachian otherness gained renewed prominence in the 1960s with the "discovery" of remarkably high levels of poverty in the region—especially in the coalfield communities of West Virginia and Kentucky—and the subsequent War on Poverty. Challenging the stereotypes that were deployed to explain either the region's presumed isolation in the nineteenth century or its very real poverty in the twentieth century is a principal objective for most of us who teach region in Appalachia.[8]

The War on Poverty not only contributed to regional stereotypes—most notably the view of Appalachia as a regionwide culture of poverty—but also led to indigenous, grass roots–based social activism. That activism spawned what many observers have termed an Appalachian Renaissance in the 1970s and 1980s, including a vast proliferation of regional arts and creative writing. Its academic expression was the creation of Appalachian studies courses and research centers; filmmaking, radio, recording, and performance, especially through Appalshop, a grassroots media center in eastern Kentucky; the birth of academic journals; and the founding of the Appalachian Studies Association. The last was designed "to coordinate analysis of the region's problems across disciplinary lines" and "to relate scholarship to regional needs and the concerns of the Appalachian people."[9] Postmodernist and poststructuralist theories encouraged the recognition of difference and diversity in the region. Their wariness of essentialism also led to self-consciousness about the politics of writing and representation. At the same time, important leaders of the Appalachian studies movement who were associated with the Highlander Center promoted a distinctive blend of scholarship and activism through participatory research that continues to influence both the content and pedagogy of Appalachian studies courses today. New attention to power, history, and activism made many of us, especially in the social sciences, critical of the objectivism of mainstream approaches, sensitive to the power relations embedded in our disciplinary knowledges, and more open to dialogue and partnership between citizens and scholars. These factors continue to influence our teaching.[10]

I have typically taught three courses on Appalachia: a multidisciplinary introduction to Appalachian studies, an upper division/graduate course on the sociology of Appalachia, and a graduate level, multidisciplinary seminar that critically examined new, cutting-edge writings on the region. I will focus here on my introductory course, APP 200. From 1978 until recently, I (and others) taught APP 200 once a year as a once-a-week, sophomore-level seminar that was capped at thirty students. It was designed to contribute to a minor degree in Appalachian studies. Since then, however, we have reconfigured the course to meet the citizenship requirement of our new university-wide core curriculum. APP 200 is now offered every semester and typically meets three times a week (with two lectures and discussion sections). Early on, my colleague Ann Kingsolver had an enrollment of 180 students in this new format, and I taught 150 students the following term. I offer these demographics as an example of adaptation and survival but not necessarily progress or evolution.

Our new learning outcomes and course objects for APP 200 are as follows:

A. Demonstrate an understanding of historical, societal, and cultural differences in Appalachia such as those arising from race, ethnicity, sexuality, language, nationality, religion, political and ethical perspectives, and socioeconomic class.
B. Demonstrate a basic understanding of how these differences influence issues of social justice and/or civic responsibility in the region.
C. Demonstrate an understanding of historical, societal, and cultural contexts relevant to the understanding of Appalachia.
D. Demonstrate an understanding of the following as they pertain to Appalachia:
    1. Societal, cultural, and institutional change over time
    2. Civic engagement
    3. Regional, national, and global comparisons
    4. Power and resistance
E. Demonstrate a basic understanding of effective and responsible participation in a diverse society.

Particular attention is devoted to representations and images of Appalachia. We compare alternative ways in which Appalachia has been pictured in fiction, Hollywood films, documentaries, music, plays, academic histories, and social science literature. The reading assignments compare contemporary works of fiction, history, and social science with the goal of conveying an understanding of the different multidisciplinary methods of understanding Appalachia. Consequently, APP 200 students are expected to meet the following *additional learning goals and objectives:*

F. Recognize the presence of stereotypes and how they serve the interests of some groups while disempowering and marginalizing others.

G. Learn to recognize the distinct but complementary ways of discovery and representation in the arts, humanities, and social sciences through readings and lectures by University of Kentucky faculty representing each of these approaches.

H. Learn to obtain and critically evaluate information from documentary films, the Internet, and library/archival sources.

As in my other two courses, I begin APP 200 with a mapping exercise. I present each of the students with an outline map of the fifty U.S. states and then ask them each to draw the boundaries of the Appalachian region. The regions they sketch are variously large and small. Some extend far north or south (or both); others spread wide from east to west. Some center almost exclusively on eastern Kentucky. Comparison of their maps leads to a discussion of the ideas students hold about what and where Appalachia is and what kind of people they imagine to live there. One objective is to remind them that there is no road sign saying, "Now Entering Appalachia." Then I show them other maps and discuss the reasons and interests behind them. One is of Appalachia's physiographic zones. Another is a map of the federally defined twelve-state Appalachian region. The latter includes more than four hundred counties from New York to Mississippi that are served by the Appalachian Regional Commission (ARC). It's the closest thing we have to an official definition of the region—its generous boundaries shaped less by commonality than by the need for broad congressional support in the 1960s, when the ARC was established. Next we examine maps by two important researchers a half-century apart, John C. Campbell and Thomas Ford, who imagined versions of Appalachia defined by cultural homogeneity, and discuss their criteria for inclusion. Another map is based on the impressions of undergraduate geography students from across the United States. I follow that with a map that traces the journey an English ethnomusicologist, Cecil Sharp, whose discovery in 1917 of long-forgotten British ballads that were still being sung in the mountain South conveyed the impression of a place where time stood still. After playing a recording of one of those ballads, I play a Hungarian folk song Sharp might have recorded had he ventured into the West Virginia coalfields—a zone identified by American geography students as the heartland of Appalachia—where half the coal-mining workforce was composed of immigrants from southern and eastern Europe and African Americans from the Deep South—change and diversity overlooked.

The thematic outline that follows after a discussion of the social and discursive construction of Appalachia includes (1) the discovery of poverty in the 1960s and how that helped give birth to Appalachian studies; (2) settlement, subsistence agriculture, and demographic and economic crises in nineteenth-century Appalachia; (3) industrial transformation (with an emphasis on coal mining); (4) mechanization, deindustrialization, unemployment, and outmigration and their effects on contemporary social life; and (5) power, public policy, and citizen activism in the current conflict over mountaintop removal (MTR) coal mining today. Along with readings by social scientists and historians, the primary texts for this historical overview are two historical novels by Denise Giardina (*Storming Heaven* and *The Unquiet Earth*) that depict life along the Tug River valley of Kentucky and West Virginia from the standpoints of several families across multiple generations from the late nineteenth century until the 1970s. Throughout the course, I make extensive use of the outstanding film resources we have on Appalachia, thanks to the Appalshop filmmakers and others, and I use Appalachian music to illustrate as many themes as possible. We engage in two in-class simulations (one of a trial resulting from Appalachian feud violence and another of a modern-day MTR permit hearing), and twice we visit the university archives to view historical documents of a 1930s coal strike in Harlan County, Kentucky, and a collection of materials depicting life in Wheelwright, an Appalachian Kentucky coal town.[11]

My stress on history in APP 200 has been influenced by Barrington Moore's brilliant demonstration in his book *The Social Origins of Dictatorship and Democracy* that social relations of the past—especially class relations in agriculture—have long-lasting effects on the processes of economic, political, and cultural development. It would be extreme to say that if slave-based plantation agriculture gives you the Deep South today, the legacy of subsistence agriculture, in part, gives you Appalachia. Nonetheless, I try to show in teaching APP 200 that nineteenth-century crises in subsistence agriculture, capitalist exploitation, and the patron-client relations of a coercive local state apparatus combined to create a perfect storm that led to the distinct pathway Kathleen Blee and I have termed elsewhere Appalachia's "road to poverty."[12]

On a final note, just as our ability to teach Appalachian studies at the University of Kentucky has been secured by our contributions to the university's concerns for enhancing citizenship learning, so too have we been able to make the case for Appalachian studies by renewing our focus on Appalachia in relation to global economic, political, social, and cultural processes. We have encountered college administrators who suspect that regional studies are tainted by the declining prestige of "area studies" as well as parochial and outdated in a world they erroneously imagine to be increasingly "flat." Nonetheless, we have been able to show that Appalachian studies complements the heightened emphasis on international studies. Consequently, our College of Arts and Sciences *Vision 2020* now promotes international studies and Appalachian studies as complementary programs that connect "world issues" and "life in Kentucky." By stressing the continuing importance of region in scholarship, pedagogy, and citizenship, we are trying to demonstrate that now perhaps more than ever—in the context of a globalizing world and an internationalizing curriculum—*place matters.*

The Making of "New England": Region as Cultural Politics

Kent C. Ryden

If you saw the view from my office window at home in Yarmouth, Maine, you could probably guess which region of the country it's in. Basically—and appropriately enough, I suppose, for someone who taught in an academic unit called the American and New England studies program—I live in a postcard, a quick visual summary of some of the central common tropes of New England regional identity. There stands the venerable meetinghouse, its coat of white paint refreshed regularly by the Village Improvement Society. Next to it are rows of gravestones bearing names like Abigail Gooch, Hiram Hatch, and Mehitabel Larrabee. Even my own house is drawn into the scene, its 177 years of age earning it a plaque that certifies it as officially Historic, a suitable companion for church and cemetery.

It's an iconic scene, one with a great deal of historical weight and momentum. But icons always invite iconoclasm, don't they? Like any such scene believed or intended to denote regional identity, it's a construction, a matter of selection and emphasis from among the historical materials available—and therefore also a matter of exclusion and de-emphasis of many, many other aspects of landscape and history. In a crucial way, it's a scenic charlatan, which is one of the important things about regional studies in New England: the creation and ongoing reinscription of what we might think

North Yarmouth and Freeport Baptist Meetinghouse (1796), Yarmouth, Maine, in 2012. Photograph by Kent C. Ryden.

The John White House (ca. 1840), Yarmouth, Maine, in 2012. Photograph by Kent C. Ryden.

of as "old New England" is a continual exercise of cultural power, of social machinery designed to elevate some groups and erase others. So it's important to look behind the familiar postcard where I live, not only to historicize it and understand where it came from, but to realize how it gives familiar visual and physical form to the kinds of power dynamics and differentials that come into play in any assertion of identity, be it regional or otherwise.

The fetishization of the white church–centered New England village didn't occur as a matter of course just because people noticed that there were a lot of old meetinghouses lying around. It was a deliberate cultural choice on the part of certain regional residents who felt that their dominance— their sense of regional ownership, if you will—was increasingly threatened. To speak briefly and simplistically: over the course of the late nineteenth century, New England was transformed, more so than other American regions, by industrialization, urbanization, and immigration, as more and more of those immigrants were Catholic or southern European (or both). New Englanders who had an imaginative stake in the older, more rural, more Anglo-Saxon region that seemed threatened with eclipse reacted by staging what we now call a colonial revival, which in part involved rearranging the New England on the ground so that it more closely matched the idealized New England of the mind, a manifestation of an ethnically and economically pure past that never actually existed. Meetinghouses and village centers acquired both fresh (and historically inaccurate) coats of white paint and new layers of symbolic significance. The structures and places deemed important became those where old Anglo-Saxon Protestant farmers had lived, or were believed to have lived. The construction of the postcard was basically a performance of the Orwellian notion that those who control the past control the present, a statement on the part of culturally powerful New Englanders that this region is ours and not yours, you newcomers and interlopers. You're not New Englanders; in fact, in our idealized landscape, you're invisible; there's no place for you; you don't exist.

In a nutshell, I've just demonstrated for you both my teaching objectives in regional studies and the way I go about trying to achieve them. Borrowing an album title from the old Firesign Theater comedy troupe, I like to joke with my students that the unofficial motto of our program is "Everything You Know Is Wrong." Well, if it's wrong, why do we know it? Why do we continue to know it; why do tourists keep coming to New England not only looking for it but finding it? Questions as complicated as these invite multiple avenues of address, the postcard being constructed not simply from history or architecture or literature or any other single aspect of our complex and tangled cultural world, which we nonetheless tend to sort into discrete academic disciplines. Multidisciplinarity and interdisciplinarity, that is, provide the best pedagogical tools for trying to gain an understanding of that multifaceted thing we call region. Fortunately, I taught in a wide-ranging regional studies program in which I was able—nay, required—to use those tools. Thus, in my teaching, I use multiple platforms to explore how and why dominant regional ideologies have arisen in New England, how those ideologies have generated contestation and counternarratives, and how multiple regional discourses can exist and converse at once.

For example: in literature, how was Robert Frost complicit in reinforcing a view of small-town and rural northern New England that was a balm for the soul, and how was his contemporary Edwin Arlington Robinson able in his "Tilbury Town" poems to portray that exact same place, in that exact same time, as constricting and tragic, and why does that matter? How does Carolyn Chute's bleak neo-naturalistic novel *The Beans of Egypt, Maine* converse with the retailing, marketing, and tourist-pleasing juggernaut the L.L. Bean Company of Freeport, Maine, a company whose ongoing success highly depends on an image of the state as being charmingly pastoral (and, as its goods imply, affluent)? In teaching about New England environmental history, I can talk about how the climate and hydrology of the region, coupled with the availability of capital in Boston and other cities, helped enable the rise of water-powered industry in New England—which, of course, sparked industrialization, which ignited urbanization once factories were freed by the steam engine from having to be located in sometimes remote river valleys, which spawned increasing immigration over time, which, as I mentioned earlier, led to the colonial revival. I can also talk about the widespread failure of agriculture in New England over the course of the nineteenth century, which not only freed up a labor force for early factories but also created a landscape of abandonment, which then had to be imaginatively and physically rebuilt and reimagined by second-home buyers, state tourism promoters, and various colonial revivalists as an idyllic retreat rather than the detritus of a played-out economic system that it actually was. Then, of course, those abandoned farms became reforested, creating the annual autumn foliage that is so important a part of the postcard and which completely hides the landscape's actual history from view. Literature, history, the natural environment, and the built environment all talk to each other, and together they show us that a region is not a place so much as it is a process, an ongoing and dynamic interweaving of pretty much every social and cultural phenomenon you can think of.

In the history of the academic and popular usage of the word, *region* has tended to be synonymous with "the sticks," the place where nothing happens. Nothing could be further from the truth; region is the place where *everything* happens, right outside your classroom, up close where you can examine highly fraught cultural concepts as real, concrete things. Issues of race, ethnicity, class disparity, economic inequality, environmental exploitation, and the reaching of natural limits—New England is a pedagogical laboratory for studying all these things and much, much more. I may see a classic meetinghouse and a charming New England cemetery when I gaze out my window, but I also see, and am inspired to talk about, the very complicated story of how that scene accrued the meanings it has, a story whose strands are regional in their particularities but national and international in their generalities. I'm looking at a New England postcard, that is, but I'm also looking directly at America—and beyond.[13]

Teaching Region: Native American Studies

Gina Caison

In many respects, it might be easy to dismiss regionalism as an outdated organizing principle for literary and cultural studies classrooms. Indeed, in the past, many regional studies models provided only a narrow view of a specific geographic space where hierarchies of race and class were enforced by what Kent Ryden notes as the "postcard" history, telling its viewers, "this region is ours and not yours." This "ours" and "yours" regionalism worked alongside narratives of settler colonialism, expansionism, and racism in erasing Native American people from the history and literature of the various regions my colleagues and I discuss in these short pieces.

With the recent transnational turn in American studies, critics and teachers seem even more eager to let go of singular spaces and instead examine a nexus of cultural and economic exchanges. I posit that teaching and examining the region as a category of analysis, however, illuminates more about transnational exchange than it occludes. Furthermore, it allows students to reevaluate what they think of as the transnational moment. While many students might think of transnationalism as a recent phenomenon akin to debates about trade, economics, and immigration, the regional perspective shows the long scope of transnational exchange. Thus, a focus on region allows students to consider places as dynamically constructed through the relationships between many groups of people over time.

Because scholars often think about Native American epistemologies, cultures, and languages in terms of regional continuities (for example, the Algonquian linguistic continuum running from the coast of New England to the Outer Banks of North Carolina), I often teach Native American literature in such a way as to facilitate students' examinations of their own regional backyards in relationship to local Native histories and worldviews. Like Laura Hernández-Ehrisman, I want students to think about how they would draw their region today and how someone could have drawn it in the past. In thinking of the Algonquian linguistic continuum that I just mentioned, today we might find that students from the Jersey Shore do not imagine that they live in a region that once shared a cultural continuum with their counterparts four hundred miles south in Virginia Beach. By highlighting this regional history, students can begin to examine the many regions that existed in their space before their "own" region. In this way, a long view of regionalism can incorporate other languages and nations that address the deep history of transnational exchange among Native nations. This in turn might address some of the potential problems that Philip Joseph rightly identifies in a focus on regional literatures that imagines the study of regional English dialects as a sufficiently diverse language curriculum. Through the recognition of linguistic and literary traditions other than English in our particular regions, we can work toward Joseph's call that "teachers of regionalism have a special obligation to ensure that literature in dialect does not supplant the study of foreign languages. The ability to engage with foreign-language speakers on *their* terms is a fundamental value in the humanities." Acknowledging Native languages from within a region and as defining characteristics of particular spaces pushes students toward the important recognition not of *foreign* languages but languages and peoples indigenous to the spaces they now call home.

Such a regional approach can also facilitate a better understanding of the diversity within Native American cultures. Sometimes students (particularly non-Native ones) can feel as if the plethora of Native nations, cultures, and languages in North America is too overwhelming to grasp in a single term. And, admittedly, it is. Thinking regionally, in this case, can help students understand that it makes more sense to think about the specific Native national and cultural vectors that inform a work rather than to homogenize all Native experience into one constructed racial or ethnic category (which can often be their first impulse). Thinking regionally prompts students to see the detailed and interrelated ways that Native cultures co-developed across present-day national boundaries and alongside their varied responses to colonial invaders and settlers. This perspective also facilitates a discussion of Native American national sovereignty, and it forwards many of the goals set forth by Native American studies scholars such as Craig Womack, who sees promise in Native literature courses focused on individual tribal and national groups such as the Creek.[14]

Additionally, this "zooming in" to think about the interrelationships in Native nations in small spaces also serves another one of the core goals of any of my regional courses, which has to do with questioning the very geographic boundaries that many students come to the course imagining as totalizing spaces. Frequently, I begin my literature courses (whether Native, southern, or even just the problematically broad "American" literature survey) with an upside-down image of a section of the Earth. I begin by asking students to identify the place. After they succeed, which usually happens because someone eventually recognizes Florida, we examine the physical layout of the space. Students make numerous observations, including the sheer number of Caribbean islands; the often ignored proximity of Cuba to the mainland United States; and the even surprising proximity of "northern" Colombia and the "southern" U.S. Gulf Coast. The initial spatial disorientation brought about by this image accomplishes three important goals of my course: it begins the term by undoing some of the colonial boundaries the students may have imagined as historically totalizing; it allows them to think about the construction of region as it pertains to precolonial cultural contact; and it reminds them of the geospatial arbitrariness of north-south identity. Once students consider spatial identifiers under this framework of contingency, they can begin the process of working out what constitutes a region, whether it be geological boundaries, shared languages, economies, cultural practices, or even historical traumas.

From there, I want students to see how any discussion of the region is already bound up with larger transnational threads. For example, it is difficult—nay, impossible—to talk about the present-day U.S. South without talking about the African, European, and indigenous peoples who contributed to the region's culture. To facilitate these conversations in my southern literature course, I have students build a collaborative map that "places" the literature we are reading for the term.

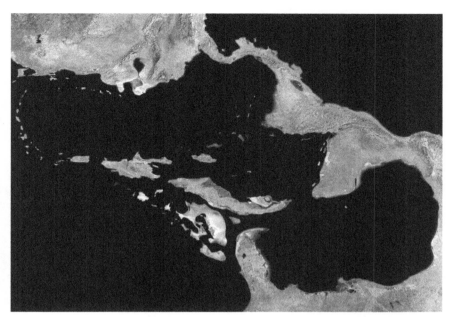

Satellite composition of the Earth's surface from NASA/Goddard Space Flight Center via Visible Earth. NASA Visible Earth.

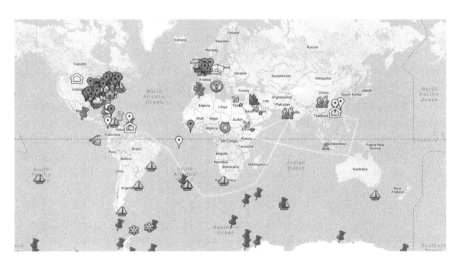

"Mapping Southern Literature," composed with and courtesy of Google My Maps/ Google Earth.

Here they begin to see where something like southern literature takes us and how much of the world might be invested in something we call the "South." When asked to reflect on a second map, one student hypothesized that all this was making her think that the South was not so much a *place* as a *time* when people interacted with and exploited one another for material benefits within a plantation economy. Thus, she concluded, we see the South "going other places" because the same social conditions and power relationships are replicated at different moments around the globe. This insight echoes David Davis's assertions about the importance of theorizing the region in recent discussions of globalization, and it gives me hope that what this student realized was that the region offered her a concrete opportunity to see the mechanisms of racial and economic exploitation as it moved across national boundaries. Reflective moments such as these are where we see students working with Dwight Billings's assertion that regional studies classes can help students think concretely and locally about universal and global issues of power, inequality, justice, and citizen agency and responsibility.

This leads me to my own reflective moment when I consider what I have learned from exchanges with colleagues from across disciplines and areas of regional study. I agree with many of my fellow authors in this volume that place is process. There are stories behind the regions we imagine, and it is important for students to learn that no region is a historical constant. I do, however, want to propose that place is more than the process of colonialism. The places we teach about have histories and languages and economies that far exceed the last five hundred years. The regions we discuss have histories that even exceed themselves as regions. This is what I want my students to know. It is heartening for me to find that so many of us are thinking through these questions. As Ryden notes, this is not a conversation that can happen within our own narrowly defined disciplinary regions. Indeed, this interdisciplinary approach can be disorienting. But, as we know, when it comes to regions, orientation has a long history that we might do well to challenge.

Notes

The authors would like to thank Molly McGehee for conceptualizing and initiating the conference panel that inspired this chapter.

1. Douglas Reichert Powell, *Critical Regionalism: Connecting Politics and Culture in the American Landscape* (Chapel Hill: University of North Carolina Press, 2007), 8.

2. Ibid.

3. Ibid., 6–7.

4. Michael Sandel, *Democracy's Discontent: America in Search of a Public Philosophy* (Cambridge: Harvard University Press, 1996).

5. E. J. Dionne, "Introduction: Why Civil Society? Why Now?" in *Community Works: The Revival of Civil Society in America* (Washington, DC: Brookings Institution Press, 1998), 8.

6. Ken Saro-Wiwa, "Author's Note," *Sozaboy: A Novel in Rotten English* (1985; repr., White Plains, NY: Longman, 1994).

7. Reichert Powell, *Critical Regionalism*, 3–31.

8. Henry D. Shapiro, *Appalachia on Our Mind: The Southern Mountains and Mountaineers in the American Consciousness, 1870–1920* (Chapel Hill: University of North Carolina Press, 1978); Allen W. Batteau, *The Invention of Appalachia* (Tucson: University of Arizona Press, 1990).

9. Alan Banks, Dwight Billings, and Karen Tice, "Appalachian Studies, Resistance, and Postmodernism," in *Fighting Back in Appalachia,* ed. Stephen L. Fisher (Philadelphia: Temple University Press, 1993), 283.

10. Dwight B. Billings, "Appalachian Studies and the Sociology of Appalachia," in *21st Century Sociology: A Reference Handbook,* ed. Clifton D. Bryant and Dennis L. Peck, 2 vols. (Thousand Oaks, CA: Sage Publications, 2007), 2:390–396, 543–545.

11. These archival materials have been made available online by Katherine Black as an archival exercise to teach students how to analyze historical materials and to provide extensive information and discussion of a touchstone event in Appalachian and U.S. labor history. See https://appalachiancenter.as.uky.edu/coal-miners-strike-archive.

12. Dwight B. Billings and Kathleen M. Blee, *The Road to Poverty: The Making of Wealth and Hardship in Appalachia* (New York: Cambridge University Press, 2000).

13. I have elaborated on many of the ideas in this essay at much greater length in two books: Kent C. Ryden, *Landscape with Figures: Nature and Culture in New England* (Iowa City: University of Iowa Press, 2001), and Kent C. Ryden, *Sum of the Parts: The Mathematics and Politics of Region, Place, and Writing* (Iowa City: University of Iowa Press, 2011). Other useful and relevant works on New England regional studies include Dona Brown, *Inventing New England: Regional Tourism in the Nineteenth Century* (Washington, DC: Smithsonian Institution Press, 1997); Joseph A. Conforti, *Imagining New England: Explorations of Regional Identity from the Pilgrims to the Mid-Twentieth Century* (Chapel Hill: University of North Carolina Press, 2001); and Joseph S. Wood, *The New England Village* (Baltimore: Johns Hopkins University Press, 1997).

14. See Craig Womack, *Red on Red: Native American Literary Separatism* (Minneapolis: University of Minnesota Press, 1999).

Contributors

Dwight B. Billings recently retired as a professor of sociology and distinguished professor of arts and sciences at the University of Kentucky. He is a past president of the Appalachian Studies Association and past editor of the *Journal of Appalachian Studies*. The author of numerous books and articles on Appalachia and the American South, he is currently at work on a study of struggles for economic and political justice in Appalachia.

Gina Caison is an assistant professor of English at Georgia State University, where she teaches courses in southern literature, Native American literatures, and documentary practices. She is coeditor of *Small-Screen Souths: Region, Identity, and the Cultural Politics of Television* (2017), coproducer of the documentary film *Uneasy Remains: The University of California and the Native American Graves Protection and Repatriation Act*, and host of the podcast *About South*. Currently she is completing a monograph about the intersection of Native American and southern history in the region's literature.

David A. Davis is an associate professor of English, director of fellowships and scholarships, and associate director of the Center for Southern Studies at Mercer University. He studies southern literature and culture, and he teaches courses in American literature and southern studies. He edited a reprint of Victor Daly's novel *Not Only War: A Story of Two Great Conflicts* (2010) and a reprint of John L. Spivak's novel *Hard Times on a Southern Chain Gang: Originally Published as Georgia Nigger* (2012). He coedited *Writing in the Kitchen: Essays on Southern Literature and Foodways* with Tara Powell (2014).

Elizabeth S. D. Engelhardt is John Shelton Reed Distinguished Professor of Southern Studies in the Department of American Studies at the University of North Carolina, Chapel Hill. Among her publications are *A Mess of Greens: Southern Gender and Southern Food* (2011), *The Tangled Roots of Feminism,*

Environmentalism, and Appalachian Literature (2003), and *The Larder: Food Studies Methods from the American South* (coeditor, 2013). She is a series editor for the Southern Foodways Alliance Studies in Culture, People, and Place Series at the University of Georgia Press and the Appalachia in Transition Series for Ohio University Press. She serves on the board and chairs the Academic Committee of the Southern Foodways Alliance.

John Gaventa is currently professor and director of research at the Institute of Development Studies, University of Sussex, United Kingdom. Previously he served as a staff member and director of the Highlander Center in the United States (1976–1994), faculty member of the University of Tennessee (1986–1996), director of the Coady International Institute at St. Francis Xavier University, in Nova Scotia, Canada (2011–2014), and as chair of Oxfam Great Britain (2006–2011). He has written widely on issues of citizen engagement, power and participation, and participatory forms of research, including his award-winning book *Power and Powerlessness: Quiescence and Rebellion in an Appalachian Region* (1980). In 2011, he received the Tisch Civic Engagement Research Prize for his distinguished scholarship on civic learning, citizen participation, and engaged research.

Mary L. Gray is a fellow at Harvard University's Berkman Klein Center for Internet and Society and a senior researcher at Microsoft Research. She maintains a tenured faculty appointment at Indiana University. Her research looks at how media access and everyday uses of technologies shape people's lives. Her book *Out in the Country: Youth, Media, and Queer Visibility in Rural America* (2009) explored how young people in the rural United States use media to negotiate sexual and gender identities, local belonging, and visibility in national LGBT politics. She also studies the social impact of digital labor on the future of employment.

John Haywood is from Risner, Kentucky, and has been doing artwork since before he can remember. He studied art at Morehead State University and the University of Louisville. He opened the Parlor Room Art & Tattoo in Whitesburg, Kentucky, so that his interests in painting, tattooing, and music could all come together. He performs old-time music solo and with several groups. His website is haywoodarts.com.

Laura Hernández-Ehrisman is an associate professor in the Department of University Studies in the School of Arts and Humanities at St. Edward's University in Austin, Texas. She teaches and administers general education requirements at the university, and she is course coordinator for a course called "The American Experience." Her research focuses on urban cultural history in south and central Texas. Her book *Inventing the Fiesta City: Heritage and Carnival in San Antonio* (2008) focuses on gender, race, and the rise of the Mexican American middle class in the celebration of San Antonio's Fiesta celebrations. Her 2016 essay "Breakfast Taco Wars: Race, History, and Food in Austin and San Antonio" was published in *The End of Austin*, a digital humanities project of the University of Texas.

bell hooks is a writer, artist, cultural critic, feminist theorist, and public intellectual. She was born Gloria Jean Watkins in Hopkinsville, Kentucky, and adopted her great-grandmother's name as her pen name. She received her Ph.D. from the University of California, Santa Cruz. Some of her books include *Ain't I a Woman: Black Women and Feminism; Teaching to Transgress: Education as the Practice of Freedom; Where We Stand: Class Matters; All about Love: New Visions; Bone Black: Memories of Girlhood; Belonging: A Culture of Place; Salvation: Black People and Love; Feminist Theory: From Margin to Center; We Real Cool: Black Men and Masculinity; Outlaw Culture: Resisting Representations; Black Looks: Race and Representation; Talking Back: Thinking Feminist, Thinking Black; Sisters of the Yam: Black Women and Self-Recovery;* and *Appalachian Elegy: Poetry and Place.* She is now based at the bell hooks Institute in Berea, Kentucky.

Philip Joseph is an associate professor of English at the University of Colorado Denver (UCD), where he teaches courses in American literature. His book *American Literary Regionalism in a Global Age* was published by Louisiana State University Press in 2006. He is the cofounder of the Colorado Center for Public Humanities at UCD (now the Public Humanities Initiative) and served as the center's director from 2007 to 2014. His current book project, *Rogues in Combat: The Deep History of the Picaresque War Narrative, 1668–Present,* examines the global migration of the rogue's narrative as a form for telling the story of a recent historical war. His articles have appeared in *PMLA, American Literature,* and other publications.

Ann E. Kingsolver is a professor of anthropology at the University of Kentucky. She has been listening for thirty years, as an ethnographer, to how people interpret capitalist logic and practice, especially all that gets called globalization, and act on those understandings. Her own books include *NAFTA Stories: Fears and Hopes in Mexico and the United States* and *Tobacco Town Futures: Global Encounters in Rural Kentucky,* and she edited *More Than Class: Studying Power in U.S. Workplaces* and coedited *The Gender of Globalization: Women Navigating Cultural and Economic Marginalities* and the *Routledge Companion to Contemporary Anthropology.*

Rich Kirby has performed, recorded, and mentored others in traditional Appalachian music since the 1970s. At Appalshop, in Whitesburg, Kentucky, he has been a staff member and producer at WMMT, produced recordings for the June Appal record label, served as music director of the Seedtime on the Cumberland Festival, worked with traditional music in schools, and produced a number of traditional music programs that have been distributed nationally. He performs with Rich and the Po' Folk and other groups. One of his recent projects has been to produce recordings of traditional Appalachian songs sung by his grandmother Addie Graham.

Carol Mason is the author of three books examining different aspects of the rise of the Right since the 1960s. Cornell University Press published *Killing for Life: The Apocalyptic Narrative of Pro-life Politics* (2002) and *Reading Appalachia from Left to Right: Conservatives and the 1974 Kanawha County Textbook Controversy* (2009). *Oklahomo: Lessons in Unqueering America* was published in 2015 by SUNY Press in its Queer Politics and Cultures series. Mason holds a Ph.D. in English from the University of Minnesota and currently is a professor and chair of Gender and Women's Studies at the University of Kentucky.

Ron Pen is a retired professor of music at the University of Kentucky, where he has also served as director of the John Jacob Niles Center for American Music and director of Appalachian studies. His research is focused on Appalachian musical culture, and his recent publications include *I Wonder as I Wander: The Life of John Jacob Niles* and "Preservation and Presentation of the Folk: Forging an American Identity," in *Music, American Made,* edited by John Koegel. Pen is also a musician, performing with the Red State Ramblers old-time string band and the Appalachian Association of Sacred Harp Singers.

John Pickles is Distinguished Professor of International Studies in the Department of Geography at the University of North Carolina, Chapel Hill. His current research focuses on the effects of changing global apparel value chains; postsocialist economies and the integration of Central and Eastern European countries into the European Union; and migration routes and Euro-Med neighborhood policies in southern Europe. He has written, edited, or coedited over a dozen books, including most recently *Geographical Dynamics and Firm Spatial Strategy in China; Articulations of Capital: Global Production Networks and Regional Transformations; The Anomie of the Earth: Philosophy, Politics, and Autonomy in Europe and the Americas; Towards Better Work: Understanding Labour in Apparel Global Value Chains;* and *State and Society in Post-Socialist Economies.*

Kent C. Ryden is professor emeritus of American and New England studies at the University of Southern Maine. He is the author of three books—*Mapping the Invisible Landscape: Folklore, Writing, and the Sense of Place; Landscape with Figures: Nature and Culture in New England;* and *Sum of the Parts: The Mathematics and Politics of Region, Place, and Writing*—as well as many articles and chapters on topics in the environmental humanities, regionalism, and literary studies.

Emily Satterwhite is an associate professor at Virginia Tech, where she teaches in the Appalachian Studies and Pop Culture programs. She is the author of *Dear Appalachia: Readers, Identity, and Popular Fiction since 1878* (2011), winner of the Weatherford Award and the Sturm Award for Faculty Excellence in Research. Her articles have appeared in *American Literature, Journal of American Folklore,* and *Appalachian Journal.* Satterwhite's current research includes a book on hillbilly horror films as well as projects on environmental and mental health in Appalachia.

Barbara Ellen Smith is a retired professor of sociology and women's studies. She lives in Charleston, West Virginia, where a portion of her Appalachian journey began many years ago. She is currently collaborating with the geographer Jamie Winders on a project on right-wing populism in the U.S. South. Her books include *Digging Our Own Graves: Coal Miners and the Struggle over Black Lung Disease* and (coedited with Stephen L. Fisher) *Transforming Places: Lessons from Appalachia.*

Index

PLACE MATTERS: NEW DIRECTIONS IN APPALACHIAN STUDIES

SERIES EDITOR: Dwight B. Billings

This series explores the history, social life, and cultures of Appalachia from multidisciplinary, comparative, and global perspectives. Topics include geography, the environment, public policy, political economy, critical regional studies, diversity, social inequality, social movements and activism, migration and immigration, efforts to confront regional stereotypes, literature and the arts, and the ongoing social construction and reimagination of Appalachia. Key goals of the series are to place Appalachian dynamics in the context of global change and to demonstrate that place-based and regional studies still matter.

CPSIA information can be obtained
at www.ICGtesting.com
Printed in the USA
JSHW032156201222
35250JS00001B/32